Where Ideas Go to Die

Where Ideas Go to Die

The Fate of Intellect in American Journalism

MICHAEL MCDEVITT

OXFORD

UNIVERSITY PRESS

Oxford University Press is a department of the University of Oxford. It furthers the University's objective of excellence in research, scholarship, and education by publishing worldwide. Oxford is a registered trade mark of Oxford University Press in the UK and certain other countries.

Published in the United States of America by Oxford University Press
198 Madison Avenue, New York, NY 10016, United States of America.

© Oxford University Press 2020

Library of Congress Cataloging-in-Publication Data
Names: McDevitt, Michael (Professor of journalism), author.
Title: Where ideas go to die: The fate of intellect in American Journalism /
[by Michael McDevitt].
Description: New York, NY : Oxford University Press, [2020] |
Includes bibliographical references and index.
Identifiers: LCCN 2019049152 (print) | LCCN 2019049153 (ebook) |
ISBN 9780190869953 (hardback) | ISBN 9780190869946 (paperback) |
ISBN 9780190869977 (epub) | ISBN 9780197519448 (on-line)
Subjects: LCSH: Journalism—Social aspects—United States. |
Journalism—Political aspects—United States. | Journalism—Study and
teaching (Higher)—Social aspects—United States. | Democracy—United States. |
Social control—United States. | United States—Intellectual life—21st century.
Classification: LCC PN4888.S6 M33 2020 (print) | LCC PN4888.S6 (ebook) |
DDC 302.230973—dc23
LC record available at https://lccn.loc.gov/2019049152
LC ebook record available at https://lccn.loc.gov/2019049153

Contents

List of Figures and Tables

Figures

Tables

Preface

Journalists at academic conferences sometimes wear safari jackets, apparently to signal that their idea of an adventure is not the university lab. I looked for the attire when I organized a panel of scholars in Montreal to discuss anti-intellectualism in news media. An Associated Press reporter in the first row stood abruptly following the final presentation. The veteran correspondent reminded everyone that reporters should be skeptical toward all forms of authority, including academic expertise. Apparently waiting for this moment for some time, panelist Todd Gitlin responded with the observation that children are notoriously defiant toward parents' authority.

I recognize that a critique of news media as anti-intellectual is not merely counterintuitive in journalism circles but an insult. I do not believe that US journalism is anti-intellectual to the bone. Much of routine newswork is simply (and realistically) non-intellectual: de-contextualized, event driven, personality focused, ahistorical, and so on. To say that journal*ism* eschews nuance, context, and contingency is not to say that journal*ists* are actively opposed to intellectuals or resent intellect in the abstract. Productive interplay of intellect and journalism is evident in the growing field of nonprofit journalism and in innovations such as knowledge-based reporting and academic journalism. Contemporary journalism does not resemble a bleak monochrome but appears more like Monet's water lilies: assertive expression of intellect in defiance of the murky shallows. I will document, for example, how reporters resist anti-intellectual pressure from editors and audiences through alliances with "dangerous professors" (Chapter 9).

This book explores journalism as cultural practice, a discursive realm in which intellect is both defended and rendered deviant. If there is a kinship of journalism with anti-intellectualism at deep levels of collective experience, we should consider the most fundamental of communicative acts in the polis, the presentation and circulation of unpopular ideas. In political theory, suspicion of cultural elites is typically viewed as endemic albeit often inchoate in public opinion. The translation of latent feelings into symbolic action directed against intellect requires a populist, proto-democratic rationale along with a medium to cohere as a punitive response. Anti-intellectualism obtains and exploits these resources in the news. This is not to say that journalism is simply a victim of appropriation. Of the many cases we will examine, some imply that the cultural status of journalism is protected, even enhanced, in the ways that it aligns anti-rationalism with populist anti-elitism.

Strains of anti-intellectualism unique to news media require the support of professional ideology, enculturation, and education. Some type of rationalization for idea suppression is required to condone or at least disguise the control of intellect. And because resentment of intellect is so antithetical to journalism's understanding of its contribution to informed citizenry, its justification is probably deeply internalized in professional socialization.

Academics, for their part, have done little to promote a healthier relationship between intellect and journalism. Anti-intellectualism is brought up at conferences when faculty grasp at a handle to express frustrations with popular culture. Nothing much has changed, at least on this score, when reading Richard Hofstadter: "One reason anti-intellectualism has not even been clearly defined is that its very vagueness makes it more serviceable in controversy as an epithet."[1] A reference to anti-intellectualism still acts as a status signifier, showing membership in an aggrieved minority. Still, academics should do more than complain about anti-intellectualism. This is, after all, no way to build theory or to compel reform. Professors and doctoral students rarely speak openly about anti-intellectualism outside academic settings, weary of being labeled "elitist." The silence is understandable at public universities in the West and in other regions with deeply rooted populism, where journalists and politicians police higher education for faculty discourse that might offend parents and taxpayers.[2]

Murmurs about anti-intellectualism mirror how people talk about the weather—plenty of complaining but no one does anything about it. A first step toward reform, and the purpose of this book, is to recognize the nature and scope of journalism's complicity in the social control of intellect.

Acknowledgments

The game in my house, with two brothers, was to see which one of us could set the record for folding, stacking, and delivering newspapers. More than one of my hastily tossed papers ended up on neighbors' roofs. I did manage to graduate from the weekly *Los Altos Town Crier* to the daily *Palo Alto Times*. I no longer relied on my Schwinn Stingray when, years later, I worked for those same papers as a reporter.

Still living in the Bay Area, I tried to leave newsrooms behind when my beat at the *Peninsula Times Tribune* was Stanford and I applied to the university's doctoral program in communication. With the application somehow successful, I switched to larger notepads, found a quiet space in McClatchy Hall, and immersed myself in the literature of family political communication. My dissertation—"Trickle-up influence of children on parents"—unintendedly tugged me back to journalism as it conceptualized what had happened in my own youth. The *San Francisco Chronicle* fueled dinner-table debates in a milieu in which Ken Kesey hosted "happenings" in La Honda, not too far from where the McDevitt kids could be found nearly every day, mostly abiding by the rules and dress code at Saint Simon School.

I wanted to teach political communication more than news writing in Albuquerque as I settled into my first semester as an assistant professor. I met my wife Angela at the University of New Mexico, however, and loved her stories about what it was like to produce news at *Univision*. She drew me back to the irreverence of newsroom culture. She became famous at the station for lacking a filter, cajoling anchors immediately after broadcasts: "Take off your makeup! We're going to the Martini Lounge."

I wrote this book as a way to reconcile my views about journalism. I want to first thank my parents, brothers, and sisters for creating a microcosm of a public sphere in Los Altos, prompting me to read the news beyond the sports pages. Paul Voakes gave me a chance to write editorials for the first time at the *Times Tribune*, and he would later chair my Journalism Department at the University of Colorado. Steve Chaffee died around the time I moved from Albuquerque to Boulder. I wish I could thank him today for giving me a chance as a scholar. I can express gratitude to another professor in Steve's department, Ted Glasser, whose work I reference throughout the book.

An inclination for the book emerged in conversations with the sociologist Brian Klocke when we watched in amazement at how *The Denver Post and Rocky Mountain News* could write so many stories about a controversial essay without describing the contents of the essay. Trained in social science, I had to catch up with cultural approaches in making sense of a media frenzy surrounding Ward Churchill. Marco Briziarelli, then a doctoral student, introduced me to the anthropology of Victor Turner, and we subsequently modeled the case as social drama in the punishment of intellectual dissent. In 2015, I took a sabbatical in the Graduate School of Education at Stanford. I am appreciative of Bill Damon for allowing me the freedom to pursue the book along with my scholarship on youth civic engagement. Back in Boulder, Jesse Been kept the project going by distributing questionnaires to journalism and mass communication majors. His diligence allowed us to develop valid and reliable measures of student anti-intellectualism. My CU colleague Patrick Ferrucci was instrumental in a textual analysis that helped me to comprehend the limits of journalistic reflexivity in populist climates. I also want to thank 25 dangerous professors. I was struck by their fondness for reporters. This appreciation contrasts with the more cynical view that often prevails in critical theory. The public scholars profiled in Chapter 9 helped me to recognize the importance of journalists rejecting the anti-elitism of media studies.

I am grateful to Hallie Stebbins for envisioning a book out of a single conference paper, and to Angela Chnapko at Oxford for her patience with a first-time book author.

Finally, back to Angela, my favorite journalists, to whom I dedicate this book.

1

Journalism and Intellect

A Vexed Relationship

Suspicion of intellect is not irrational. A free-floating intellect is always on the offending side in the morality of sanctity/degradation, loyalty/betrayal, and authority/subversion.[1] In journalism, social control comes down to the suppression, ridicule, or distortion of ideas accompanied by a repression of the capacity to recognize complicity. This interpretation aligns with how Glasser and Gunther think about self-censorship in the US press: "Given the nature of self-censorship, and the consequences of acknowledging it, little literature exists that documents in any systemic ways instances of it."[2]

Anti-intellectualism operates like dark matter in journalism, a presence inferred by its effects rather than directly observed or acknowledged. When journalists anticipate agitated audiences, reified sentiment is no more real than the fiction of omnipotent citizens in democratic theory, yet the audience imagined compels how intellect is rendered in the news as nuisance, deviance, or object of ridicule. The demos hold intellect accountable, and journalism's complicity remains muddled in affirmation of a punitive public. Journalism's contribution to the policing of ideas is poignantly democratic—audiences are cast in consequential roles that affirm their wisdom in a closed, self referential system.

Forthcoming chapters illuminate dimensions of anti-intellectualism that structure observable content but are generally not subject to reflexivity. My premise is that the social control of intellect *by* journalism is accompanied by social control *of* journalism in newsrooms and in classrooms where norms are cultivated. I will demonstrate how the cultural authority of newswork is reinforced, sometimes enhanced, by its sensitivity to ideas that offend. While journalism often operates at an analytical deficit in encounters with expertise, it is formidable in social control by amplifying and aligning feelings toward intellect. Journalism helps to rationalize (so to speak) anti-intellectualism as otherwise inchoate and latent sentiment.

Where Ideas Go to Die. Michael McDevitt, Oxford University Press (2020). © Oxford University Press.
DOI: 10.1093/oso/9780190869946.001.0001

Reporters and editors acknowledge that they simplify ideas to enhance clarity but are unlikely to recognize their participation in the social construction of intellectual deviance. An accusation of anti-intellectualism comes close to blasphemy when directed at a profession that claims quasi-priestly status in the public exercise of reason. As a topic of scholarship, the trouble with antipathy toward intellect is that this sentiment is tangled up with democratic commitments, with journalism's egalitarian ethos, its identification with "the public," ambivalence toward experts, and pleasure in holding up the haughty and highbrow to ridicule.

A few tangible episodes illustrate how democratic virtue is blended with bemusement, insincerity, resentment, and ridicule during journalism's encounters with intellect.

Exhibit A.[3] Reporters in the prestige press signal to readers the futility of the intellectual as activist. Every now and then they check in with aging, comic figures. A *New York Times* portrait of a sociology professor begins:

> THERE he was, one of New York City's last old-time Marxists, propped in a lunchtime den of wealthy Wall Street types, shaking a forkful of Irish sausage as he delivered prophecies of doom . . . No one at the Beekman Pub was listening . . . "Is everything O.K.?" asks the cheery waitress, interrupting Mr. [Stanley] Aronowitz's rambling manifesto.[4]

A reviewer for the *Times* seems surprised when linguist/activist Noam Chomsky "never raises his voice" in the documentary *Requiem for the American Dream*, an "easy listening jeremiad."[5]

> Mr. Chomsky concludes that "there's a lot that can be done if people organize, struggle for their rights as they've done in the past." You get the feeling, though, that, given all the challenges he lists, Mr. Chomsky no longer quite believes that.

Exhibit B. Evan Kindley, a founding editor of the *Los Angeles Review of Books*, heralds "a lively journalistic public sphere" of little magazines such as the *Boston Review* and the revised *Baffler*.[6] Larger publications such as *Slate*, *The Washington Post*, and *The Atlantic* have become more welcoming of academic voices with the emergence of influential blogs among public scholars. Still, Kindley picks up "ambient" tensions between the two worlds. "Often these tensions are expressed in aesthetic terms, as a criticism of styles of

writing; journalists frequently repeat the canard that academics 'can't write.'"
Academics are likely to "dismiss journalism touching intellectual matters as
underthought,"[7] leaving journalists with smiles of recognition as they pause
on words such as "underthought."

Exhibit C. In more commercially driven media, academic pundits are still
attractive to news producers, who usually know the story they want to present before professors are called. The presence of academics gives the impression of impartiality. Intellect is thereby tamed, rendered as common
wisdom in a paradoxical translation. A certain class of scholar goes along
willingly. "Political scientist [Norman] Ornstein, typical of many experts,
promotes himself in the news, hawking his largely descriptive commentary to the mass press in publications like *TV Guide*."[8] Ornstein's
centrist viewpoint "both ensures his audience appeal and certifies his
suitability."[9]

Exhibit D. Ben Goldacre, physician and science writer, observes the recyc-
ling of "sciencey-sounding" stories.[10] "Such news items tend to be of particular kinds, such as 'wacky' stories (about, for example, the scientific formula
for the perfect penalty kick) which play on the public's idea of scientists as
eccentric boffins, or medical scare stories which tend to be quickly and con-
fusingly refuted (red wine is good for you, or bad for you)."[11]

In interviews of 25 scientists and journalists, Hartley explored what
transpires when "Homo Academicus meets Homo Journalisticus."[12] One
journalist assured Hartley, a media sociologist: "We love the experts."[13]

Exhibit E. Social scientists, to be sure, are increasingly aligned with the elite
press in explanatory packages and data visualization, and in platforms such
as Monkey Cage, a political science blog sponsored by *The Washington Post*.
Editors at many news outlets, however, are still unimpressed by reporters
with advanced degrees. Dane Claussen, editor of *Newspaper Research
Journal*, explains:

> When news executives are asked why reporters don't have more expertise in
> their subject matter, they typically say that such reporters are not available,
> would cost too much money, would be difficult to edit . . . would have lim-
> ited flexibility to be moved to other beats, would not stay very long before
> moving on, and/or would be biased about their areas. All of these reasons
> are either nonsense or can easily be accommodated. The last one is partic-
> ularly rich: it suggests that news executives think that a knowledgeable art
> critic has biases while an ignorant art critic doesn't![14]

City-desk reporters were shuffled from beat to beat at newspapers I worked for in the San Francisco Bay Area. I believe my editors were concerned that reporters with substantive knowledge would become difficult to manage.

Exhibit F. According to a front-page feature in *The Denver Post*, "The Flat Earth movement is growing in Colorado, thanks to technology and skepticism about science."[15] The reporter insists: "They're thousands strong—perhaps one in every 500—and have proponents at the highest level of science, sports, journalism and arts." The *obviously insincere* reporting is surpassed only by learned helplessness: "(All scientists and educators consulted for this story rejected the idea of a flat earth.)"

Claussen describes an intellectually vacuous objectivity.[16] "In this approach to reporting, the story is balanced, seems fair, accurate, etc., but the journalist has neither really sought the truth nor communicated it." As Sartre might say, journalists act in bad faith by failing to live up to their deepest commitments in deliberative communication.[17] Or is this critique not quite apt? If anti-intellectualism is inevitable in journalism, moral and ontological questions about authenticity seem beside the point. The Flat Earth feature managed to be oddly deferential to scientific authority and patronizing to readers, submissive in one sense, elitist in another. The relationship of journalism to intellect is anything but straightforward.

Exhibit G. When I arrived at the University of Colorado as an assistant professor, Boulder students delighted in the ritualistic burnings of sofas. The University's administration doused that tradition, but undergraduates now tell me that Halloween has become "Halloweek." Later, I document whether journalism majors are more or less intellectual than other students (Chapter 8).[18] Comparisons aside, adjunct faculty are slapped in the face when they teach a course for the first time. They come to understand that many news majors are not particularly interested in reading the news and resent quizzes that ask about public affairs. But journalism schools deserve the students they attract. The history of professional education is marked by repeated failures to elevate journalism as a learned profession (Chapter 2).

Exhibit H. Textbooks urge students to extract bits from interviews but not to signal to sophisticated sources how the game is played lest the interviewees object. In *Beyond the Inverted Pyramid,* instructors from the University of Missouri offer advice for the end of interviews.

Go over any tricky spellings. Recheck any mathematics or technical information. Reconfirm—if you're not afraid of alerting the source to some unwitting admission—your understanding of the central points.[19]

The instructors essentially advocate what McGlone refers to as "contextomy," the art of *de*-contextualization followed by *re*-contextualization against the intentions of a source.[20] Much of student (and professional) work amounts to a collage of de-contextualized bits mashed together. The consequence is that students fail to internalize a sense of rhythm and flow. I ask students to write idea-centered essays; otherwise they run after quotes like squirrels scrambling for acorns.

The University of Missouri is home to the world's first school of journalism. Its widely used, current textbook perpetuates a professional legacy of scorn toward experts.[21] Students should not hesitate to dismiss long-winded responses as social science blather.

> "Why is it that our fourth-graders score below average on these reading tests," you ask the school superintendent. He may reply, "Let me first conceptualize the parameters of the socioeconomic context for you." The real answer probably is, "I only wish I knew" . . . Listen politely for a few minutes while the school superintendent conceptualizes his parameters.[22]

Some of these exhibits could be viewed as harmless eccentricities of newswork and professional identity. A postwar observation from Richard Hofstadter applies to contemporary journalists: "Men do not rise in the morning, grin at themselves in their mirrors, and say: 'Ah, today I shall torment an intellectual and strangle an idea!'"[23] I will document, nevertheless, the prowess of news media in systemic control of intellect. Control extends beyond suppression of ideas and ways of thinking to the aggressive rendering of dissent into deviance.

My intent is not to develop a typology of journalism forms most hostile to intellect nor to present a map of where irrationalism most readily ignites across media markets. I will make distinctions such as the elite press, quality media, and parochial newspapers, but only to illustrate contingencies for the premise that containment of intellect is intertwined with submission of journalism itself. Journalism, that is, becomes an object of its own agency. The book assembles findings from qualitative and quantitative methods, directly comparing news text with interviews from the same editors and reporters who produced the content. A survey of undergraduates implies developmental trajectories in how professionals internalize sensitivity to ideas that might offend audiences.

This first chapter explores the vexed relationship of journalism and intellect. A defender of common sense, the press is irked at intellect yet often dependent on its critical autonomy.[24] The profession alone is not responsible for intellect's fate in a mediascape receptive to punitive populism. That said, a tactical relationship to intellect is innate to journalism. Communication is constitutive of community, which is bound by core beliefs, which are inevitably probed and dissected by intellect. While democratic solidarity is grounded in shared discourse and interpersonal tolerance, moral validity claims reach into the prelinguistic sacred.[25] Journalism's response to transgressive ideas could be viewed, then, as a cultural appropriation of media in the actualization of anti-intellectualism. But this does not get us very far in disentangling journalism's unique contributions. The introduction begins an explication, carried forward throughout the book, of journalism's role in the reification and rationalization of a punitive public. A final section outlines the plan for the book.

From Awkward Accommodation to Aggression

Journalism understands its mission as "the coming to judgment of public intelligence."[26] The profession identifies with an informed citizenry and increasingly justifies its methods through transparency in ways that invite metajournalistic reflection.[27] Subsequent chapters nonetheless document how US journalism operates in the regulation of intellect—that part of reasoning with the autonomy to unsettle foundational beliefs.

The claim that journalism cultivates resentment toward intellectuals (populist anti-elitism) and suspicion of intellect (anti-rationalism) must overcome the objection that the news simply conveys cultural sentiment.[28] Leaving aside the bluster of academics when they see their expertise misrepresented, we should acknowledge that many reporters, editors, and columnists are fairly described as public intellectuals. With anti-intellectualism intertwined in the nation's cultural history,[29] journalism's contribution is relatively benign if news media disregard perspectives the general public is unwilling to engage. In routine circumstances, ideas are not strangled so much as packaged as commodities in a commercially driven press.

A vexed relationship with intellect is explained, in part, by the disorientation that arises in newswork when knowledge is not pre-rendered for ease of use. Reporting is source dependent—interpretive schemes grounded in intellect are subsidized by think tanks, policy advocates, academic centers, and other intermediaries.[30] Journalists embrace the duty to inform citizenship but not as autonomous brokers of ideas. If anything, journalism is wary of the incitement of ideas, an occupational ideology distinct from the pragmatics of whether news conventions can accommodate sustained, intellectual discussion.[31] In *Democracy for Realists*, Achen and Bartels run through an inconvenient history for intellectuals in politics.

> In the antebellum era, prominent southern professors and university administrators often defended slavery . . . Brilliant 19th-century German professors helped give shape to German nationalism and the racial identity theories that led to Nazism, and German university students in the 1930s were often enthusiastic supporters of Hitler . . . More recently, 20th-century communism attracted highly educated people around the world. Numerous French intellectuals supported Russian communism well after its crimes had been exposed . . . In the United States, prominent political science professors became advisors to the American government during the disastrous Vietnam War, while others naively favored Ho Chi Minh in his ultimately successful effort to establish a repressive communist state in that country.[32]

The salience of this historic record in journalistic thinking has yet to be explored in surveys of reporters and editors. From a cultural perspective, however, a reticence to engage with intellect is shaped by the obligation of mainstream media to defend moral foundations of sanctity, loyalty, and authority.[33]

Neither the nature of news nor its hegemonic function imply a crude or inevitable anti-intellectualism. We can think of journalism as mediating interactions between intellect and the public, intervening when necessary. Resentment works both ways. Episodes of professors lashing out at the public or popular culture are rare, but no one should be surprised if references to H. L. Mencken gain currency in academia. To take just one example from the quotable Sage of Baltimore: "On some great and glorious day the plain folks of the land will reach their heart's desire at last, and the White House will be adorned by a downright moron."[34]

Quality news media are often protective of political discourse as a reason-giving enterprise, particularly when the polity is confronted by mobilized irrationalism. Columnist Maureen Dowd, for example, characterized debt-ceiling negotiations with Tea Party freshman as the "Washington Chainsaw Massacre."

> They were like cannibals eating their own party leaders alive. They were like vampires . . . like zombies . . . like metallic beasts in "Alien" flashing mouths of teeth inside other mouths of teeth, bursting out of Boehner's stomach every time he came to a bouquet of microphones.[35]

Other times journalism itself is more than willing to show teeth, an instinct that becomes predatory when intellect is the transgressor.[36] Journalists routinely dismiss a great deal of intellectual dissent as mired in obfuscation, as an annoyance perhaps, but hardly newsworthy. Depending on the ideological climate, however, we should expect journalists to be quite sensitive to subversive discourse in patrolling boundaries between legitimate and deviant ideas.[37] Sensitivity should be acute in media proximate to an intellectual breach,[38] as when the Detroit press took the lead in fixing public attention on Dr. Jack Kevorkian, an early advocate of a patient's right to die.[39] An iconic photograph reveals the pathologist a bit too gleeful in showing off his "suicide machine." On the other side of Lake Erie, Pennsylvania media pounced when Drexel political scientist George Ciccariello-Maher tweeted on Christmas Eve 2016: "All I Want for Christmas is White Genocide" (Chapter 9). Much of the commentary echoed Drexel administrators in a literal interpretation of the obvious satire, further evidence of bad faith.

Anti-intellectualism flourishes in American society, transcendent of news media,[40] but subsequent chapters explain how particular strains resonate with the ideology and epistemology of journalism. This symbiosis protects and sometimes enhances the profession's authority when journalists imagine audiences as restive and angry.

Control of Intellect in the News

Anti-intellectualism is not reducible to overt episodes of social control. It lurks in latent antipathy ingrained in cultural milieu and reinforced, generation by generation, in contexts such as religion, business, politics, and media.

This book represents the first sustained effort to comprehend journalism's unique contributions to the policing of intellect. If anti-intellectualism in the news seems like it should be aptly understood, this is only because we have learned to live with the problem for so long. In 1922, Walter Lippmann came close to capturing anti-intellectualism by evoking an epistemology of diversion.

> [The news] is like the beam of a searchlight that moves restlessly about, bringing one episode and then another out of darkness into vision. Men cannot do the work of the world by this light alone. They cannot govern society by episodes, incidents, and eruptions. It is only when they work by a steady light of their own, that the press, when it is turned upon them, reveals a situation intelligible enough for a popular decision.[41]

Lippmann was ultimately interested in the inherent limitations of news, not the most egregious practices. His work reminds us that any critique of journalism as an institution that contributes to anti-intellectualism should acknowledge the nature of news while showing what is still possible. An inelegant term—*non*-intellectual—must suffice as a description for the bulk of US journalism. *Anti*-intellectualism, however, is not entirely explained in terms of epistemological deficits. The agency of journalism is formidable in periodic mobilization of irrationalism. We will examine the aversion of news to intellect in everyday reporting and the antagonistic relationship of journalism to intellect when core beliefs are at stake. In those latter circumstances, the restless searchlight that Lippmann conjures becomes more like a prison tower light, fixing public attention on ideational deviance so that it does not wiggle away.

Explicit scrutiny of journalism's contribution to the regulation of intellect remains scarce a century after Lippmann's portrayal of a distracted press[42] and a phantom public.[43] Scattered scholarship is often agonistic about complicity. News media reflect cultural features such as hedonistic celebration of triviality[44] and expectations for vocational training in college.[45] Theorists do recognize that anti-rationalism and anti-elitism in popular media are formidable expressions of disaffection in established democracies. MacGregor, for example, describes "a channeling" of public mentality that eradicates "all but populist positions."[46] Populist anti-elitism is typically understood as an inchoate style of thinking in a climate of opinion,[47] a syndrome more than a doctrine.[48]

Krämer recognizes the imagery of gathering, atmospheric forces is more suggestive than definitive in identifying affinities of populist anti-elitism with media-centered politics.[49] Mass media are favorable to populist positions when they circumvent elected leaders to speak directly for "the people." Populist media such as talk radio and tabloid newspapers rely on the schemata of the "common people" and their presumed wisdom as an "antidote to the knowledge of elites alienated from the everyday world."[50] The ideology of the Fourth Estate, as a countervailing power to government and party politics, is often manifest in an anti-institutional attitude. Meanwhile, audiences revel in the crude and clownish performances still deemed inappropriate (as of this writing) in official, government proceedings. Hall, Goldstein, and Ingram explain: "The exaggerated depictions of the sociopolitical world that [Donald] Trump crafts with his hands to oppose political correctness and disarm adversaries accrue visual capital in a mediatized twenty-first-century politics that is celebrity driven."[51] A gallery of photographs document pistol hand in action, followed by firing squad, script-reading Hillary, stiff Mitt Romney, low-energy Jeb, and wrist-flailing reporter. The quality press dips into the performance while signaling its anti-populist sensibilities, as when correspondents documented candidate Trump at the Iowa State Fair in late summer 2015, chewing pork chop on a stick.[52]

The earthquake election of 2016 awakened scholars to the specter of populist anti-elitism as consequential in political communication, including disproportionate press attention to an unqualified candidate early in the primary season.[53] Journalism's unique contributions to actualized anti-intellectualism are revealed in the reification and rationalization of a punitive public. My intent is to explicate journalism's complicity, keeping in mind that attitudes toward intellect are typically latent in public sentiment, in journalism, and in the relationship of journalism to the public.

If the profession periodically benefits from upsurges of resentment and suspicion, its understanding of these sentiments as mercurial and outside its jurisdiction helps to explain why the problem does not motivate reform. This is not to say that journalism lacks the facility to think beyond deadlines, incidents, and soundbites. The boundaries for reflexivity discussed in subsequent chapters are explained more by professional ideology than any cerebral ceiling. The science journalist Jim Holt, for instance, was able to write brilliantly about the darkest question in metaphysics—Why is there something rather than nothing?[54] Holt's comfort with Heidegger notwithstanding, the possibility that the press might benefit from a crisis of democracy exists somewhere beyond the realm of nothingness.

The attention cable news lavished on Trump in pre-primary coverage of the 2016 presidential race seemed reasonable to many journalists: incidents would eventually out him as unacceptable, as Sarah Palin was exposed in 2008 during interviews with Katie Couric. Journalists will acknowledge that they benefit from audience engagement during times of crisis. A bridge too far—along the road to reflexivity—is the premise that journalism is co-producer in a crisis of democracy. Yet Katz and Liebes are persuasive in arguing that cynicism and audience fragmentation explain a retreat from ceremonial "media events" such as anniversaries and patriotic holidays.[55] News media and anti-establishment agents are now invested in disruptive events.

Many normative questions in democratic theory address dilemmas that reporters and editors acknowledge. This is, strikingly, not the case with anti-intellectualism. A collapse of reflexivity elevates journalism's complicity in a media sphere where authoritarianism takes hold. Agitated audiences imagined by journalists absolve the profession from its role in mobilized irrationalism. Apart from a failure to confront illiberal advances in media and politics, journalism is also culpable when guarding absolutist beliefs against intellectual breaches. These transgressions offer opportunities for journalism to accrue cultural capital in the rendering of dissent into deviance.

This book, however, is not dystopian. Several chapters document circumstances that engender resistance to anti-intellectual sentiment within and beyond news media. While journalists rarely use the term "anti-intellectual" in the context of media,[56] they do recognize the problem when they see it in politics,[57] as evident in Dowd's nightmare of metallic beasts bursting out of Boehner. The willingness of reporters to call out politicians—and perhaps more importantly the public—represents a healthy expression of autonomy in an authoritarian zeitgeist.

Plan for the Book

The book is organized around the idea of journalism mediating the relationship between intellect and the public. Both intellectuals and sectors of the public can breach a cultural understanding—a long-standing but frayed social contract internalized in ways that keep hostility in check. Intellect is generally admired when instrumental, convenient when funneled into predictable partisan binaries, but suspect when free floating. Forthcoming chapters reveal the adaptability of news media in responding to transgressions across the cultural hierarchy: from ordinary citizens who revel in post-truth spectacle, to populist candidates, to radical intellectuals who offend mainstream beliefs.

Part I explores the relationship between news media and democratic decline. The disruptive force in this context is the punitive populism at play in the rise of Trump. Part II examines how news media respond when intellect is the aggressor. Part III focuses on professional education and reform to identify what might bring about a healthier relationship of journalism with the public.

Part I: News Media and Democratic Decline

Literature on democratic backsliding originated in political science but must now consider media-led weakening of norms. A juxtaposition of the contemporary climate with the postwar period illustrates the importance of grappling with the relationship of journalism to democratic decline. Media politics became the successor to party politics in this transition,[58] bringing forth new forms of participation but also setting loose irrational forces in contempt of the liberal order. In *The Paranoid Style in American Politics*, Hofstadter observed at midcentury: "Although American political life has rarely been touched by the most acute varieties of class conflict, it has served again and again as an arena for uncommonly angry minds."[59] In *Anti-intellectualism in American Life*, he documented the anti-rationalism of evangelical religion, the populist anti-elitism of politics, and the unreflective instrumentalism of business and education.[60] Other historians recognized that the book, published in 1963, did not anticipate the scope of media power in mobilizing resentment toward intellect.[61]

Political institutions participate in backsliding through the rhetoric of popular sovereignty and in maneuvers such as executive aggrandizement and harassment of the electorate.[62] Chapters 2 and 3 examine how journalism undermines its democratic commitments through appeals to its own values. In gatekeeping political messages, reporters and editors value conflict and tolerate incivility to highlight disagreement.[63] Yet incivility, broadly speaking, "involves a violation of norms of respect for other people or the democratic process."[64]

Journalists preside over the news as discursive space, in many circumstances still exerting control in the digital era. Steven Levitsky and Daniel Ziblatt, authors of *How Democracies Die,* explain what can happen when norm breaking becomes contagious.

> When a politician receives applause when threatening the press, other like-minded politicians are encouraged to do the same . . . As language becomes more extreme, the opponents of demagogues grow frightened and feel compelled to respond in kind. A tit-for-tat extremism can be unleashed. The results are not good.[65]

Levitsky and Ziblatt urge party leaders to act as candidate gatekeepers before campaigning begins. The problem is that media politics long ago succeeded party politics. Blumler and Kavanagh characterize the first two decades after World War II as the golden age of parties.[66] Today, anti-intellectualism is more authentically participatory than the animus Hofstadter chronicled. This disposition *should* compel journalism to protect the news as a venue for the public exercise of reason, especially during campaign season, when democratic norms and institutions are most at risk.

Chapter 2 proposes that journalism invests in democratic decline through the representation of grievance, at times benefiting from anti-elitist insurgence at the expense of other institutions. A brief history of professional education foreshadows how journalism would accommodate the rise of Trump. A discussion of how anti-intellectualism manifests in US culture then underscores how the failure of journalism to develop as an intellectual profession makes it vulnerable to illiberal sentiment.

Chapter 3 contemplates whether news media have internalized a proto-democratic duty to represent public mood in ways that redeem a politics of retribution. The chapter compares the near-instant commentaries of media scholars to interpretations of journalists following the startling election of 2016. While journalists were quite willing to recognize audiences as intolerant of quality news, they appeared unwilling to consider how this perception shaped their reporting. Disproportionate attention to candidate Trump was not so much justified as large sectors of the electorate were imagined as intolerant of reason-based reporting.

Part II: Social Control of Intellect

Many ideas go to die in the academic-media nexus, and no doubt many deserve that fate. Public scholars, however, seek audiences beyond higher education. Chapter 4 traces a web of controls at the interface of academia and media, where intellect is subject to populist sanction. Ideas that challenge orthodoxies must overcome the self-imposed instrumentalism of careerist faculty; a vigilante infrastructure primed for activation in response to transgressive discourse; and the risk-aversive communication of university administrations. Chapters 5–7 follow ideas that manage to navigate through the academic-media nexus. Additional hazards await, particularly from news outlets proximate to an intellectual breach.

Chapter 5 explicates a recursive regime to model how news media operate in a three-stage process—mobilization of resentment and suspicion; alignment of anti-rationalism with populist anti-elitism in symbolic action; and return to equilibrium. Activation of anti-intellectualism leaves behind residual antipathy, submerged in the next phase of equilibrium and available for reactivation when another breach occurs. The next two chapters illustrate recursive dynamics in a predatory (game on!) response to Ward Churchill, a University of Colorado ethnic studies scholar who mocked American innocence following the attacks of September 11, 2001. Chapter 6 chapter applies "social drama"—adapted from the anthropology of Victor Turner[67]—to portray a performance of media ritual in redress of an intellectual breach. Social drama would take years to play out—with Churchill finally banished from the Boulder campus—yet the outcome was foretold in a microcosm of initial story leads.

The power of journalism in patrolling boundaries of acceptable ideas is most clearly evident in media close to where a breach occurs. Chapter 7 documents how a Churchill essay was subject to rampant decontextualization as a precursor to social drama. Newspapers proximate to the CU Boulder campus proved unwilling to host any sustained critique of American innocence vis-à-vis 9/11. This finding implies that local journalism carries much of the burden for defending ideology at the national level. A dramatic case of idea rendering should, however, prompt a reparative response. Op-ed and letter writers challenged editors by engaging directly with Churchill's essay. Opinion writers rejected news frames by contemplating Churchill's ideas in their original context.

I confronted Front Range journalists with the same evidence of decontextualization reported in Chapter 7. In interviews, many expressed denial and ambivalence about their newspapers' refusal to engage Churchill's ideas. But journalists are not simply conscripted into the rendering of ideas into deviance, even in climates hostile to dissent. Several reporters described tactics of resistance. One Denver reporter poked back at editors in news copy, quoting sources who said they were sick of the media circus.

Part III: Education and Reform

Chapter 8 explores how journalism's dysfunctional relationship with imagined audiences is rooted in professional education. I worked with a research team from five colleges to measure anti-intellectualism among journalism students for the first time. The chapter documents experiences conducive to critical thinking, along with formative attitudes that engender resentment and suspicion of intellect. Digital natives who instinctively desire affirmation from social media are likely susceptible to self-censorship. In a corollary hypothesis, news majors eager to please audiences should be receptive to transparency as a principle of responsible practice. While transparency is heralded in media ethics textbooks,[68] affinity for transparency in this sample predicts *support* for journalistic anti-rationalism and anti-elitism. Students comfortable with subjecting their work to audience approval agree with survey items such as "Journalists should acknowledge that all opinions are equal in a democracy."

Chapter 9 returns to the academic-media nexus to ask whether dangerous professors could make journalism safe for intellect. I view the nexus as a field of fields in the sense that journalism relies on knowledge from disciplines across the scholarly landscape. A multitude of interacting, epistemic communities implies disorientation, not clear rules of engagement, but these conditions induce creative tension. I interviewed 25 professors targeted by vigilante watchlists to explore how risk-tolerant scholars cultivate relationships with reporters to convey dissent and to challenge orthodoxy. Successful brokering of ideas hinges on scholars and reporters jointly recognizing the constraints of newswork. Editors can still spike stories, but reporters motivated to challenge conventional narratives seek alliances with critical scholars.

The book concludes with a discussion about what intellectual journalism would look like. Earlier chapters examine aftershocks of the 2016 election, professional education, and other contexts that might engender a rethinking of media engagement with intellect. Drawing on these insights, Chapter 10 identifies where to look for intellectual journalism as an emerging ethos. Intellectual journalism asserts itself in a shift from public-oriented to craft-oriented accountability; the wisdom to reject misguided reform; alliances with risk-tolerant scholars; and forms of resistance that reject the bad faith of objectivity.

PART I
NEWS MEDIA AND DEMOCRATIC DECLINE

2

Peopling of the Journalistic Imagination

Four Kinds of Anti-intellectualism

News values enumerated in textbooks remain strikingly similar across a century of professional education, taking on the feel of oral history.[1] A deficit in reflexivity would explain why journalistic contributions to anti-intellectualism and democratic decline do not register as a critique. Journalism's folk theory of itself is distilled in the idea of a Fourth Estate, the people's representative, a role most evident when the formal branches of government fail.[2] Yet the aspiration to redeem democracy and to divine public will can lead news media into some dark places depending on the milieu imagined.

In the pre-digital era, representation of feeling and belief in mass media provided the primary, day-to-day proxy for public opinion. Kunelius and Reunanen contend that the coordination and command of public attention persists as a powerful resource in a fractured media environment. Toward the end of the twentieth century, journalists in Western democracies "detached themselves from the 'political' (i.e., choices facing political leaders), representing public opinion not so much as the *content* of what the public believed" as an "*attitude* toward the performance of powerful institutions."[3] Media in this interpretation portray audiences as an emotive, restive force. More troubling still is the view of journalism as not simply a medium of unfocused anger but as a streamline for irrational will formation demanding recognition and retribution of some sort.[4]

The anthropologists William Mazzarella interprets populism as "an intensified insistence of collective forces that are no longer adequately organized by formerly hegemonic social forms: a 'mattering-forth of the collective flesh.'"[5] Impolite guests at the civic dinner party would flaunt the low in the new millennium. "Yes We Can! Secede" T-shirts greeted Governor Rick Perry at a Don't-Mess-with-Texas rally in 2009. A decade after *Fox News* host Glenn Beck offered "FREE Rules for Patriots," the Donald Trump re-election campaign rolled out ozone-depleting hair spray. More is at stake in symbolic politics than spectacle, however. The angry carnival exemplifies Ernesto Laclau's claim that the universality of populist reason is always contaminated by "the peculiarity of the 'people' as a historical actor."[6]

This chapter contemplates the implications of a journalistic imagination populated by the semi-erudite[7] the mindset Adorno characterized as entitled yet intellectually impoverished. Today, anti-intellectualism is enculturated beyond journalism in echoing enclaves where confirmation of belief feels like thinking.[8] I posit that news media contribute to democratic decline through representation of grievance, benefiting from anti-elitist insurgence at the expense of other institutions. Political scientists refer to democratic backsliding as decline in support for norms that foster responsive governance and consent of the governed.[9] This literature, however, has not considered the role of intellect in the protection of democratic order. Expertise in political communication is corrupted in a myriad of ways, most notably in the rationalization of entrenched power, but when political regimes are undermined by disinformation,[10] an autonomous intellect becomes more pivotal as a check against both elitism and anti-elitism. Looking past the peculiarity of MAGA hats, Tea Party costumes, insults, and mind candy, some strains of punitive populism are motivated by valid grievances against elite exploitation. The fate of intellect, consequently, is the key to understanding the conditions in political communication that engender backsliding.

Reification of anger toward institutions of liberal democracy cripples the capacity of news media to work effectively with those same institutions in setting a policy agenda supportive of those left behind by neoliberalism. The result is a failure of responsiveness in both journalism and governance. A brief history of professional education followed by a discussion of how anti-intellectualism manifests in American culture help to explain why journalism is vulnerable to incursions of illiberal sentiment. Anti-rationalism, populist anti-elitism, and other strands of anti-intellectualism intertwine in the news, resistant to reflexivity, churning up contradictions of democracy, inviting further decline. I hope to explicate this dynamic in the following sections, although I want to avoid imposing a narrative arc on historical change. Journalism historian Kevin Lerner cautions that our current moment could be more cyclical than entropic.[11] While further backsliding is not inevitable, the moment calls for an interrogation of the Fourth Estate identity in journalism ideology. The chapter concludes with a critique of the normative theory that urges students and professionals to view themselves as handmaids of the people.

Development of Journalism Education

Journalism historian Jean Folkerts explains that the American press was anchored from the beginning "in both the printing trades and the world of intellectuals who recognized the value of newspapers in shaping public opinion."[12] After the Civil War, reporters sought professional standing to distinguish themselves from the public, but their editors and publishers were leery of college-educated men. Horace Greeley pleaded, "Of all horned cattle, deliver me from the college graduate."[13] Another publisher, Joseph Pulitzer, pioneered melodramatic reporting but sought a different legacy. "My idea is to recognize that journalism is, or ought to be, one of the great intellectual professions."[14]

The professional identity of the press crystallized in the Progressive Era of the late nineteenth and early twentieth centuries, expressed most forcefully by the conviction that journalists serve the citizenry in ways that compensate for the self-interest of politicians. In this view, later recognized as altruistic democracy,[15] there is nothing inherently wrong with US governance other than *current*, corrupt actors. The notion gives journalists credit for exposing scoundrels while ignoring *innate* contradictions of democracy, a system made more vulnerable by peopling of the journalistic imagination with angry audiences.

Journalism schools profess that reporters and editors are faithful servants of the people. Reporters are not phased, consequently, when sources complain: No one elected you. Schudson writes that there is "little in journalistic thinking today but contempt for political parties, yet no idea of what alternative associational forms could adequately organize political representation."[16] He notes that liberal northern newspapers in the 1960s criticized Martin Luther King Jr. for organizing protests that might spark violence. If parties, interest groups, and social movements are all suspect, journalism must find ways to represent citizens in ways that restore democracy.

Unlike other professions, journalism does not possess a monopoly on a body of esoteric knowledge, which complicates the claim of professional status. One solution is the principle of democratic inclusion made possible through clarity of expression. Journalists would become experts not in knowledge per se but in how to translate complexity. Translation without full comprehension imprints the interests of powerful actors keen on exploiting the piety of democratic inclusion. The National Press Club adopted the 1914

Journalism Creed of Walter Williams, founder of the world's first journalism school at the University of Missouri. Among the principles:

> I believe that the public journal is a public trust; that all connected with it are, to the full measure of their responsibility, trustees for the public; that acceptance of lesser service than the public service is betrayal of this trust.
>
> I believe that clear thinking and clear statement, accuracy and fairness, are fundamental to good journalism.[17]

News writing courses proliferated at US colleges through the early 1900s, but the vocational approach drew criticism from academics outside journalism, including University of Chicago President Robert Hutchins. In response to a Hutchins speech delivered at the Inland Press Association in 1938, the dean of Northwestern's journalism school insisted that his students possessed the capacity to evaluate issues and events superior to liberal arts graduates, especially those trained in "medieval classicism which President Hutchins would prescribe."[18] Journalism educators resisted assimilation of intellect when directed at the press itself, but Hutchins would have more to say.

Thirty years old when he became a university president, a philosopher of education, Hutchins was not impressed by the piety of journalism nor inspired by its creed. In 1944, he directed a team of 13 intellectuals to explore how mass media should function in democracy. The result of the deliberation—*A Free and Responsible Press*—warned that journalism can "debase and vulgarize mankind," inviting government regulation.[19] Media should provide citizens with "a truthful, comprehensive, and intelligent account of the day's events in a context which gives them meaning."[20]

Bates writes that the commission's intellectual self-regard did not inspire much deference when the report was published in 1947.[21] With the notable exception of H. L. Mencken, journalists expressed immense faith in ordinary citizens to inform themselves. The news was not some kind of public pedagogy and did not need to serve that function. Many reporters, in fact, recoiled from the word "journalist" and the implication of professionalism. They were newspaper men. Democracy would take care of itself if reporters were allowed to work unimpeded. To be sure, textbooks on occasion cautioned that news outlets carry responsibility to protect democratic norms and institutions. In *Newspaper Reporting of Public Affairs*, published in 1940, Bush explained that a chief function of the press is "to stand vigil for the public to guard it against unscrupulous exploiters, demagogues, and other real public enemies."[22] Many contemporary journalists nevertheless fall short of a synoptic understanding of how news functions in political communication, as evident in restrained reflexivity following the 2016 election (Chapter 3). Journalists located deviance in Trump supporters rather than consider whether epic news attention condoned the deviance.

The Hutchins Commission's critique lives on in professional education as the social responsibility theory of the press, and while it survives in newsrooms only as a slogan about "the public interest," many reporters accepted a culture of press criticism during the societal discord of the 1960s.[23] Decades earlier, Lippmann depicted the news as incapable of conveying truth;[24] by 1965 he was ready to endorse news reporting as an intellectual discipline.

> This growing professionalism is, I believe, the most radical innovation since the press became free of government control and censorship. For it introduces into the conscience of the working journalist a commitment to seek the truth which is independent and superior to all his other commitments—his commitment to publish newspapers that will sell, his commitment to his political party, his commitment even to promote the policies of his government.[25]

This radical independence became elitist and anti-democratic in much of the normative theory of cultural studies.[26] I return to this theme below in a discussion of intellectual prostration.

Journalism's identity in higher education is still contested, and while reporters and editors are notoriously disinterested in scholarship about their craft,[27] they sometimes take notice of the divide between professional and research faculty. In the 1960s, this became known as the "green-eye shades" of the copy desk at odds with the "chi-squares" of social science. News organizations and universities have learned to live with a skillset-mindset dissonance for strategic reasons, not because of an authentic fondness for each other.[28] In my experience, the green-eye-shade mentality persists in instructors assuring students that (1) journalists are already their own worst critics; (2) one has to practice journalism to truly understand it; and consequently (3) academic study of news media is mostly irrelevant.

As Reese observes, academic journalism "is organized with an interdisciplinary liberal arts focus, yet must address a professional constituency," making it "vulnerable to attack from all sides."[29] Media concentration and philanthropic clout led the industry to assert itself more aggressively in academia in the 1990s. This became evident, for example, in the Freedom Forum's larger presence at journalism conventions, when it warned against journalism losing its identity in communication studies.

The profession today struggles with an erosion of prestige and scores of failed newspapers. It turns to the academy for guidance on how to navigate the digital revolution. At the same time, backed by foundation money, media organizations seek leverage to influence curricula. Foundations sensed a new vulnerability for journalism schools in the vortex of digital disruption. In a statement not intended as ironic, Howard Finberg at the Poynter Institute explained in 2012: "Journalism education cannot teach its way to the future."[30] Eric Newton, then senior adviser to the president of the Knight Foundation, characterized journalism schools as "the caboose on the train of American media."[31] Web journalist Robert Hernandez appeals directly to students, prodding disciples to "hijack your school's assets."[32] As in professional practice, journalism in higher education has entered a betwixt-and-between phase of ambiguity and uncertainty, allowing for creative possibilities but also an unleashing of destructive impulses (Chapter 10). The unreflective instrumentalism of digital media "thought leaders" is justified, in part, by an inclination to democratize the training of journalists. And while mythology of the digital sublime conveys inevitable progress, hostile interventions into journalism education are also free to mine veins of aggression, resentment, and suspicion that run deep in American history.[33]

Anti-intellectualism in American Culture

Richard Hofstadter found trace elements of anti-intellectualism in the Great Awakening; in the migration of revivalists to "saddlebag and bear-meat country"[34]; and in more contemporary movements such as "life adjustment" in public schooling.[35] Published in 1963, the landmark *Anti-intellectualism in American Life* was embraced by artists and academics stung by the House Committee on Un-American Activities.

Anti-intellectualism in the American experience is endemic because of its deep connections with a democratic ethos.

> It first got its strong grip on our ways of thinking because it was fostered by
> an evangelical religion that also purveyed many humane and democratic

sentiments. It made its way into our politics because it became associated with our passion for equality. It has become formidable in our education partly because our educational beliefs are evangelically egalitarian.[36]

Hofstadter advocated a loose definition of this concept because it is at once an idea, a feeling, an attitude, and a notion. "The common strain that binds together the attitudes and ideas which I call anti-intellectual is a resentment and suspicion of the life of the mind and of those who are considered to represent it; and a disposition constantly to minimize the value of that life."[37]

Curiously, Hofstadter ignored mass media for the most part, although he corrected for that a year later in a *Harper's Magazine* essay. Broadcast media provide a "vast theatre" for the paranoid imagination, casting light on otherwise shadowy villains, among them Jesuit agents of the Vatican, international bankers, and Masons.[38] Suspicion of intellect and resentment of intellectuals require cultural support in latent forms and periodic activation in overt episodes to remain endemic (Chapter 5), implying a hegemonic role for journalism. Anti-intellectualism is not so much a constant thread as a fluctuating force, "drawings its motive power from varying sources."[39]

The sociologist Daniel Rigney teased out three themes in Hofstadter's understanding of what makes intellect unpopular: *religious anti-rationalism, populist anti-elitism,* and *unreflective instrumentalism.*[40] Anti-rationalism registers an instinct to protect the moral foundations of sanctity, loyalty, and authority against intellect's relentless critique. The intrusiveness of intellect—its probing in places it does not belong—might help to explain the flaunting of the low in response. The cultural milieu today is characterized by distrust of authority and experts, coupled with an extension of anti-rationalism from fundamentalist religion to secular areas of political expression. For large sectors of the citizenry, friendly media have supplemented if not replaced religious organizations as venues for confirmation of belief and identity.[41]

In social media, a spreading of the faith is practiced in collective misintelligence, bridging anti-rationalism with populist anti-elitism. This interpretation echoes recent scholarship showing that as network-supported extremity in opposition to policy rises, objective knowledge plummets. Zollo et al. conducted a massive content analysis of Facebook to show how conspiracy theories diffuse in homogeneous and polarized communities.[42] As motivation for the study, the research team noted the case of Jade Helm 15. Observers of a routine military exercise in the summer of 2015 perceived the beginning of civil war.

Rigney writes that populist anti-elitism encompasses, among other traits, "a mistrust of claims to superior knowledge or wisdom on the part of an educated elite."[43] In reactionary inflections, populist anti-elitism is often directed at intellectuals, a social category viewed as subversive and disloyal. A rebellious populism, meanwhile, is crucial to the identity of progressive politics, as I discuss below with reference to academic anti-elitism as cultural critique.

An unfortunate legacy in Hofstadter's midcentury portrayal of anomie is the reduction of populism into an irrationality of the masses. Historians since the 1950s have discredited the etiology in which demographic support for Senator Joseph McCarthy was somehow rooted in the agrarian populism of the 1890s.[44] Populism is a frequent topic of contemporary news and commentary, but writers tend to focus on style rather than the historic and economic contexts from which populist movements arise. This creates a disorientation in which almost any idea, initiative, or candidate is labeled populist. On the other hand, Hofstadter was prescient in his view of populist anti-elitism as isotopic, its egalitarian inclinations too often breaking down into nativist aggression.[45] The punitive populism of contemporary politics is actualized, confident in its ability to extract punishment from elites and to intervene in their institutions. Hofstadter's isotope seems more stable in "convergence culture," a form of populism that joins the lesson-giving and lifestyle instruction of television with the do-it-yourself disaffection of web-based media.[46]

Returning to Rigney's typology, unreflective instrumentalism devalues "forms of thought that do not promise relatively immediate practical payoffs."[47] The disposition is concerned with rewards and costs, "and does not imply a hostility to reason per se." If not hostility, Rigney conveys manipulation in the instrumental production of media content.

The effects of mass media on attitudes toward intellect are certainly multiple and ambiguous. On the one hand, mass communication greatly expands the sheer volume of information available for public consumption. On the other hand, much of this information comes preinterpreted for easy digestion and laden with hidden assumptions, saving consumers the work of having to interpret it for themselves. Commodified information naturally tends to reflect the assumptions and interests of those who produce it, and its producers are not driven entirely by a passion to promote critical reflection.[48]

Commodified information implies linkages among anti-intellectualism, the manufacturing of consent, and other critical perspectives in which news media perpetuate the internalized assumptions that support prevailing ideology.[49] News as a commodity provides a departure for how I portray the rendering of intellectual dissent into deviance, beginning in Chapter 5. My analysis here and throughout the book is distinct from a political economy approach, however, in the view that anti-intellectualism serves the interest of journalism first in preserving or enhancing its cultural authority.

Rigney recognized that Hofstadter failed to articulate *unreflective hedonism* as a fourth kind of anti-intellectualism, a dominate force in mass communication following World War II that would become, for many theorists, a sedative in the postmodern condition.[50] The contemporary crisis of attention, in this reckoning, is rooted much deeper than the popularity of digital technology.

Rigney observed that "the power of media to define the terms of public discourse" captured the imagination of social critics following Hofstadter.

> Postman (1985), for example, examines public discourse in an age dominated by entertainment industries, concluding that the electronic media have not produced Orwell's dark vision of an externally imposed oppression after all, but rather something more akin to Huxley's vision of a brave new world, a trivialized culture that creates an almost limitless appetite for amusement and diversion. News and education are now essentially popular forms of entertainment, competing with situation comedies and video games for the fun-consumer's shortened span of attention.[51]

Authoritarian messaging in campaign seasons and other contexts recognizes that these visions are not a binary in post-truth politics: oppression without overt intimidation is possible when critical thinking wallows under relentless distraction.

Claussen illustrates the affinity of instrumentalism with hedonism in *Anti-intellectualism in American Media: Magazines and Higher Education.*[52] In the analysis of publications since the G. I. Bill of 1944, he finds superficial portrayals of college life: parties, fraternities, tailgates, hazing, hippies, binging, prospects for marriage. Magazines rarely showed interest in the life of the mind—the actual work of higher education. Media consumers, not surprisingly, evaluate colleges based on vocational and hedonistic expectations. Unreflective instrumentalism is not benign, not simply lacking in curiosity, but embodies impatience with a free-floating intellect that can manifest in the intolerance of anti-rationalism and the vengeance of anti-elitism (Chapter 4).

Editors and reporters are unlikely to recognize the news as I characterize it: a product that trivializes intellect up until intellect is recognized as dangerous. My goal in the next section is to explain how strands of anti-intellectualism are intertwined in reporting, and how these sentiments are condoned by journalists *in their own terms*. This hidden curriculum of the news, in turn, justifies representation of grievance while ensuring that the profession's complicity in democratic decline remains incomprehensible to itself.

Anti-intellectualism in the News

Press historians have observed how the ideology and epistemology of US journalism reinforced each other in a genuine alliance with populist sentiment. Rutenbeck chronicled a "triumph of news over ideas" during the late nineteenth century and early twentieth century, an era marked by "the passing of personal, partisan, idea-centered journalism."[53] The transition represented not just the ascendance of commercial logic but an assertion of professional identity and craft, with the capacity to exhibit and to expose prized over nimbleness in conceptual exchange. Pride in the unmasking of power reflects an epistemology of essentialism, whereby nuance is viewed as dissemblance. The unmasking role is thereby vulnerable to anti-intellectual appropriation. Neo-McCarthyism and memes of the intellectual as traitor persist as a threat to an independent press but not because of external, overt intimidation.[54]

A suspicious populism resonates at deep levels of journalistic conviction. Sociologist Herbert Gans argued that American journalism should be understood as a "paraideology" to distinguish "an aggregate of only partially thought-out values" from an "integrated, more doctrinaire set of values usually defined as ideology."[55] In participant-observation of newsrooms in the 1970s, he documented eight enduring values that underscore a "vision of the good nation and society."[56] Among these, altruistic democracy, small-town pastoralism, ethnocentrism, moderatism, and respect for social order readily play into the populist narrative of "the pure people" spontaneously aligned against cultural elites.[57]

Journalistic objectivity is in several respects conducive to a disciplined and humble epistemology—moderatism in the terminology of Gans. In a survey of newspaper journalists and academics, Post found that the former expressed more doubts about objectivity as a basis for identifying causes and consequences.[58] Journalists typically confront unique circumstances and without the systemic methods of science, are reluctant to speculate about causality.

A constrained epistemology aligns with a professional ideology of moderatism in the engagement of ideas. Journalism's assertion of professionalism through impartial news in the nineteenth century helps to explain its suspicion of theories as systems of thought.[59] The knowledge work of journalism depends on the immediate observation of incidents, circumstances, and people. Theory would seem to wipe a translucent film over these observations or, conversely, to clarify reasons for anarchy and extremism.

With the rise of electronic media in the twentieth century, fear of propaganda and "brainwashing" implicated journalism in a conundrum of democracy. Hogan writes that the "central paradox of America's constitutional tradition lies in a persistent tension between our commitment to popular sovereignty and fears that 'the people' might be too easily distracted or manipulated to govern themselves."[60] To the extent that journalists are suspicious of intellectuals, they are unlikely to make the effort to comprehend their methods and motives. In a protective (and perhaps patronizing) relationship, journalism shields the public from systems of thought, leaving media consumers more receptive—not less so—to distraction and manipulation. In a media ecosystem that some view as increasingly hospitable to populist rancor aligned with creeping authoritarianism,[61] journalists forgo tools of comprehension for themselves and their audiences.[62]

Practices associated with objectivity establish the appearance of authenticity, impartiality, and trustworthiness. Journalism presents itself as simply a medium from which external sources are granted access. Attribution and other protocols could be described as non-intellectual in that they substitute formalism for critical judgment. Sources with privileged access know the rules of the game and consequently subsidize reporting with predigested information. The same routines in news production help to overcome intellectual deficits when reporters interact with sources with greater technical proficiency or substantive knowledge. Under deadline pressure, the challenge for journalism is to fit facts, data, and interpretive schemes into story templates rather than to engage with a free-floating intellect. In this respect, intellectual deficits of American journalism—or perhaps the withholding of intellectual proficiency in the case of quality media—constitute strategic assets in efficient newswork.

All of these tactics arguably serve journalism first, with some ideas left intact to nourish the public sphere. Scholars of political economy typically characterize the news paradigm as deferential if not submissive to elite power. I view news media's complicity in anti-intellectualism, by contrast, as *serving the interest of journalism itself* in preserving or enhancing its cultural status as an arbiter of legitimate discourse.[63]

Prior to the 2016 election, scholars began to challenge whether moderatism still applies in reporting, which often favors polarization in representations of advocacy groups[64] and extremists in coverage of Congress.[65] Quoting lawmakers who reliably toss ideological bombs is hardly welcoming of intellect. If anything, the practice confirms populist contempt for systems of belief that seemingly consume elites. For audiences already predisposed to dislike the establishment, the impression left by political news is that to give ideas free rein is to invite chaos. Reporters' reliance on ideological extremists is consequently damaging to intellect's reputation even as the practice might perpetuate within journalism the delusion that it accommodates a broad spectrum of political thought. A caveat, in an era of post-truth politics, is that the news has enlarged its sphere of legitimate discourse by including authoritarian rhetoric, a dynamic the next chapter explores in the massive attention to candidate Trump in 2015–2016.

This unsettling development reveals the power of populist anti-elitism to undermine not just institutions but also theory itself. Hallin's widely cited model of journalism protecting boundaries between legitimate and deviant discourse did not anticipate the mainstreaming of illiberal rhetoric.[66] The 2016 election might have confirmed a loosening of journalism's hold on Enlightenment principles—in particular a duty to guard conditions for reason-giving discourse.

A fundamental revision of theory is needed to account for journalism's relationship to irrationalism as an emotive, fluctuating force. With this goal in mind, the next section juxtaposes Hofstadter's era with postmillennial politics. The dimensions of anti-intellectualism fall into a framework that helps to explain journalism's contribution to democratic decline.

Representation of Grievance

Left free, there is nothing intellect "will not reconsider, analyze, throw into question."[67] By contrast, anti-rationalists cradle their beliefs; Hofstadter characterized the paranoid style as "almost touching" in its concern with factuality.[68] Indeed, this literature seeks to be more coherent than the real world. But angry minds do not constitute a caucus. Anti-rationalists do respond to offense, however. Instrumentalists, by contrast, are too focused, and hedonists are too distracted, to bother with disagreeable ideas. Populist anti-elitists stand out among the four as politically productive. They operationalize and further entwine anti-rationalism, unreflective instrumentalism, and hedonism (Chapter 5). Populism relies on a thin ideology of the pure people versus the corrupt elite, making it adaptable to a range of ideologies and grievances.[69] It can affix not only to its anti-intellectual cousins but also to journalism as a carrier. Without a populist insurgence, and without journalism as an accomplice, anti-rationalism wallows in resentment. Instrumentalism and hedonism are not yet politicized.[70]

This discussion draws from Catherine Liu's history of antipathy toward intellect since the postwar period.[71] She recounts how cultural populism became the nation's consensus politics, embraced by the left and right, a project pioneered by progressive academics in the 1980s and subsequently taken up by conservative intellectuals. With cultural studies as its headwaters, academic populism flowed through discourse attacking Hofstadter, Adorno, and other midcentury thinkers, casting them as elitist in their defense of aesthetic autonomy. Hofstadter, for his part, judged popular culture as hospitable to an otherwise inarticulate authoritarianism. In more elaborate critiques, Adorno depicted mass media as a resource that allows consumers to indulge in a democratic irrationalism less dependent on despotic entrepreneurs.

In 1952–1953, Adorno studied the astrology column introduced by the *Los Angeles Times*.[72] Liu writes that for Adorno, "believing in the irrational connection between celestial bodies and one's personal fate represented a cognitive shortcut and a leap into the abyss of the mystical and magical systems that defied the out-of-touch experts and eggheads who did not, after all, know it all."[73] Through horoscopes and letters to the editor, newspapers signaled that anyone could be an expert, if not in science then in consumption, lifestyle, and politics. This constituted a radical and rapid democratization of knowledge.

Liu explains that popular astrology conferred dignity on readers whose formal education and labor had become increasingly administered by forces beyond their control. Mass testing for intelligence turned high schools into "holding tanks for social triage," ensuring class reproduction and inequality.[74] Against such powerlessness, academic populists viewed reason as deformed in technoscientific oppression. In subjective experiences of media entertainment, they imagined "a world of ordinary people with popular tastes and deep passions who, as fans and amateurs, could finally create a culture of their own that eluded the experts."[75] In *No Respect: Intellectuals and Popular Culture*, for example, Ross celebrated the carnivalesque of low culture, including the skeptics who stood up to the preening science of global warming.[76] Anti-elitism as cultural critique resonated beyond higher education in the seeding of populist politics. Conservative intellectuals reworked cultural studies themes to direct resentment against the same scholars who gifted them with the polemic.

News media—an institution with obligations to represent public opinion—must somehow adjust to this intermingling of hedonism, anti-rationalism, and populist anti-elitism. Some indulgence in these sentiments could be viewed as benign if Madisonian, mediating institutions modulate affect. In the decades leading up to the Trump presidency, sectors of journalism might appease or resist anti-liberal forces as they intertwine and gain strength. In a more aggressive, populist posture, the press might draw on the profession's faithful servant conceit to protect its standing at the expense of other institutions.

Political scientists have recognized the press as a political institution at least since the publication of Douglass Cater's *The Fourth Branch of Government* in 1959.[77] Direct sponsorship of the press by political parties prevailed through the mid-nineteenth century. Modern journalism relies instead on subsidies that extend beyond press releases and soundbites to themes, frames, and policy agendas promoted by elected officials. In *Governing with the News*, Cook argues that policymaking and newsmaking "are increasingly intertwined to the point of being indistinguishable."[78] What journalists perceive as a ploy to make news might be viewed by officials as an effort to shape policy.

Cook defines institutions in terms of organizations perceived within society to reliably preside over a particular sphere. Scholarship generally confirms a "homogeneity hypothesis" in political news.[79] Across modalities, news outlets preside over politics in ways that reduce uncertainty under deadline and reinforce professional consensus over the most important issues and actors on any given day of coverage. Like the rest of us, journalists enjoy a good fight and are consequently receptive to populist elements. But populism is also compatible with the ideology of critical professionalism, a stance that distances journalism from established parties while assuming the role of a superior representative. A team of scholars analyzed styles of populist news in 11 countries, and while they documented lowbrow and highbrow genres, the interpretive schemes of *upscale* magazines were more people-centric and *anti-elitist* compared with the content of commercially driven media.[80] As noted above, journalists apparently pick up in professional training the notion that they must represent the public in ways that compensate for the self-interest of parties, elected leaders, and interest groups.

From an ontological perspective, "the people" do not exist a priori but are constituted in and through discourse. The tone and pitch of voices heard in the news are shaped by how reporters and editors imagine audiences. Broadly speaking, nations exist in the minds of their members in "imagined communities,"[81] and while these social constructs are philosophically impoverished, a horizontal comradeship spreads through nationalist feeling. Contemporary theory understands imagined communities as unstable depending on macro-level conditions such as perceived opinion climate and micro-level factors such as the motivations of message senders and receivers.[82] Brubaker explains that the people as a political subject can take on at least three meanings in populist discourse.

> It can refer to the *common* or *ordinary* people, the people as plebs, to whom recognition, respect, or resources should be redistributed; to the *sovereign* people, the people as demos, to which power should be restored; or to the *bounded* and *distinct* people, the people as a moral, cultural, or political community, which should be protected against various threats.[83]

Polysemy of "the people" allows news media to assert cultural and political authority, as when the plebs deserve respect, the demos demand change, or the community requires support against some offense. Journalism can directly and immediately rectify respect and acknowledge insult, showing off its power in the face of other political institutions, but it cannot deliver policy on its own. Populism as an expression of authoritarian instinct subordinates socioeconomic cleavage to intra-political conflict.[84] Confined to symbolic politics, populism in this mode takes flight from the material world of working conditions, exploitation of labor, and deaths of despair. News media contribute to policy incoherence, frustration, and anger when objective class interests are not articulated, leading to a crisis of journalistic and governmental responsiveness.

Lebow writes that if the policy sector is perceived as a dead end, consumerized citizenship is reduced to "a disjointed assortment of privatized simulacra of a public."[85] And when the entire political system is viewed with contempt, media are incentivized to distance themselves from other institutions. In these atmospherics, journalism benefits by disassociating itself from the issue-party-policy nexus, again suggesting that news media gain political status by undermining legitimation of other institutions. Reification of a punitive public implicates journalism in democratic decline, and not just in the portrayal of institutions as currently corrupt or dysfunctional, but also in the amplification of contradictions innate to democracy. As Mazzarella explains, populism "expresses the structural scandals of democracy: the presumptive sovereignty of the unqualified, the tension between liberty and equality, the apparently lockstep parallel growth of mass enfranchisement and administrative opacity."[86]

The immediacy of an affective news stream allocates to journalism a power not available to other institutions.[87] Populism is a genuinely collective phenomenon, allowing news media to reclaim a leading role in mass communication. But when groups with valid grievances are not constituted in *policy* aspirations, journalism's representative function obliterates its capacity to collaborate with elected leaders in advancing remedies. News media can make up for complicity in failed policy with affirmation of frustration. Since publication of Cook's *Governing with the News* in 1998, journalism may have shifted as a political institution from policy collaboration with government to a pathological regime of affective representation.

The contemporary climate reminds some historians of the world of the 1930s and 1940s; they reference themes, devices, and tricks of false prophets.[88] Journalism, for its part, cannot claim innocence when it reifies anger beyond the capacity of institutions to productively represent and channel affect. Tyranny is enabled by the abandonment of rationality in its vision of progress. It crystallizes in oppressive governance. The immediacy of viral frustration overcomes the rhythms of delegation and the delays of deliberation.[89] In the worst outcome, the populist leader becomes the internalized drone for the body politic, sensing what people want directly, organically, preempting conflict.

Intellectual Prostration

The assimilation of irrationalism into news production situates journalism in democracy as a peculiar and paradoxical institution: news media provide an expanded representative function but are not formally responsible for ensuring system stability. This perspective seeks to make sense of a Manichean defeatism in news media as a political institution, such that expectations for rational restraint are matched by a cultural force seemingly beyond journalism's control. Populist energies rise up through many sectors of media: in talk radio, the tabloid press, and in social media as engines of conspiracy and vitriol. Populism with punitive motives nevertheless requires uptake in mainstream and elite media to achieve some measure of respect.[90] Sustained news attention, particularly during election cycles, ensures democratic contradiction if not crisis.[91]

The Fourth Estate as trustee of the public is more salient to journalists than the Fourth Estate as trustee of democracy. Responsibilities of news organizations should extend, at the very least, to do no harm. Ostensibly this applies to media not representing public sentiment in ways that accelerate democratic decline. Journalism is at once *tolerant of anti-intellectualism* in representation of illiberal sentiment (Chapter 3) and *intolerant of intellect* when the parochial press protects moral communities (Chapters 5–7). No doubt these attitudes are internalized rather than taught explicitly. Journalism students become carriers of anti-rationalism by internalizing the duty to stand guard against ideas that might offend audiences (Chapter 8). In a survey I supervised at my campus and four other colleges, news majors who agreed with anti-rational sentiments such as "Journalists should include religious beliefs as much as science in debates about public policy" also endorsed anti-elitist statements such as "Journalists should expose professors who undermine American values."

Something is amiss in the normative theory that shapes professional identity. The vexed relationship between intellect and journalism implies a self-defeating epistemology: *intellectual prostration,* a concept that highlights how knowledge institutions undermine themselves. Hofstadter reflected on the predicament of intellectuals in democracy.

> The intellectual class, whether or not it enjoys many of the privileges of an elite, is of necessity elite in its manner of thinking and functioning. . . . [Intellectuals] have thus found themselves engaged in incompatible efforts: They have tried to be good and believing citizens of a democratic society and at the same time to resist the vulgarization of culture which that society constantly produces. It is rare for an American intellectual to confront candidly the unresolvable conflict between the elite character of his own class and his democratic aspirations.[92]

As I noted in Chapter 1, many reporters, editors, and columnists are fairly described as public intellectuals. The conflict Hofstadter describes is felt acutely in the press, where intellectual prostration takes forms such as the willingness of writers to humiliate themselves in sciencey-sounding stories and the learned helplessness of reporters checkmating scientific authority with science denial. Prostration toward the public is also signaled in aggressive responses when journalists perceive a need to defend virtuous audiences against treasonous intellectuals (Chapters 5–7).

The form of intellectual prostration I have in mind does not succumb to economic temptation, an outcome most often associated with unreflective instrumentalism. As a subclass of anti-elitism, intellectual prostration conforms instead to a political imperative. Expressions of solidarity occur through a negation of autonomy, method, and privileged knowledge. This democratic strain of anti-intellectualism could be situated in the history of American ideas, as it resonates with some articulations of intuitionism, romanticism, and pragmatism.[93] Suffice to say for our purposes, intellectual prostration falls under democratic anti-intellectualism rather than the aristocratic anti-intellectualism in which only priests, theologians, and metaphysicians can divine transcendent truth.

Liu writes that academic anti-elitism "allows us to believe that what is important for intellectuals and academics is not refining or communicating knowledge by using substantive arguments to persuade our interlocutors."[94] All we have to do is "create some kind of affective and epistemological 'accessibility' in order to have done something politically effective." Academic anti-elitism is, ironically, often untranslatable to the people from whom solidarity is sought. "Who wants to hear a bunch of professors and graduate students flagellate each other and themselves for their 'normativity'?"

Intellectual prostration is particularly pernicious in journalism, where there is more at stake. Intellect renounces its elite status, feeding on itself in an effort to show allegiance toward ordinary citizens. Media scholar Robert Manoff, for example, affirms the sentiment in his vision of professional education: "Because the journalist is the handmaiden of the citizen, citizenship must be on the table as we consider the future of journalism and journalism education."[95]

Compared with cultural studies, anti-elitism in elite journalism is less esoteric and, as a consequence, less narcissistic in the display of hallow gestures. Journalism's contribution to government responsiveness could model the kind of empathy Barbara Ehrenreich evoked in *Nickle and Dimed: On*

Getting by in America[96] combined with expertise to bolster policy agenda setting. Collaboration of journalism with intellect in this fashion is *not* anti-democratic—it articulates a devotion to equality by comprehending and narrating the conditions in which human dignity might thrive.

Intellectual prostration might have reached its peak in civic/public journalism of the 1990s. Academic advocates portrayed the public in eclipse, alienated from civic life, reduced by media to passive spectators. Journalism in this vision should convene conversation rather than simply unload facts. Rosen assured journalists that experts are no "substitute for the public's best judgment."[97] Public journalism preceded meaningful innovations in areas such as crowdsourcing, citizen journalism, and solutions journalism. It deserves credit for promoting reflexivity in the recognition that because journalism participates in the construction of social reality, it is obligated to advocate in the public interest in practices such as purposeful agenda setting and deliberative framing.

Public journalism sought only thin grounding in communitarian ethics, however.[98] It did not anticipate the viral populism enabled by digital media. The public emerged from eclipse with a vengeance, setting the stage for the Trump presidency. A healthy skepticism of experts in the civic-engagement literature was not accompanied, for the most part, by an embrace of intellect as a corrective to parochial media. Direct partnerships with audiences, including the promotion of a common good, threaten journalists' ability to question the very consensus about what constitutes the common good.[99] Consensus-seeking journalism is too often complicit in suppression of dissent, particularly in parochial media (Chapter 7).[100]

In a textual analysis of trade magazines, Ferrucci and Nelson find that the "engaged journalism" popular today is remarkably similar to public journalism in the way that audiences are imagined: they are eager to participate in civic life, possess wisdom that news outlets ignore, and view journalists as remote elitists.[101] Imagined audiences are, in turn, remarkably similar to how citizens are perceived in the "folk theory of democracy." Achen and Bartels describe this mythology in *Democracy for Realists*.[102] The book interrogates the belief that rational voters control policy and that government is consequently responsive to thoughtful citizenship. In the centerpiece example, New Jersey voters punished Woodrow Wilson for not preventing shark attacks in the summer of 1916.

Schudson acknowledges that while "expertise is a permanent embarrassment to democratic theory,"[103] the solution is to imagine a leash long enough so that public policy benefits from knowledge discovery without experts becoming toadies of politicians. I would only caution that the leash not extend to intellect. The meager interest in normative theory about how to accommodate intellect in journalism implies that intellect and expertise are easily conflated. The intellect defended by Hofstadter in the wake of McCarthyism strangles on a leash. Normative theory that seeks to hold intellect accountable to the public does not comprehend the nature of intellect in the first place. Intellect does not respond well to showdowns, to being exposed; it is not accountable to the public.

This lack of accountability does not sit well in American news media,[104] nor in anti-elitism as cultural critique in the academy,[105] but without an accommodation for intellect, journalism spirals into a self-referential pathology. In a recursive regime, journalism seeks to preserve its diminished authority by condoning anger directed against itself (Chapters 5, 10). As a first step toward accommodation of intellect, reporters and editors should shed their sensitivity about being perceived as elitist. Professional education and normative theory should advance an unapologetic defense of independent, critical thinking. An aspirational profession would anticipate new manifestations of reflexivity as motivation for resistance to anti-intellectual forces. Meanwhile, theorists in democratic communication should take intellectual journalism seriously; I can say that my keyboard does not cue a laugh track when I type "intellectual journalism."

We should not be distracted by fascist attacks on news media to recognize that democracy is undermined by appeals to its own values. At least some of the conceptual preconditions for crisis are likely articulated in critiques of journalism. Cultural studies, for example, is often offended by the "aura of scientism and rationality" that the quality press evokes.[106] Outcomes that advocates of communitarian journalism hoped for at the end of the millennium—a strong public combined with a humbled press—are defining features of the post-truth era. Symmetries are striking. Initiatives to revitalize community in the 1990s depicted citizens as isolated, mere spectators of journalism as a powerful institution that serves its own ends. In a mirror reversal, anti-media populism today looms as a powerful force that exploits the vulnerability of journalism, a loosely confederated field without the collective will and normative commitments it must possess to defend itself.

3

Eclipse of Reflexivity in the Rise of Trump

Journalists evoke "the public" in language at once celebratory and obeisant, a dynamic captured by James Carey: "The god term of journalism—the be-all and end-all, the term without which the enterprise fails to make sense, is the public."[1] The god of Romans 12 ("Vengeance is mine . . .") comes to mind for how journalists might view sectors of the citizenry when the press is viewed as an enemy of the people. Populist anger in election seasons constitutes both a threat to reason-based reporting and an opportunity for journalism to command public attention in ways reminiscent of the pre-digital era. While anti-intellectualism is often characterized as a diffusive and latent sentiment, it is periodically mobilized when populist rhetoric opposes virtues of "the people" against privileges of the ruling elite.[2] Digital and legacy news media doubtlessly motivate grassroots movements in an oppositional sense (e.g., Tea Party against the quality press). Journalism nevertheless reasserts a central role in mass communication when it provokes attention back toward itself, thereby enhancing its relevance as a gatekeeper of candidates and their liberal/illiberal pronouncements.[3]

This chapter focuses on punitive populism as a type of antipathy at play in campaign politics and condoned in news media even as its resentment extends to the press. Block and Negrine propose that while news media are not solely responsible for the advance of anti-elitist sentiment in the United States, the United Kingdom, and Venezuela, contemporary populism relies on a distinctive style of political communication to "connect with the political feelings, aspirations, and needs of those who feel disenchanted, excluded, aggrieved, and/or disadvantaged by conventional center-ground politics."[4]

In 2015–2016, the eventual Republican nominee for president obtained the blessing of Fox News but also "free" and substantial coverage from the quality press, including *The New York Times* and *The Washington Post*.[5] Neither Trump's poll numbers nor fundraising ability nor endorsements explains the pre-primary level of attention. Polls, fundraising, and endorsements are the criteria that journalists themselves use when cornered to justify attention to one candidate more than another. These represent, in journalistic thinking,

Where Ideas Go to Die. Michael McDevitt, Oxford University Press (2020). © Oxford University Press.
DOI: 10.1093/oso/9780190869946.001.0001

objective measures of candidate viability. I want to emphasize how minimal this rationale is for allocating the fiercely contested resource of news attention. By contrast, news outlets could lay down explicit, policy-oriented criteria, such as the coherence and financial integrity of candidates' proposals.[6] Leaving aside any higher aspiration for campaign coverage, Trump still failed to meet journalism's criteria for recognition as a serious candidate during the "invisible primary"—the period when candidates jostle before votes are cast in the first primaries and caucuses.

In the words of political scientist Thomas Patterson, "Journalists seemed unmindful that they and not the electorate were Trump's first audience."[7] With no credentials and no substantial constituency at the time, Trump understood instinctively that respectable media would cooperate. Campaign correspondents and their editors apparently imagined a populist response to Trump as a precursor to actual evidence of widespread public support. In this view, populist sentiment takes on a looking-glass quality in newswork, existing as a narrative template because journalists, along with those adept at media manipulation, anticipate its activation.

Affirmation of anger in conjunction with downplaying of policy expertise is antithetical to journalism's understanding of its contribution to an informed electorate. The contradiction motivates an appraisal of how journalists critiqued their work in the rise of Trump. I took advantage of a rare opportunity to compare the near-instant analysis of media scholars to the interpretations of journalists following the election. Textual analysis documents the limits of reflexivity when journalists articulate concerns about reporting, their audiences, and, most importantly, the relationship between the press and the public. The chapter concludes with a discussion as to whether news media have internalized a proto-democratic duty to represent public mood in ways that justify a politics of retribution.

Boundaries of Reflexivity

A *Judge* magazine cartoon from 1896 depicts the populism of William Jennings Bryan as a snake swallowing a mule, the latter representing the Democratic Party. Populism considers society "to be ultimately separated into two homogeneous and antagonistic groups, 'the pure people' versus 'the corrupt elite.'"[8] Media indulgence in imaginary of the *volonté générale* (general will) is at once opportunistic in election campaigns, sustaining a mesmerizing drama, and destructive to journalism itself when populism becomes predatory toward its host. To the extent that journalism imagines and represents the public as an illiberal force, some form of reflexivity is needed as a corrective.

Journalists are increasingly willing to criticize their work in digital spaces and through interactions with critics, signifying a shift from objectivity to transparency in the discourse of legitimation.[9] Media sociology portrays journalism as adaptive in forms of reflexivity such as paradigm repair,[10] paradigm change,[11] and boundary work.[12] Professional reflexivity refers to "journalists' capacity for self-awareness; their ability to recognize influences and changes in their environment, alter the course of their actions, and renegotiate their professional self-images as a result."[13]

Anti-intellectualism, however, is rarely up for discussion in newsrooms or classrooms where the profession is taught. Claussen writes that news media

> have rarely covered intellectuals *as intellectuals* or even employed the word "anti-intellectual." Its relatively recent coining aside, mass media surely have been unlikely to use such a clearly negative-sounding word to label themselves, their readers, their advertisers or their news sources.[14]

While reflexivity allows journalists to negotiate the boundaries of responsible practice, transparency is itself subject to boundaries for the types of critiques that become salient.[15]

Notwithstanding journalists' resistance to a critique of their work as anti-intellectual, commodified information influences the public's capacity for critical thinking, tolerance for complexity, and receptivity to new ideas.[16] Still, anti-intellectualism in news judgment is difficult to conceptualize and to operationalize because it entails opportunities not taken, context not provided, ideas otherwise not engaged. The problem persists as a murky presence in journalism as an interpretive community, rarely recognized in metajournalistic discourse, not readily subject to measurement, and difficult to isolate from other forces.

News commentators, to be sure, were more likely to allude to anti-intellectualism with the advent of conservative populism in the modern presidency, beginning with Dwight D. Eisenhower.[17] A "renaissance of anti-intellectualism" is perhaps most salient to journalists on the campaign trail.[18] In the fall of 2015, CNBC moderator John Harwood asked Donald Trump if he were running a "comic-book version" of a presidential campaign.

Reporters and editors doubtlessly recognize anti-intellectualism in their audiences when it flares up. Following the "comic-book" question, no one missed the positive feedback Marco Rubio received from the audience when he quipped: "We need more welders and less philosophers."

Conditions that compromise newswork periodically induce paradigm repair, although not necessarily in ways that embrace professional responsibility, as when "pack journalists bash pack journalism."[19] As a theoretical perspective, paradigm repair itself seems problematic if the public is viewed as more moralistic than deliberative. The textual analysis below anticipates articulations of reflexivity in which practice is not so much justified to the public as the public is imagined in ways that justify problematic practice. I consequently propose *professional realism* as a form of reflexivity to account for how audiences are viewed from a populist prism.

Professional realism could be viewed as an adaptation of paradigm repair for circumstances in which journalists lower their expectations of the public. Professional realism refers not to repair of normative or deviant practice but to a retreat from principles of deliberation. Journalists insist on realistic boundaries for what is possible in ideologically charged climates. The public, not the press, is in need of repair in this tactical form of reflexivity, a sign of the bad faith I reference in Chapter 1. If professional realism is an accurate representation of journalistic thinking in the context of Trump coverage, we should not expect much effort to defend newswork to audiences. Critiques would instead focus on limitations of those same audiences.

Textual Analysis and Findings

The thin ideology and confrontational style of populist discourse in 2015–2016, on top of the election outcome, would nevertheless prompt reflexivity on some aspects of campaign coverage. Patrick Ferrucci and I conducted a textual analysis of metajournalistic discourse to identify boundaries of reflexivity about the relationship between reporting and the popularity of Trump.[20]

Through metajournalistic discourse, actors within and outside media challenge assumptions for what is desirable and realistic. This form of pragmatic discourse delineates journalism as cultural practice and strikes "a subjunctive tone about what the news should be."[21] Practices that produce news content, the news itself, and conditions for audience reception are critiqued in ways that ensure the provisional status of journalism as knowledge work. Routines of journalism are, however, anchored by doxic news values, including gut feelings about public mood. Imagined communities can be widely internalized in the press without becoming objects of reflexivity.[22]

A comparison of the discourse of scholars and journalists provides leverage for tracing the limits of reflexivity. The intent is to map the regions of *possible* themes—those articulated by scholars plus journalists—and then compare those viable interpretive schemes to those *actually* articulated by journalists. For commentary of scholars, we analyzed *US Election Analysis 2016: Media, Voters and the Campaign*, a volume produced by Bournemouth University in the United Kingdom.[23] The tight time frame and brevity of analyses required for inclusion were not conducive to theory-laden perspectives, putting journalists and academics to some extent on the same footing in making sense of the Trump victory.[24] Four editors from communication disciplines at Bournemouth invited 82 scholars "in the US and around the globe" to comment on journalistic performance; campaign rhetoric; policy platforms of Trump and Democratic nominee Hillary Clinton; diversity and division in identity politics; social media in campaign strategy; popular culture and populism; and global perspectives on the reputation of US electoral politics. Entries were submitted within 10 days of the election outcome. Editors described the contributions as short and accessible but also authoritative. We examined commentary of both the editors and the invited authors ($n = 86$).[25]

For discourse produced by journalists, we relied on a purposive sample of 212 articles published in the 35 most-circulated newspapers in the United States. The time frame—November 9 to 28—extends beyond the deadline given to scholars (November 18). The additional 10 days allowed for a larger sample of text while recognizing that the deadline constraints of newswork require more time for reflexivity to crystalize. A larger corpus from journalists is also needed given the inclusion of news stories ($n = 121$) as well as commentary ($n = 91$). We anticipated that a relatively small amount of news about the election would be sufficiently interpretive and evaluative to warrant comparisons with academic discourse on the same topics. We conducted a Factiva search using the following terms: "Trump," "journalism," "media," "journalist," "populism," and "election." These parameters netted more than 8,000 articles, but only the 212 that discussed journalism's role in the election were subject to textual analysis.[26]

Journalistic discourse generally asserted that Trump's victory occurred due to media illiteracy in the public; social media propagation of fake news and allowance of filter bubbles; and failure of the press to understand the depth of voter anger. Scholars viewed the rise of Trump as predictable when considering long-established routines of the press; journalists' misunderstanding of both the public and populism; and the dire economics of legacy journalism.

Discourse of Journalists

Journalists argued fairly consistently that much of the public ignored respectable news outlets—those that value truth and accuracy—and instead sought out fake news that fit ideological preferences. Many media consumers did not understand the difference between authentic and fraudulent news, according to this perspective. A columnist for the *Austin American-Statesman* wrote:

> One of my great sadnesses of this past election cycle is the villainization of the press corps. I chafe at the insistence, even in my own social circles, that the great and evil media are out to get the "other" side. I also object to the idea that if a story doesn't appear in someone's social media feed, then clearly the mainstream media are ignoring it. Readers and consumers vote with every mouse click. News organizations have a duty to provide balanced and complete coverage, but consumers have a duty to seek it out, which means reading and subscribing.[27]

In a similar interpretation, Trump supporters relied on "news" from conspiracy theorists such as Alex Jones. One story quoted former Trump advisor Roger Stone:

> I think he's emerged as the single most powerful voice on the right. Elitists may laugh at his politics (but) Alex Jones is reaching millions of people, and they are the foot soldiers in the Trump revolution.[28]

The article noted that Jones forged his reputation by disseminating fake news such as the #Pizzagate story. John Herrman, who covers media for the *New York Times Magazine*, suggested that audiences weighted fake news the same as mainstream, quality news. "Major news organizations, household names trusted for decades, lost a great deal of ownership over audiences."[29]

Respectable news sources were reduced to noise "among many contributors in infinite feeds."

This lament cautioned against giving in to a mobilized irrationalism. Dana Milbank, columnist for *The Washington Post*, wrote:

> This is a time of self-flagellation in the media, as we scold ourselves for being out of touch with the anger in the country and failing to hear the beleaguered white working class. But this is both misleading and potentially harmful.[30]

Journalists targeted social media, Facebook in particular. In this retelling of the election, the public fell prey to a technology conglomerate that cared only for profits. Journalists posited that Facebook disseminated fake news; the public did not understand the content was fake; and the result was Trump's victory. Purveyors of fake news illustrate "how websites can use Facebook to tap into a surging ideology, quickly go from nothing to influencing millions of people and make big profits in the process."[31] Facebook knew it was publishing fake news and chose not to act. Twenty-five of the 35 newspapers sampled quoted Mark Zuckerberg after the election. When the CEO spoke at a press conference, a media columnist for *The New York Times* condescendingly applauded him for acknowledging Facebook's role. "It was heartening to hear, especially after his earlier assertion that it was 'crazy' to believe that misinformation on Facebook had affected the presidential election in any real way—despite copious evidence that it was disturbingly in the mix."[32]

While 18 reporters and columnists emphasized Facebook's profit-driven decision to not remove fake news, others blamed the platform for allowance of filter bubbles and echo chambers.

> The problem with Facebook's influence on political discourse is not limited to the dissemination of fake news. It's also about echo chambers. The company's algorithm chooses which updates appear higher up in users' newsfeeds and which are buried.[33]

Explicit criticism of the social media giant tended to excuse its users as bystanders not expected to understand the nuances of News Feed. "The most influential sources of political misinformation on Facebook are not Macedonian fake-news sites or satirical pages but the thousands of partisan news outlets, pages and blogs that derive their traffic from News Feed."[34]

Slightly more than 88% of the articles we examined did not address the role of the press, although some journalists observed that news media did little to understand middle America. A public editor detailed a group in North Carolina after Election Day to illustrate the problem.

> There is a group of 10 friends in Charlotte, N.C., all women, all in their 50s, all white. They're college educated with successful careers, and they have a message for *The New York Times*: Come visit us.[35]

Media columnist Jim Rutenberg wrote that reporters failed "to capture the boiling anger of a large portion of the American electorate that feels left behind by . . . establishment Washington, Wall Street and the mainstream media."[36]

In other instances, journalists argued that the press overestimates both its cultural authority and comprehension of public sentiment. In the words of one *USA Today* contributor, "The media ideologically aligned itself not just against Donald Trump but with the demographic groups that made up its audience."[37] Some journalists proposed that their colleagues' misread of the public could be traced to overreliance on polls.[38] A columnist for the *Pittsburgh Post-Gazette* characterized mainstream journalism as elitist and "unbearably smug" for how it covered the election.[39] The overall theme seemed to be that "journalism took a hit" on Election Day "and rightly so."[40]

Discourse of Scholars

A striking difference between journalists and academics concerns normative practice as part of the solution or the core problem. Newspaper reporters and columnists contended that journalism failed to adhere to principles, including a commitment to understand the public on its own terms. Scholars asserted that news media, in fact, followed routines of professionalization established in the early twentieth century. In the media studies view, journalists gather and report news in a specific manner, using specific routines that did not translate well in 2016. Massive attention devoted to Trump "is not the fault of the mainstream media, nor of their journalists, who are simply applying the professional codes and practices with which they have been raised."[41] Journalists, in fact, were loyal to tradition as they adhered to "a set of institutionally defined values, procedures and practices."[42] Mazzoleni asked:

> How could the media ignore such a bizarre presidential hopeful? . . . They just couldn't! So, they covered his triumphant march toward the nomination, using the horse race frame, the one that they are long accustomed to.[43]

Trump relied on news media to spread messages initially sent only to supporters.[44] Thus, journalists would return a news subsidy with a campaign subsidy—the favor of newsworthy oddities would be rewarded with amplification and diffusion of Trump's messages. Twitter posts "were information subsidies for the global media—free content that is accessible and easy to reuse."[45] Candidate Trump exploited the appeal of soft news against journalism itself by luring campaign reporters out of their comfort zone, the realm of undisputed facts and analysis.

While journalists acknowledged that they failed to understand the heartland *in 2016*, scholars emphasized that the quality press had for many decades shown little interest in rural communities. Journalists were consequently ill-equipped to comprehend the power of populism once mobilized.[46] Political scientist Lance Bennett explained:

> Most of the press and party elites missed the scale of angry emotion aimed at them by white working and middle class Americans. Indeed, the cosmopolitan press had long rendered these folk nearly invisible, brushing off the early warning signs of the Tea Party as a minor disturbance. And so, most media experts and party insiders engaged in knowing discussions of how impossible it would be for anyone to be elected with Trump's combination of inexperience, shady business dealings, and inability to manage his emotions and stay on script.[47]

Lacking empathy for the concerns of disenchanted voters, repoters failed to adequately confront Trump on policy details. "[H]is candidacy became an ill-defined canvas onto which disgruntled and fearful voters could project their hopes and assuage their anxieties."[48]

Still, most academic discourse seemed to assume that US political journalism could be remedied. The dissent of media scholars Seth Lewis and Matt Carlson was thus sober in its uncertainty:

> Much of the post mortem criticism now being levelled at the news media assumes that basic terms like "news" have some shared understandings

attached to them, some agreed-upon normative expectations for journalism in public life. We shouldn't be so sure anymore.[49]

Much of the academic analysis proposed a connection between public antipathy toward the press and disruption of the news industry caused by economic turmoil. The press could not produce insightful content because "newspapers, shrunken by the onslaught of the digital revolution on their revenues, with fewer journalistic resources and in a constant scramble for 'hits' and 'eyeballs,' amplify 'news' without troubling with time-consuming verification."[50] Rural America in particular suffers from the gutting of newsrooms.

> [N]ewspapers that served as key community institutions have been hollowed out, much like the factories and church pews, and the print-to-digital shift has only accelerated the concentration of power to coastal news elites—the same elites who mostly responded to Trump and his ilk with snark and scorn, either explicitly on Twitter or implicitly in their framing of news coverage.[51]

Other academics disagreed with the notion of "coastal news elites." In this view, the entire news industry suffered irrevocably from cost-cutting measures. Robert McChesney, a scholar of political economy, posited that while many have criticized journalists' coverage of the election, they are missing the bigger point:

> But there was a far greater problem in 2016 that got almost no mention: there is very little coverage of political races by journalists any longer. The US model of commercial journalism has collapsed and when people go to the polls they have almost no idea who the candidates are and what they stand for aside from what they might have seen in the TV ads.[52]

Hermida emphasized more subtle impacts of market-driven journalism. He placed most of the blame for superficial coverage on cable news, arguing that the "news" in that term is a "misnomer" and that "these networks are not in the business of evidence-based reporting."[53]

> They are in the emotion business. And emotion sells. Ratcheting up anger and outrage on cable makes business sense.

Geoffrey Baym, a scholar of broadcast news, contended that reporters covered Trump incessantly, especially during the Republican primaries when the attention was not warranted, because Trump recognized the "mutual interests" of his campaign and a struggling news industry.[54]

Front-Stage Reflexivity

This chapter was motivated in part by recognition of the 2016 election as an opportunity to identify emergent forms of journalistic resistance to punitive populism. With journalism's celebrated suspicion of political elites in mind, I would expect reporters to show more willingness to recognize crude populism in speechmaking than to acknowledge this sentiment in the public itself. Reporters nevertheless took stock of episodes such as being scolded to "Tell the truth!" as they were herded into pens at rallies. Correspondents at stump speeches found ways to signal deviance in crowd behavior. In Beaumont, Texas, *The Washington Post* reported Trump's assertion that strict gun control added to the death toll from terrorist attacks in Paris. When Trump emphasized the danger of taking in Syrian refugees, "the crowd booed Syrian refugees for several seconds."[55] The reporter's attention is drawn away from gun policy to document the spectacle of Americans booing an ethnic group when most deserving of compassion. Efforts of journalists to distance themselves from an abrasive populism signify productive reflexivity in how professionals think about audiences, a theme I return to in the final chapter.

Alternatively, journalists' evaluation of their work could be interpreted as a calculated defense of tainted news, particularly the disproportionate attention to Trump in the pre-primary season, when media coverage is so valuable to anti-establishment candidates.[56] Many journalists implicitly argued that the rise of anti-elitist populism and Trump's eventual victory were aided by media illiteracy of citizens unable to resist or even detect fake news as fake. This sector of the electorate presumably voted for fake news and against respectable journalism.

Academics and journalists overlapped to some extent in criticism of the press as elitist. The "snark and scorn" described by Lewis and Carlson implies a need to better connect with disenchanted citizens. If we grant, however, that punitive populism is already a defining feature of media-based politics in the United States,[57] the remedy for journalism is not to infuse its style and interpretive schemes with a down-home sensitivity. A nuanced journalism of empathy and expertise—an "elite" journalism without apology—would better capture the substantive concerns of rural America.

Boundaries of reflexivity observed are in some respects an artifact of this study's time frame and the content sampled. Textual analysis with a broader period would capture a wider range of perspective from journalists and academics on the 2016 election. This chapter is nevertheless focused on the limits of reflexivity. My goal was to document journalistic thinking in the moment, to reveal how the imagined public shapes both the news created and rationalization for that work.

Reliance on large-circulation newspapers prevented a comparison with perspectives of editors, reporters, and columnists working in rural and small-town communities. The textual analysis of journalists is also confined to audience-facing critiques. Metajournalistic discourse includes not just front-stage criticism of the news with readers as consumers but also back-stage perspectives in which reporters and editors are sometimes more critical of their work (Chapters 7 and 9).[58] Front-stage reflexivity could be quite subtle. A dynamic in which journalists are unlikely to expose themselves and their readers as anti-deliberative implies a third-person effect. Journalists in this scenario would signal that Americans (OTHER Americans) don't read newspapers and are unable to distinguish real news from fake news.[59]

The evidence here for how journalists imagine the public is indirect, reliant on textual analysis. On the other hand, reflexivity in normative theory is viewed as accountability through transparency, and thus meaningful reflexivity must manifest in what the press expresses openly to its readers. Textual analysis in this respect generates evidence for how journalists, in their own words, view the public's receptivity to substantive, policy-centric news.

Dark Side of Reflexivity

News outlets patrol boundaries of acceptable and deviant discourse.[60] Journalists appeared to place Trump and his supporters in the realm of deviance. Academics, by contrast, indirectly advanced the view that journalists did not simply characterize Trump as deviant; *they widened legitimate debate to include the ideology of a punitive populism.* Juxtaposing the two interpretations helps to diagnose a condition of contemporary political communication: the disorientation that arises in the legitimation of deviance.

Leaving aside the possibility that news media might misread public opinion—and taking anti-rational temptations as an authentic feature of post-truth politics—the depiction of widespread disaffection is advantageous to journalism in a tactical sense. In "strategic ritual" as originally proposed by Gaye Tuchman in the 1970s,[61] balancing of opinions, reliance on official sources, and other practices that signal objectivity ward off partisan attacks. Routines in the objectivity paradigm are put aside during periods of war, when journalists show allegiance to binding beliefs.[62] The emergence of punitive populism in how journalists portray audiences constitutes another type of crisis, one internal to representative democracy.

I noted in the previous chapter that the press at midcentury—in response to criticism from the Hutchins Commission[63]—expressed confidence in ordinary citizens to inform themselves. Contemporary journalists are criticized from all angles, but they are not naïve. While recent scholarship identifies affinities of news media with populist ideology,[64] the evidence here suggests that correspondents and commentators have not internalized a view of the public as innocent and virtuous. On the other hand, populism is compatible with critical professionalism,[65] the sentiment that distances journalism from established parties while assuming the role of a superior representative. Where does this leave the idea of a Fourth Estate if parties, government, and now the people are all suspect? I argue in the final chapter that the profession can and should reshape a professional identity by shifting from public-facing to craft-oriented accountability.

Much is at stake in how journalists make sense of their contribution to Trump's success. Did news media co-produce the Trump campaign? Did they co-produce a crisis of democracy in the condoning of retribution as one of the spoils of victory? Katz and Liebes warn that while journalists benefit from audience engagement in periods of crisis, they can lose control of coverage to anti-establishment actors.[66] The lavish attention to Trump before and during the presidential primaries was apparently less threatening to journalism's self-image under the assumption that he would never actually occupy the White House.

This scenario points to a dark side of reflexivity. Professional realism departs from paradigm repair in the perception that newswork must adjust to limitations of the public. Deviance is located in imagined audiences in ways that obscure problems inherent in practice. Journalists, for example, repeatedly referenced the public's appetite for fake news. Downplaying the public's expectations is accompanied by a foreclosing on the aspirations of deliberative journalism. Reform of campaign reporting is consequently contingent on recognition of journalists that their work is shaped by audiences they imagine.

The correction is not simple, however, when considering contradictions of *anti-intellectual journalism*. Professional enculturation must somehow rationalize this sentiment and obscure the dissonance. While journalists were quite willing to recognize audiences as intolerant of quality news, they appeared unable, or at least reluctant, to contemplate how this critique shaped their reporting. In an analysis of 75 introductory textbooks, Parks reveals how generations of reporters and editors have been taught that "they have substantial freedom of judgment," but they must constrain this judgment to the "common-sense expectations" of peers and the public.[67] Journalists exercise disciplinary power over themselves by anticipating the judgment of audiences,[68] a vulnerability increasingly evident in a digital age of constant surveillance. Neither the imagined public nor the anticipation of its judgment is subject to reflexivity when journalists assume that the tone of their work simply mirrors public sentiment. Chapter 8 will explore how support for journalistic anti-intellectualism is inculcated in the views of college students (i.e., digital natives) as they develop attitudes toward their epistemic authority with audiences in mind.

Future research on how journalists reify public sentiment is vital in the wake of the 2016 election. Subjunctive sentiment becomes consequential to the extent that it finds voice and validation (Chapter 5).[69] The inconvenient question for journalists as they anticipate future campaigns is the extent to which media rationalize a punitive populism such that the news becomes a medium for mobilized irrationalism. A deviant in the White House would ideally prompt reflexivity on how the epistemology of newswork shapes how audiences are imagined. If newsworthiness as a doxic value is resistant to reflexivity,[70] and newsworthiness orients journalists to the perceived feelings of audiences,[71] the perception of an agitated and incompetent public constitutes a crisis for both journalism and democracy.

PART II
SOCIAL CONTROL OF INTELLECT

4

The Academic-Media Nexus

The co-founder of a university, Jane Lathrop Stanford was fond of inspirational sayings, and this explains the inscription in the nave of Stanford Memorial Church, completed in 1903.

> There is no narrowing so deadly as the narrowing of man's horizon of spiritual things . . . No widening of science, no possession of abstract truth, can indemnify for an enfeebled hold on the highest and central truths of humanity. "What shall a man give in exchange for his soul?" [Mark 8:37, Matthew 16:26]

Sandstone is more aesthetically appealing than structurally sound at a campus so close to the San Andreas Fault, but so far it has preserved Mrs. Stanford's caution toward the full embrace of intellect. Apart from any religious legacy, the contemporary university is instrumental and strategic—for the most part—rather than anti-rationalist in the social control of intellect. Still, mistrust of intellect remains a secular preoccupation at private and public universities, institutions entrusted with preservation of cultural heritage. When faculty take risks in the public sphere to challenge orthodoxy, they should not assume that university administrators will support them against populist blowback.

The nexus of academia and news media is a contradictory space for knowledge work, where exchanges of ideas are constrained in an intricate system of internalized norms and risk-averse communication. Stanford greets the public most prominently at Memorial Church, a place where weddings, masses, and other ceremonies affirm core beliefs. Universities writ large seek to preserve a legacy of grandeur and gravitas even as they interact routinely with the public in the academic-media nexus, a space where intellect is potentially most disruptive.

Journalists produce news in defensive practices to deflect criticism.[1] By contrast, Shils suggests that it is "practically given by the nature of the intellectuals' orientation that there should be some tension between the

Where Ideas Go to Die. Michael McDevitt, Oxford University Press (2020). © Oxford University Press.
DOI: 10.1093/oso/9780190869946.001.0001

intellectuals and the value-orientations embodied in the actual institutions of any society."[2] The academic-media nexus consequently represents a liminal space where intellectual work is regularly held up to public judgment. We will consider not just the fate of lone-wolf professors but also how the university is portrayed in response to ideas that offend. The university's regulation of intellect is itself subject to surveillance and possible intervention when students, alumni, trustees, and other stakeholders question how controversies involving freedom of expression are handled.[3] In many circumstances, journalists are ultimately in control of the boundaries for what counts as acceptable ideas, that is, those worthy of widespread circulation.[4]

Journalism is unusual as a profession in that it does not possess an esoteric body of knowledge. It nevertheless asserts authority in policing intellectual dissent.[5] "One of the hallmark characteristics of journalism is that, unlike other professional domains such as law, mathematics, or geography, it is not a self-standing and autonomous profession." Journalism depends on "an adjunct referential domain without which it cannot exist."[6] The profession appropriates from science an image of objectivity—or perhaps a thin implementation of scientific method—but not the ideational substance of expertise.[7] Journalism consequently operates at an intellectual deficit in encounters with the academy, but typically has the upper hand in shaping how academic labor is presented to the public.[8]

This chapter argues, first of all, that interactions of journalists and academics deserve more scrutiny with respect to both media sociology and normative theory on the circulation of ideas. We then examine three sources of social control that impinge on the nexus as a space for ideas that challenge orthodoxies: the self-imposed instrumentalism of intellectuals; a new form of anti-intellectualism that features systemic surveillance of academic discourse; and the strategic communication of university administrations. A final section contemplates the implications of risk-averse communication in higher education for public perceptions of intellect and its contributions to policy and politics.

The Study of Idea Circulation

In the universe of human thought—sometimes referred to as the noosphere[9]—journalism would seem to orbit as a lonely little planet. The larger sphere of ideas in academia (and beyond) can appear irrelevant to the view of news as hegemonic practice, a perspective that looks for recursive and reinforcing content. Koopman writes that the public sphere "is a *loosely* bounded space, but at any particular time and place it is a *bounded* space nonetheless."[10] Media theory on the flow and management of ideas is perhaps realistic in a bias toward endogeneity in the sense that journalists typically lack time and resources to research beyond the topical circulation of content. "Churnalism" is the product of gutted newsrooms and the dictates of deadlines in conjunction with a tendency of an echoing press to adopt the frames of official sources.[11] Journalists "routinely look over their shoulders to validate their sense of news by observing the work of their colleagues, especially the work of elite members of the press, such as the *New York Times, Washington Post* and national networks."[12]

Media sociology often operates within a tidy universe of events, circumstances, and information readily observable or available to journalists, political actors, and the public.[13] These are the issues that matter at any given time in a system of political communication that has become increasingly competitive in the professionalization of issue advocacy.[14] However, a focus on frame contestation and the competitive management of issue salience can obscure the cultural forces that determine what ideas circulate or fail to circulate in the first place. In traditional conceptions of gatekeeping, influences on newsmaking are viewed as reflecting prevailing norms and audience expectations.[15]

In the media effects paradigm, salience is arguably the most generative concept, bridging agenda-setting theory with priming, framing, and issue ownership.[16] The transfer of issue salience from news media to the public (agenda setting) influences criteria citizens use to evaluate political leaders (priming), and the highlighting of some facets of an issue or problem over others (framing) promotes "a particular interpretation, evaluation, and/or solution."[17] Political parties and candidates benefit from issue salience by emphasizing issues in which they hold a reputation for competence (issue ownership). These theories have launched hundreds of peer-reviewed articles. As someone who has contributed to a few of these studies, I sense that the reduction of concepts and themes to issue relevance, as well as the need to operationalize salience into countable bits, forecloses on comprehension of how ideas flow across knowledge domains.

With the exception of science journalism, media sociology in the United States has generally failed to explore the academic-media nexus as a context for idea circulation despite the many ways public intellectuals experiment with digital technology and public pedagogy.[18] Granted, most of the time the discourse of faculty and independent scholars operates as a parallel universe, lacking news value, beyond the comprehension or interest of journalists and their audiences. The academic-media nexus is nevertheless a vital area of normative theory in imaging how public intellectuals might contribute to the origination, migration, and framing of ideas in legacy and digital news media. This space is also generative of innovation in the repair of provocative ideas when rendered deviant in mainstream media (Chapter 7).

The academic-media nexus for the present analysis refers to the sphere where scholarship and pedagogy seek a larger audience and where journalism obtains expertise and commentary. As knowledge workers, journalists, pundits, professors, and independent scholars, among others, are all reasonably classified as "intellectuals."[19] Contemporary public intellectuals strive to overcome traditional distinctions between academics and journalists in exploring the possibilities for public pedagogy in new communication platforms. The academy and news media represent distinct fields with cultural capital unique to each realm,[20] but they integrate cooperatively in forms such as knowledge-based, literary, solutions, and developmental journalism.[21]

Collaboration is normatively appealing in many respects. Working with journalists or as journalists, academics might enhance the frame repositories available for interpretation of issues and events.[22] They might call into question the partisan binaries that contribute to legislative gridlock.[23] In periods of national crises, they challenge a subservient, patriotic press.[24] Academics might intervene in election cycles to challenge the presentation of politics as a horse race or a strategic game.[25]

From the perspective of field theory, however, the autonomy of cultural production is compromised by intellectuals' interaction with mass media.[26] Rules of the game vary considerably depending on the academic and media context, particularly as they relate to audiences. We can imagine the spatial ecology as an ecotone, the place where two biomes meet and integrate; the transition between communities can produce a diverse ecosystem of comingled species. New forms of public scholarship will doubtlessly thrive in the evolving mediascape of information technology. Public intellectuals will continue to figure out ways to work effectively with social media and news media, and some will create their own fora for civic or activist pedagogy. But an ecotone is also subject to aggressive migration, which can impose uniformity.

Intellectual autonomy is undermined when knowledge work undergoes *mediatization*[27]—when media logic migrates into the academy, such that actors adopt news values and the boundaries for acceptable discourse established in popular media. While mediatization has been developed theoretically at the intersection of media and politics, the concept is also useful for anticipating the social control of academic labor. The adoption of media logic compromises the cultural authority of the academy when its work is reduced to commodities in news production.

In political journalism, intellectual discourse tends to be recognized and validated to the extent that salient ideas are funneled into sanctioned debates and schema readily understood by audiences.[28] Public intellectuals favored by news media as sources or as stand-alone commentators are often not those with the most unique and challenging perspectives, but those with predictable views that resonate with audiences and journalists themselves.[29] Thus, mediatization favors a form of knowledge work that is instrumental in adapting and conforming to the imperatives of mass-market media.

Mediatization is most pernicious *within* the university when faculty, students, administrators, and regents internalize boundaries of acceptable discourse at play in mass-market journalism. In 2013, University of Colorado regents voted to expand CU's anti-discrimination policy to include "political philosophy" (beyond established categories: race, sexual orientation, veteran status, etc.). In journalism, this notion of fairness helps to explain the intellectually vacuous, false balance associated with objectivity. In academia, an instructor of political philosophy would commit malpractice by polling students for partisan identity and adjusting class discussion time and assigned readings to cover every cranky idea.

Classroom interactions, conference panels, and polemic essays interpreted as provocative in scholarly settings can appear incendiary when subject to de-contextualization and re-contextualization in social media, tabloid news media, doctrinaire think tanks, and other institutions suspicious (or envious) of independent academic work. This dynamic suggests that higher education will become increasingly strategic and defensive, both in terms of communication policies and in the internalization of norms for how faculty should interact with journalists.

Retreat into Instrumentalism

Academic contributions to news media and public dialogue hinge on scientific literacy and goodwill, or at least some level of consent to deliberate, along with some respect for the rules of the game. Lyotard discusses the incommensurability of scientific and narrative knowledge while emphasizing that the pragmatics of science requires nevertheless a narrative function. Science and narrative knowledge are both

> composed of sets of statements; the statements are "moves" made by the players within the framework of generally acceptable rules; these rules are specific to each particular kind of knowledge, and the "move" judged to be "good" in one cannot be of the same type as those judged "good" in another, unless it happens that way by chance.[30]

Lyotard offers "crude proof" for the reliance of science on narratives of legitimation:

> [W]hat do scientists do when they appear on television or are interviewed in the newspapers after making a "discovery"? They recount an epic of knowledge that is in fact wholly unepic. They play by the rules of the narrative game; its influence remains considerable not only on the users of the media, but also on the scientist's sentiments.[31]

We might expect acumen from scholars in comprehending risks and rewards in the academic-media nexus, but critical discourse is potentially inflammatory depending on how it is rendered by journalists. The capacity of intellectuals to secularize the sacred is a recurring theme in social theory, reflecting what Barrow describes as an "unstable accommodation between intellectuals, capitalism and the state."[32] Whether as priests, teachers, philosophers, or specialists in law, intellectuals offer "some especially salient set of normative prescriptions for human and social conduct other than ritual as such."[33]

While intellectuals are sometimes perceived as seers of a better society, the integration of academic intellectuals in the university system complicates their identity.[34] Universities were founded as the material locations for the creation of universal knowledge, yet evolved as places for the splintering of knowledge into fragmented spheres beyond the comprehension of non-experts.[35] Enlightenment thinkers auspiciously confronted the church and state as monopolies of knowledge and in the end became guardians of university-based monopolies.

In Europe and later in the New World, intellectuals sought to create intellectual capital for viability apart from industrial and trade capital, but this effort to institutionalize an autonomous system of exchange never crystallized. Bourdieu maintained that intellectuals are in continuous negotiation with capitalists for a better exchange rate between the cultural capital of the former and the economic capital of the latter.[36] The cultural status constituted by knowledge, educational credentials, aesthetics, and other trappings of intellectual life translates efficiently into economic returns only to the extent that intellectuals channel expertise into instrumental ends.

Nevertheless, intellectuals rely on private and public institutions for funding and the infrastructure necessary to preserve academic freedom. Further, they depend on a political economy in which market dynamics establish the value of publications and other academic products.[37] Molnar concluded that professors are obligated to negotiate between patronage and autonomy, in most cases at the expense of the latter.[38] In this view, hegemonic control consists in the institutional capacity to regulate intellectuals through market forces rather than to regulate their work directly.

Criticism of intellectuals is not rooted entirely in populist resentment and suspicion. Said chastised faculty for sheltering themselves in campus sanctuaries.[39] In chorus with Said is a cadre of critical theorists who view the professionalization of intellectuals as inculcating a policy-oriented, instrumental rationalism.[40] Liu writes that the demise of nonacademic intellectuals "has been hastened by the rise of the professional academic, a decidedly nonheroic figure who polishes his resume while keeping an eye on his bank account."[41] An authentically free and questing intellect is stifled in assembly-line pedagogy of higher education itself;[42] in the standardization of primary education;[43] and even in the supposedly book-worm domain of professional librarians.[44] The impression left by this literature is that anti-intellectualism is self-perpetuating and internalized, even in the most unlikely places.[45]

Giroux comes close to asserting that academics are complicit in perpetuating a culture of anti-intellectualism, inviting derision when their work is not simply ignored.[46] "If critical thought, sometimes disparaged as theory, gets a bad name, it is not because it is inherently dogmatic, jargonistic, or rigidly specialized, but because it is often abused or because it becomes a tool of irrelevancy—a form of theoreticism in which theory becomes an end in itself."

The idea of the public intellectual "has as its core the Emersonian mission of helping people to think better about the circumstances that confront them."[47] In Hauser's distinction, academics "usually plough through a narrow disciplinary patch, whereas intellectuals roam ambitiously from one discipline to another."[48] Mass media became sites of intervention for public intellectuals in the postwar era. In *Power, Politics, and the People*, C. Wright Mills argued:

> Fresh perception now involves the capacity to continually unmask and to smash the stereotypes of vision and intellect with which modern communications [i.e., modern systems of representation] swamp us. These worlds of mass-art and mass-thought are increasingly geared to the demands of politics.[49]

The premise that mass media are crucial sites for intervention highlights the irony of mediatization in the academy. Media logic infiltrates higher education as activist intellectuals strive for influence in the opposite direction, in extending an ethos of critical thinking to the "worlds of mass-art and mass-thought."

Today, activists increasingly rely on alternative media to curate ideas that might mobilize action,[50] sometimes intentionally resisting engagement with mainstream media.[51] However, the feeling of solidarity that social movements cultivate relies on a shared cultural legacy in the civil sphere.[52] In the tradition of Mills,[53] Arendt,[54] and Said,[55] Peschek argues that public deliberation requires "an engaged intelligentsia of genuine independence" in conjunction with "a media of open and genuine communication."[56] Put another way, the legitimacy of critical scholarship hinges on overlapping values with the public; otherwise dissident ideas fail to resonate with opinion leaders potentially sympathetic. The mission of the public intellectual thereby implicates journalism as a carrier of mass-thought and as a powerful actor in the civil sphere.[57]

Surveillance in and of the Academy

Outside the university, accusations of elitism resonate with particular force when historic circumstances expose the contradiction between academics' critical function—proclaimed proudly as independence from the corruption of power—and their desire for privileged status.[58] Intellectuals dependent on academia and aligned with other institutions in the civil sphere must periodically demonstrate deference to the citizenry. This can manifest as rituals of public humiliation, evident in the Joseph McCarthy witch-hunts of the 1950s and in contemporary cases discussed below and in subsequent chapters. The rules of the game in the academic-media nexus are contingent rather than secure, suggesting that activist interventions must adhere to a strategic logic even as its practitioners might loathe the risk-averse communication of university administrators. Liu argues that by the 1980s, anti-elitism as cultural critique had become consensus politics. "While the Left denounced critique and negativity as the true usurpers of the sovereignty of the people's will, conservatives construed public goods such as public universities oxymoronically as socialist luxuries that had parasitically attached themselves to the aggrieved 'American taxpayer.'"[59] The old-guard, cultural conservatives "made their peace with the philistines of the Christian Right by attacking universities."[60]

Ideological opportunists—"moral entrepreneurs" as they are described in the moral panic literature—are sensitive to circumstances that might reawaken memes of intellectuals as subversive. The haughty professor, for instance, is reimagined as treasonous, no longer simply an annoyance. The intellectual and the public are consequently both liminal constructs in the nexus of media and academia. Social hierarchies are reversed, in some respects, when intellectual work is subject to public judgment in an era of viral populism. An unfortunate comment is easily taken out of context in social media if a student with a mobile phone believes that she is duty bound to expose a professor.

Academic conferences and publications are mined by moral entrepreneurs for tropes, themes, and imagery. In an illustrative case, conservative critics recognized how symbols used at a Christian feminist gathering in Minneapolis could be deployed to discredit its leaders. Hoover and Clark suggest that when the newsworthiness of an event corresponds to ritual structure, conflicting factions evanesce into a larger drama, which transcends "the practical realities and actions of the various constituent parts."[61] I would add that a correspondence of a situation to ritual structure does not erupt spontaneously but is enabled by the dramaturgical agency of journalism. Chapter 6 documents the role of parochial news media in the alignment of anti-rationalism with populist anti-elitism through social drama.[62]

Redress in the academic-media nexus implicates perhaps most clearly what is at stake in populist challenges to intellectual autonomy. Who draws the boundaries for acceptable discourse? What many journalists might consider an ideological breach occurs regularly in seminars, conferences, and published papers. Journalism's ideological agency is evident in its capacity to transform an abstract provocation into a sociocultural breach and to rapidly marshal a crisis through media ritual.

A recasting of faculty as subversive—not simply suspect—is practiced with the greatest indulgence by David Horowitz in *The Professors: The 101 Most Dangerous Academics in America*, published in 2006.[63] In the conservative imagination, the antiquated hippies that populate sociology, women's studies, and ethnic studies departments deserve another look. Horowitz and his research team cherry-pick through literature and campus activism reaching back to the 1960s. "Guerilla decontextualization" illustrates the vulnerability of intellectuals to ritualistic mocking.[64] When a trope, premise, analogy, or other rhetorical device is extracted from a discourse of legitimation and juxtaposed to common sense, audiences are invited to join in the ridicule. As Lippmann observed, a salient stereotype gives readers a foothold into a news story.[65] The guerilla characterization seems appropriate in the sense that ideologues extract and retreat from contextualized discourse in opportunistic strikes. While popularizers of academic labor such as Malcolm Gladwell could be critiqued as carpetbaggers, opportunists such as Horowitz are more aptly recognized as vigilantes.

More recently, Turning Point USA launched Professor Watchlist.[66] According to the website, "TPUSA will continue to fight for free speech and the right for professors to say whatever they wish; however students, parents, and alumni deserve to know the specific incidents and names of professors that advance a radical agenda in lecture halls."[67]

Echoes of McCarthyism reverberate in the post-9/11 era with intellectuals readily depicted as soft targets and enemies of the people. Intellectual discourse can be deeply offensive to citizens, particularly during moments of national grieving or when core beliefs are dissected. News media are periodically tasked with protecting the national grieving process. Fritch et al. write:

> Understandably, Americans do not wish to see evil in themselves, and certainly not in the victims of 9/11. They/we resist the very possibility of a (reasoned) account of the tragedy; perhaps this is why we remember the Twin Towers but conveniently forget the Pentagon.[68]

After terrorist attacks in Paris, columnist George Will noted that presidential candidate Chris Christie "sounded a new theme" while campaigning in Florida: "There are all too many people in academia and in global business that aren't really interested in America as a nation-state anymore."[69] A few years earlier, a freshman Tea Party activist in Arizona introduced a bill stipulating that public high school students must "recite an oath supporting the U.S. Constitution" to receive a diploma.[70] These incidents highlight the dilemma of intellect in politics: high school instructors, professors, artists, independent journalists, and other cultural workers are most resented when they have the most to offer as a check on nativism and nationalism. In the logic of authoritarian populism, cultural elites represent sources of subversion rather than comprehension in addressing problems such as terrorism, illegal immigration, and gun violence.

Hofstadter observed that intellectuals affect the public mind in their roles as experts and ideologues.

> In both capacities they evoke profound, and, in a measure, legitimate fears and resentments. Both intensify the prevalent sense of helplessness in our society, the expert by quickening the public's resentment of being the object of constant manipulation, the ideologue by arousing the fear of subversion and by heightening all the other grave psychic stresses that come with modernity.[71]

Thus, a retreat into expertise and a rejection of the public intellectual role would not entirely diffuse the public's resentment toward being objects of manipulation. One of the composites of anti-intellectualism described in Chapter 2—religious and secular anti-rationalism mixed with media-mobilized populism—poses risks for public scholars at the same time that universities increasingly seek brand identity through marketing of higher education.

Faculty with dissident views enter the public realm at some peril. Rowe and Brass write: "There is a pattern of criticism in the media and public sphere of universities for being 'out of touch,' disconnected from the 'real world' outside the ivory tower, complacently and indulgently oblivious to 'ordinary people's' needs and priorities."[72] Absent the pall of blatant anti-intellectualism, faculty labor is still subject to co-opting by way of "contextomy": de-contextualization and re-contextualization in news narration against the author/speaker's wishes.[73]

This opportunism implies that journalism is on occasion parasitic to intellectual culture.[74] Kunelius argues that while elite sources retain control over expert knowledge, largely setting the agendas of public life, journalists "control the genres that frame the *style* of the flow."[75] Echoing Bourdieu,[76] he predicts escalating tension between expert systems and media as journalism exercises dramaturgical agency as a "moralistic and moralizing force."[77] The domain in which media and the academy meet, consequently, represents a nexus ripe for explorations into how journalism exercises cultural authority by fixing public attention on intellectual provocations. Outcomes can include the damaged reputations of intellectuals and the academic institutions that support them.

Typical encounters in the academic-media nexus are initiated by reporters contacting academics. Rowe observes that "these micro-encounters exhibit a clear inequality of discursive power in favor of journalists, who are well positioned to select, reject, or otherwise discipline academic language and discourse."[78] Rowe interviewed an editor, for example, who explained that he looks for academics who would "not quibble" about how much they would be quoted.[79] Academics generally know what they are getting into, of course, and often accept a subservient relationship as a necessary annoyance in contributing their expertise to a larger audience. Routine encounters do not describe what occurs, however, and what is at stake, when news media confront a prominent challenge to core beliefs and respond by rendering dissent into deviance.

Strategic Communication

A retreat into instrumental work is in some respects a rational response to a new and vibrant expression of anti-intellectualism. Compared with Hofstadter's analysis of cultural features in the postwar McCarthy era, the media system today features not just a smoldering resentment but also a vigilante infrastructure primed for activation in response to transgressive discourse. Strategic communication in the control of intellect is most readily apparent at public universities, particularly in states where regents are partisan officials elected directly by the people. While Ivy League chancellors worry about how parents and alumni might respond to bad press, their counterparts at public universities must also contend with taxpayers and editorial writers who expect that state-funded colleges will affirm loyalty and reflect the values of citizens.

At my campus, for example, University of Colorado administrators have tried to shake a party-school image with a "Be Boulder" rebranding campaign. The administration successfully snuffed out an annual 4/20 marijuana smoke-out by spreading fish-based fertilizer over the quad. Meanwhile, the president's office eliminated a faculty and staff newspaper, the *Silver and Gold*. Editorially independent but financed by the administration, the publication strived to preserve the ethos of a news bureau. The *Silver and Gold* did not survive a CU system-wide initiative in 2009 to make university communication more "efficient and effective." The president's office explained that CU was not in the business of producing newspapers.

The protectors of CU's image appeared proud of the fish-fertilizer tactic.[80] University spokesman Bronson Hilliard explained: "It's not toxic, it's not harmful, it's totally organic, it doesn't have any chemicals in it, and it's not pleasant to breathe." Other maneuvers offer comic relief. During the Jerry Sandusky scandal at Penn State, *The Onion* led Page 1 with a photograph of three boys at a press conference and the headline: "Nation's 10-Year-Old Boys: 'If You See Someone Raping Us, Please Call the Police.'"[81] *On the same date*, December 1, 2011, the CU Office of the Chancellor circulated a memo to all Boulder campus faculty, staff and students: "If you see or hear about possible sexual abuse or any criminal victimization of another person, you should immediately contact the University Police at . . . . "

We might speculate that if faculty could communicate more directly with students and citizens—free from the apparatus of university communications—a healthier relationship with the public would be possible. Innovations in digital media offer new models for public scholarship and outreach, some with their own take on postmodern humor. A professor at the College of Saint Rose in Albany is accepting $12.50 "bribes" for the Museum of Political Corruption.[82] Visitors are asked "to pay a bribe instead of an admission fee," Professor Bruce Roter explained. The cafeteria serves pork.[83]

The "decline of the public intellectual" is nonetheless a long-standing narrative, explained from a myriad of critical viewpoints.[84] To the extent that it exists, the decline is at least partially a symptom of risk-averse communication internalized by faculty, staff, and administrators.

In Australia, Brass and Rowe observe a reconfiguration of the academic-media nexus marked by risk management, self-consciousness in promoting university brands, and "public comment" policies to regulate faculty statements.[85] Universities increasingly deploy a suite of strategies to "maximize positive media outcomes."[86] Anti-intellectualism is endemic to both Australia and America, perhaps due to similar cultural histories in frontier settlement. We should not be surprised, then, when policies pioneered across the South Pacific are adapted for use here. The University of Kansas regents adopted a provision under which faculty can be fired for "improper use of social media."[87] The policy extends to expression in an employee's official duties that is deemed "contrary to the best interest of the university."

Controversies over academic freedom are increasingly negotiated in social media. The American Association of University Professors appears intent on protecting faculty rights in new-media contexts through the public shaming of university administrators and through the documentation of best and worst practices in reports such as "Academic Freedom and Electronic Communications."[88]

Strategic communication could be interpreted as universities avoiding interaction with the public on ideologically charged issues because the risk of backlash is too great to justify foreseeable benefits. To the extent that journalism mediates the relationship between the public and academics, this interplay carries risks when circumstances make salient the incompatibility of intellect with egalitarian sentiment.

In engagement with the academy, journalists encounter ideas and discourse hovering between accepted expertise and deviance. Academic dissent is consequently combustible in news practices depending on the ideological climate. In routine circumstances, the news helps to mask tension between intellect and democratic sensibilities by simply ignoring critical, academic discourse. While the public might judge a great deal of faculty labor to be subversive, disloyal, or even dangerous, in most cases this work fails to meet conventional criteria for newsworthiness. Of course, dissent ignored by news media also forecloses on possibilities for ideas to challenge assumptions and orthodoxies in public thinking.

When the Rules Shift

Strategic management of university communication brings to mind Robert Beyers, a legendary figure at the Stanford News Service. Beyers ran the office like a news bureau. He grilled university presidents and provosts in mock press conferences. He dismissed promotional news as "administrivia." Upon retirement, he warned of internal pressures at the university against straight news. When he died of pancreatic cancer in 2002, an obituary from the campus news service foreshadowed a time when it would be important to remember the Beyers legacy.

John Dreyfuss, former education writer at the *Los Angeles Times,* recalled that Beyers once alerted him to a plan by students to take over the campus administration building, an extraordinary act for a university "PR" person. Beyers reasoned that reporters would write stories anyway, so it would be best if they had all the facts. "He always discussed both sides of any situation, even if one side reflected badly on his school," Dreyfuss said. "And he loved that school."[89]

While veteran journalists covering higher education might look back fondly at an era of spontaneity and tolerance for controversy, university tactics are rational from a strategic perspective. They are in place to forestall mutual hostility: the contempt of many intellectuals for the public, and the public's periodic desire to humiliate cultural elites. The academic-media nexus constitutes a discursive field that adjusts for—and helps to conceal—the unpredictability of intellect, particularly its impolitic expression on culturally sensitive topics. An activist scholar enters this space at considerable risk, and she should not expect the support of regents, provosts, and chancellors if she probes ideas held sacred.[90]

Chapter 9 documents contributions of "dangerous professors" to what I believe is an emerging ethos of intellectual journalism. This agency, however, is best understood as resistant and adaptive to norms of newswork typically unreceptive—if not overtly hostile—to discordant ideas. Specialization and instrumentalism in academia domesticate scholarly discourse for the most part, guiding it away from provocations in mainstream media. Risk-averse communication of universities provides backup protection, and when these arrangements fail to contain a breach, journalism adjudicates confrontations of intellect with binding beliefs. When the rules of the game shift from academia to news media, intellectual dissent becomes vulnerable to exploitation in the social construction of deviance.

University preventive measures are harmful in two respects. First, they reinforce a chilling effect, internalized calculation of public scholars that they face formidable risks when intervening in mainstream debates. Initiatives not pursued are difficult to document short of retrospective interviews. Still, the long-standing perception of a "decline of the public intellectual" supports the inference that incentives in academia work against direct engagement with news media. Second, risk-averse communication reinforces a perception of intellectual dissent as gratuitous, exotic, or worse. Claussen argues that news magazines since World War II have reinforced public expectations that universities should serve instrumental ends in faculty research and in preparation of students for employment.[91] Anti-rationalist and anti-elitist criticisms of the American university are thereby conditioned by instrumentalist thinking.

Universities invite attack when they view their campuses as sand sculptures—arches and spires shaped to mirror the sublime but fragile depending on climates of opinion. Defensive tactics are self-defeating in the long run as they contribute to an implied social contract: colleges are useful for applying expertise to industry and instrumental education but should stay out of the people's business when it comes to politics and policy.

Interplay of academia and journalism in the control of ideas deserves more attention with respect to research and reform. Normative theory critical of instrumental communication is itself constricted when it fails to account for the opportunity costs of ideas potentially relevant but not taken up in the news.[92] Digital media constitute not just carriers of populist suspicion but also platforms for innovation in how intellect engages with publics beyond the academy. Scholars, for instance, could document emerging forms of resistance in efforts to repair ideas. Occupied space of on-site resistance is accompanied by space occupied online—discursive space less subject to rendering or distortion of ideas—offering opportunities for public intellectuals to gain traction for ideas rather than see them torn apart.

5

Policing Intellectual Transgressions

News as a Recursive Regime

News conceived in a populist mindset activates schema in which "normal" parts of the population confront one damn thing after another.[1] Feedback loops between media ritual and audience engagement reinforce familiar, simple, and convincing expressions of banal nationalism.[2] In online platforms as plebiscite, audiences upvote articles to share on social media while metrics provide editors with immediate data on popular content.[3] Recursion in political communication reveals itself like fractal geometry— seen everywhere once the initial pattern is recognized.

Recursion scales up and down levels of analysis, but social control of ideas is never seamless. Neither the systems of controls at play in the academic-media nexus nor the recursion embedded in news fully accounts for what happens during *overt confrontations* of intellect with journalism. One way to think about the purpose of intellect in an open society is to recognize the obligation to challenge recursive thinking itself, to make recursion subject to critique. Consequently, we should expect restraints on intellect to be an elaborate undertaking in media. Public intellectuals in democratic theory "float freely in social space."[4] At a still more abstract level, Hofstadter described intellect as resistant to control. Intellect "examines, ponders, wonders, theorizes, criticizes, imagines."[5] Intelligence, by contrast, is tamer, it "seeks to grasp, manipulate, re-order, adjust." The problem of abstraction—from a social control perspective—is that ideas are potentially subversive in the way they migrate from less restrictive realms of knowledge production to mainstream venues.

Social science lacks a framework to account for news media's distinct contributions to policing intellectual transgressions. From journalism studies, we do know that "symbolic annihilation" often awaits social movements when they seek publicity to advance alternative discourses in mainstream media.[6] Symbolic annihilation occurs through three processes: trivialization, omission, and condemnation. These activities are most

Where Ideas Go to Die. Michael McDevitt, Oxford University Press (2020). © Oxford University Press.
DOI: 10.1093/oso/9780190869946.001.0001

clearly standardized in the "protest paradigm."[7] Reporters deploy a toolbox of techniques to depict deviance: focusing on the appearance or mental abilities of protestors, portraying protests as carnivals, and use of eyewitness accounts to cast moral judgment.[8] A favorite motif is the portrayal of radical reformists as hot-blooded when acting collectively. The materiality of political resistance—"from tents to tear gas"—is conducive to depictions of proximate danger in community journalism.[9] Portrayals of collective action abolish "the political rationality of rebellious social subjects through their representation in terms of atavism, boundless violence, lack of will, ignorance, and so on."[10]

An offense of intellect requires a different set of tactics for the reporter in social control mode. She must expunge rationality, while conveying deviance and danger, but without mob behavior. In comparison to the protest paradigm, ideas themselves must be dealt with directly in the portrayal of intellectual deviance, through distortion, de-contextualization, or other means. This chapter examines how the ideology and epistemology of US journalism afford a rationale for the encoding of retributive anti-intellectualism in news as a medium for symbolic action.

Antipathy toward intellect embedded *in the news* should help to explain how this sentiment is mobilized and aligned *through the news* in configurations such as moral panic, social drama, and reification of a punitive public. The news, that is, provides the grounding from which resentment and suspicion outside journalism gain traction in redress of ideational transgressions. A cyclical dynamic emerges in phases of latency and activation. I propose a recursive regime to account for journalism's role in the activation of antipathy, alignment of anti-rationalism with populist anti-elitism in symbolic action, and return to equilibrium. Long after news media respond to an intellectual breach, residual resentment is left behind, awaiting reactivation when the climate is ripe. The chapter concludes by elaborating the thesis introduced in Chapter 1: journalists foreclose on their own capacity to deliberate by subjecting intellect to populist sanction.

A Recursive Regime

The news functions as a technology of social control in a recursive regime,[11] a populist state of mind in the streamlined processing of provocations that give offense and demand retribution. The relationship between journalism and populism of this sort can be modeled as recursive in a system marked by three phases: cultivation of latent attitudes in routine circumstances, redress of an intellectual breach, and return to an equilibrium of diffusive sentiment primed for activation in the next cycle (Figure 5.1).

Applicable to systems as varied as mathematics, linguistics, logic, and music, recursion arises in the repeated application of rules or procedures to "successive results of a process."[12] Recent applications of recursion to political communication stress immediate feedback in a reflexive system, as when memes during election campaigns circulate across blogging and micro-blogging sites, social media, and video-sharing platforms.[13] Recursion, however, implies a fractal geometry in the reactivation of social control across time and place, and consequently its full manifestation requires a careful consideration of temporal dynamics. The model developed here links newswork in real time, punishment of intellectual transgressions by institutions beyond media, and long-term protection of collective memory.

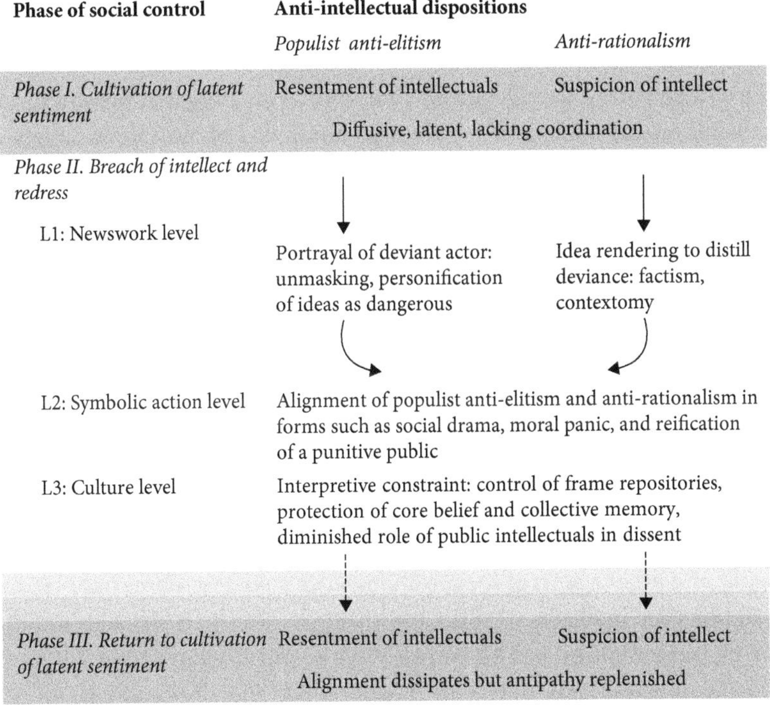

Figure 5.1 Recursion in journalism's control of intellect

This formulation allows for testing construct validity of the model across micro and macro levels in three respects: time, space, and symbolic structure. Chapter 6 documents how story leads in the initial response to an intellectual breach foretold a social drama that would take years to play out, finally resulting in the banishment of Professor Ward Churchill from academia. Put another way, the microcosm of a lead within the microcosm of a single story enacted a script for the symbolic annihilation of unacceptable ideas within and outside journalism. Focusing on spatial aspects of recursion, Chapter 7 continues the study of Churchill as deviant in residence. Tactics deployed by local newspapers to render his views on American innocence vis-à-vis 9/11 were mirrored in the national press, with the latter also picking up the feel of proximate danger. These chapters will illustrate the heuristic value of news as a recursive regime in social control of intellect. The next sections lay out the model.

Phase I. Cultivation of Latent Sentiment

Recursion in news production recognizes a nonlinear, reverberating dynamic with successive periods of latency and activation reinforcing routines that cohere as a system of social control. That said, many potential breaches in the academic-media nexus and elsewhere go unnoticed by most news outlets. An equilibrium remains undisturbed for the most part, most of the time. Some transgressions will cause outrage here and there, motivating an op-ed in a college-town newspaper, for instance, but fall short of the kind of offense that triggers a concerted media response. Journalism nonetheless contributes to anti-intellectualism as an enduring feature of American culture.

In the cultivation of latent sentiment (Figure 5.1, Phase I), journalism helps to perpetuate disregard for intellect through instrumental thinking. Consumers of US news media are familiar with a domesticated version of intellect, one filtered into technical expertise or the binaries of partisan discourse. An unbound intellect might come as a surprise, perceived as odd, or simply rejected as an annoyance. In conjunction with schools, entertainment media, and other agents of socialization, news media reinforce base-level expectations for intellectual work, and this occurs in part through unreflective instrumentalism and hedonism.[14] Ideas and discourse that fail to give pleasure or a pragmatic payoff are downgraded. When breaches occur, cultivated impatience with obscurity can fuel hostility.

Sourcing patterns in the elite press illustrate that the social control of intellect is not confined to tabloids and talk radio. Welch, Fenwick, and Roberts compared the frequency and context for sources in a content analysis of *The New York Times, The Washington Post, Los Angeles Times*, and *Chicago Tribune*.[15] State managers in criminal justice were quoted in connection with crime control and policy options, while professors and non-academic researchers were typically confined to explanations about the causes of crime.

> In fact, many state managers quoted in our sample vehemently ridiculed criminological research while engaging in crass anti-intellectualism: "I was not hired to be Arizona's chief social theorist. I was not sent here to sit meditating on Freud or on the latest 'root causes' of criminal behavior. The criminal law deals not with theories but thugs."[16]

Welch et al. described a striking similarity of policy proclamations from state managers, suggesting policy prescriptions are ideologically "pre-packaged."[17] They found "no genuine radical voices" about crime causation in the sample.[18]

When intellect is not domesticated through sourcing and other tactics, journalism affirms the public's weariness and wariness of intellectuals. In the quality press, reporters and pundits are presumed to know what other intellectuals are up to. Most likely these media figures are credible when they signal to audiences that citizens need not bother with the obscurities and eccentricities of intellectuals. Case in point, the Rev. Jeremiah Wright at the National Press Club on April 28, 2008. Wright was defiant following months of criticism. Earlier that year, ABC News reviewed dozens of his sermons, excepting parts that would guarantee outrage. In one extract, Wright conveyed his reading of the Gospels as they relate to the treatment of African Americans.

> The government gives them the drugs, builds bigger prisons, passes a three-strike law and then wants us to sing "God Bless America." No, no, no, God damn America, that's in the Bible for killing innocent people. God damn America for treating our citizens as less than human. God damn America for as long as she acts like she is God and she is supreme.

Alessandra Stanley reviewed Wright's appearance at the press club for *The New York Times*.[19]

> The Rev. Jeremiah A. Wright Jr. has wriggled out from under sound bites and screen-grab loops to put himself into context in that most American of ways: on television.
>
> And he went deep into context—a rich, stem-winding brew of black history, scripture, hallelujahs and hermeneutics. Mr. Wright, Senator Barack Obama's former pastor, was cocky, defiant, declamatory, inflammatory and mischievous, but most of all, he was all over the place, performing a television triathlon of interview, lecture and live news conference that pushed Mr. Obama aside and placed himself front and center in the presidential election campaign.

The reference to "hermeneutics" was apparently too delicious to resist. Notice also the justification for the rampant de-contextualization that preceded the press club talk; readers are invited to imagine what happens when intellectuals are allowed to speak uninterrupted.[20]

The cultivation of latent sentiment in Phase I incorporates two of three processes of symbolic annihilation referenced earlier: trivialization and omission. The portrait of Rev. Wright illustrates the ease with which intellect is belittled, while Robert Gutsche's "authorized knowers" highlights a practice that ensures omission. In his reading of news coverage of the Boston Marathon bombings, Gutsche characterizes omission in a forceful sense, as proactive suppression in protection of journalism's cultural authority.

> I argue that the press covering the bombings operated quickly to institute immediate explanations for the event by turning to what would hold the most resonance with audiences—that the event was caused by foreign terrorists. In turn, the initial coverage began an immediate process of marginalizing alternative explanations—or ignoring those explanations—as the story progressed and allowed dominant articulations of what caused the bombings to filter to the local press level for further indoctrination of US Exceptionalism.[21]

Six days after the two homemade bombs detonated, NBC's *Meet the Press* trotted out Tom Brokaw. Gutsche captures recursion in microcosm—the journalist as source reciting an authorized, cultural script: " 'With the death of Osama bin Laden, Islamic rage did not go away,' said Brokaw, apparently an expert on Islamic rage. 'In fact, in some ways, it's more dangerous.' "[22] Reliance on journalists themselves and other reassuring knowers contributes to the irrelevance of intellect during trauma, precisely those moments when independent, expert knowledge has the most to offer in comprehending how individuals and institutions might respond.

Phase II. Breach of Intellect and Redress

Stanley's takedown of Wright at the National Press Club reveals how an intellectual could be treated as an object of amusement by the elite press, while portrayed as dangerous or deviant in more commercially driven media. The latter outcome coincides with condemnation in Tuchman's symbolic annihilation. Climate of opinion, partisan orientation of news outlets, and proximity to an offense also factor in whether a significant breach of intellect occurs.

A dramatic transgression of intellect—a breach impossible to ignore or suppress—compels an intervention of journalism into intellectual discourse. Phase II signals a rapid transition from an equilibrium of latent resentment to overt redress. As diagrammed in Figure 5.1, response to a breach connects newswork to symbolic action beyond journalism in the protection of core belief and collective memory. My intent with Phase II is to explicate journalism's response with sufficient precision such that complicity in mobilized anti-intellectualism is neither mercurial nor deniable. The nitty gritty of this phase demonstrates how anti-intellectualism embedded in the news creates a medium from which anti-intellectualism is mobilized and aligned through the news.

In a rare study of ideas in the news, Caudill examined Darwinism in the press. An idea "typically has no clear boundaries, no distinct points in which it is born, lives and dies, no physical limits on its time and place of existence."[23] On the other hand, "any idea, however noble or humble, intelligent or inane, provincial or universal, is filtered through the press." By contrast, the recursive model recognizes that transgressive ideas can *tear through* routines of news production, and when this happens the journalistic response is more aggressive. Ideas are not contained or caught as much as they are dis-configured to mark deviance and to facilitate punishment.

The nature of intellect as a source of provocation suggests that journalism does not simply recognize an insult to binding belief. Journalism must proceed despite an intellectual deficit and without the option of describing action as dangerous, illegal, or bizarre. Shoemaker and Reese observe that "those with less power must break through into the news via deviant acts,"[24] a scenario that would *not* apply to intellectuals in possession of cultural capital and the will to confront orthodoxy.

Journalism is well equipped to cope with conventional politics as portrayed in "strategic ritual." Through practices such as reliance on official sources, attribution, balancing of opinions, and verifying facts, objectivity is deployed to "anticipate attack" and to "deflect criticism."[25] With privileged access to media, political and economic power is imprinted in the news as a result of this deferential and defensive objectivity. The routines of objectivity are put aside during ceremonies, anniversaries, and other situations rich in cultural resonance, and during periods of war and crisis, when journalism demonstrates allegiance to consensual belief.[26] Media sociology, however, has mostly ignored redeployment of objectivity in social construction of intellectual deviance. In the nation's civil religion, absolutist beliefs represent dangerous territory for news that conveys critical perspectives in areas such as American exceptionalism, the meaning of the September 11 attacks, or the use of sacred symbols in collective memory.[27] Routine protocols of news production are not adequate. Use of quotes might fail to sufficiently distance reporters from reviled sources; vetting of intellectual positions might imply tolerance when journalists instead sense a need to show allegiance to offended audiences.

In response to a breach, journalism ideology directs newswork in the activation of populist anti-elitism and anti-rationalization (Phase II, Level 1). Populist resentment is condoned in portrayal of deviants through the practice of unmasking. As discussed in Chapter 2, unmasking of power derives from the epistemology of essentialism, such that nuance is viewed as dissemblance, perspective as distraction, and context as shield. A journalistic version of democratic populism thereby justifies anti-rationalism in the news. While unmasking inspires investigative journalism and justifies intrusion into the private lives of politicians, it is at play in confrontations with intellectuals as members of the cultural elite. From a storytelling perspective, a punitive public reacts to an object of resentment, a requirement that would apply whether anger is simply imagined by journalists, animated spontaneously, or mobilized by actors outside media. Personification of ideas is also useful in populist reporting, a technique that transfigures abstraction into activity and agency of some kind.

In concert with the affirmation of populist resentment, *idea rendering* contributes to the activation of anti-rationalism. I propose idea rendering as a way to crystallize, theoretically, the process in which journalists translate intellectual provocations into deviance, advancing social control through symbolic action. The hegemonic purpose is to distill discourse to clearly isolate intellect as an object of public attention, juxtaposing dissent with moral consensus. In the study that best encapsulates rendering (but without using the term), MacGregor examined news coverage of Dr. Rowan Williams, the archbishop of Canterbury.[28] Williams proposed that diversity and inclusion could coincide in a multicultural legal system without damaging principles of UK law. Beyond describing his ideas as "obscure," the British press mostly ignored the speech, delivered in London. Instead, journalists pounced on a remark in a BBC interview, when Williams suggested that incorporation of Sharia law "seems unavoidable."[29] MacGregor hints at what I refer to as rendering:

> [U]nder the guise of "jargon-busting," a prime element of journalism is that much of its output is in some ways superior to that of the civic communicators whose output it handles. All sources of discourse are "put through the mill."[30]

Simplification of complex ideas is endemic to journalism, systemized in training through the "nut graph" in news writing and stylistic imperatives to shun jargon. The craft of clarification also serves journalism in a boundary-maintenance role. Nuance and context can blur distinctions between normative and deviant beliefs. Even as idea rendering distorts an intellectual perspective, it clearly signals when an ideological breach has occurred. By contrast, intellectual provocation relies on nuance to bridge conventional belief with new ways of thinking. Appeals to the civil sphere—to a shared cultural legacy[31] are undermined by the shedding of subtlety, a move that reinforces the view of intellectuals as alienated from society with little to offer in the pragmatics of policy or the building of social movements.

Journalists traffic in "contextomy" by excerpting words "from their original linguistic context in a way that distorts the source's intentions."[32] When a concept, trope, or other rhetorical bit is extracted from a linguistic context, it is not just de-contextualized but re-contextualized into a story frame whose purpose differs from the intent of the source. Contextomy could be interpreted as a form of "factism" in the rendering of intellectual discourse. Johnson-Cartee writes that journalists "are obsessed with uncovering, discovering, or collecting facts, since producing 'facts' in their news stories legitimizes the account and establishes its objectivity."[33]

In Tuchman's acclaimed ethnography from the 1970s, news is combustible, depending on the ideological contexts in which journalists negotiate social reality. "Every story entails dangers for news personnel and for the news organization."[34] She portrayed news production as a defensive, ritualistic performance: reporters "invoke their objectivity almost the way a Mediterranean peasant might wear a clove of garlic around his neck to ward off evil spirits."[35] In the paradox of strategic ritual, journalists seek credibility by absolving themselves from interpretation and their responsibility, in the first place, for de-contextualization.

The factism that guides rendering of intellectual dissent is arguably more interventionist than the processing of facts from state mangers and other official sources as described above. Journalists typically do not explain why they focus on a particular passage when mining through discourse, but to the extent that they are sensitive to violations of core belief, an extract can appear as self-evident in its deviance. An extract might circulate widely in the news in contexts many degrees of freedom away from its native discourse. This repetition confirms the collective experience of journalism,[36] promoting a naturalized view of an intellectual discretion as an obvious offense. In another irony, the extract circulates as a fact, protecting the authority of anti-rationalism in the news.

Story templates are also guided by how journalists imagine audiences. During episodes of moral panic, for example, journalists hold deviance accountable to judgment of the citizenry. In such circumstances, public opinion "is 'the group' that is 'doing the accepting.' "[37] A public of social consensus and social sanction is similarly invoked in the protest paradigm,[38] while a public of impatience and contempt is conveyed in the "public nuisance paradigm."[39] Reification of a punitive public portrays audiences as active participants in democratic populism. MacGregor describes this process as channeling a public mentality "that is condoned through the anti-intellectualism of its techniques."[40] Anti-rationalism and populist anti-elitism are thereby tightly bound in the relationship between idea rendering and a reified public.

Intellect stirs suspicion by subjecting absolutist belief to systemic critique.[41] Ideas reinforce each other in a coherent structure, in ways that disturb conventional thinking. An intellectual breach consequently constitutes a distinct form of transgression in that deliberation itself is more directly at stake compared with "talk scandals" that might arise, for example, from a politician's gaffe.[42] Recognition of a provocation in fully contextualized discourse is not necessarily obvious in the way that overt behavior is readily portrayed as a threat. Intellectual discourse must be rendered in some way to clarify ideas as threats to widely held beliefs, as evident in the Sharia law episode discussed earlier.

Newswork coordinates populist anti-elitism with anti-rationalism in symbolic action beyond journalism, representing a shift to the next level of analysis (L2). Populist retribution directed at intellectual elites, condoned by unmasking or personification of ideas as dangerous, is further justified by practices such as contextomy and factism. In this alignment of anti-elitism with anti-rationalism, the news provides a guide for mobilization of antipathy through story arcs that end in sanction rather than deliberation. Coordination helps to rationalize resentment outside journalism in domains such as the do-it-yourself justice of social-media vigilantes.[43]

Symbolic action is triggered when provocations are not easily or simply ignored in news media through trivialization and omission. This might occur when individuals or institutions—usually ignored or assumed to be in allegiance with normative belief—are exposed as guilty of a breach. Social drama might describe what Bill Maher experienced shortly after the 9/11 attacks when he argued, as host of the ABC talk show *Politically Incorrect*, that the hijackers were not cowards. Options for redress beyond media included the White House press secretary warning that all Americans "need to watch what they say and watch what they do."[44] Social drama, modeled in the anthropology of Victor Turner,[45] bridges storytelling with social action. For our purposes, social drama takes the form of media ritual,[46] giving shape and structure to anti-intellectualism (Chapter 6). Reification of public sentiment demonstrates journalistic alliance with populist anger, distancing news media from offensive ideas while depicting audiences as active participants in social drama.

News as a script for symbolic action applies to breaches committed by other journalists, pundits, religious leaders, and actors more broadly categorized as intellectuals. For example, consider normative medical practice. White chronicled the moral panic that accompanied news coverage of Jack Kevorkian in the 1990s.[47] Depictions in the news amplified deviance of "Dr. Death" as an advocate of physician-assisted suicide,[48] setting the stage for ritualistic punishment.

To be sure, journalism's response to breaches in the academic-media nexus is distinct in some respects from how media might subject a non-academic to intense coverage.[49] Many remarks and sound bites are raw material for contextomy,[50] but rendering in the control of ideas is more systematic when an extract was originally embedded in a body of academic work or situated in an entire intellectual paradigm. Higher education is also distinct in how intellectuals are portrayed in news and social media, as when moral entrepreneurs circulate memes of subversive professors. The activist/scholar Dana Cloud drew from her personal archive of hate mail to identify three frames attributed to her: gender traitor, elitist intellectual, and national traitor.[51]

In cultural practice, the final (L3) level of analysis in Phase II, journalism acts as a trustee of collective memory and a guardian of binding belief. Anti-elitism lacks a foil when offending intellectuals are no longer salient in the news, but anti-rationalism remains embedded in news in routines described above and in Chapter 2. While dissenting views that emanate from intellectual discourse are still available outside mainstream media, they are effectively cut from the news agenda when idea rendering occurs. The interpretive constraint imposed by agenda cutting limits the capacity for media consumers, pundits, and journalists themselves to negotiate alternative frames when future events implicate themes and heuristics confined to intellectual discourse.[52]

Journalists draw on frame repositories—interpretive schemes that are "culturally and cognitively available" to them.[53] Frames travel in a competitive environment,[54] and while a simple Google search nets a multitude of perspectives on a given issue, frames with cultural resonance spread most quickly.[55] When frames preferred by public intellectuals are rendered deviant or impotent, they are unlikely to compete well in the news.

Phase III. Return to Cultivation of Latent Sentiment

A transition to latent sentiment occurs gradually, unlike the detection and response to a breach. Activation of anti-intellectualism in symbolic action leaves behind resentment and suspicion, submerged in the next phase of equilibrium and cultivated for reactivation when the climate is ripe and the next breach occurs. The alignment of populist anti-elitism and anti-rationalism dissipates over time, but antipathy is replenished.

A residual effect of news media protecting collective memory and binding belief is a refreshing of memory about how audiences should feel about intellectual dissent. Episodes of virulent anti-intellectualism are likely consequential as socializing experiences for media consumers primed for outrage.

Punishment of dissent should also leave a mark on future generations of reporters and editors in the internalization of retributive drama. Chapter 8 connects these two ideas by revealing a hidden curriculum in professional education. A survey of students at five US colleges shows that majoring in journalism does not guard against support for journalistic anti-rationalism and anti-elitism. Anti-intellectualism as cultural sentiment appears to seep into professional training without much resistance.

Agents and Objects of Social Control

Figure 5.1's aerial view suggests an efficient and systemic regime, but I do not want to give the impression that all of the news practices identified are deployed in every case of redress. I do want to emphasize that the ideology and epistemology of journalism provide a formidable arsenal that almost effortlessly connects the logic of newswork with the logic of social control. Conversely, this modeling is not presented as exhaustive. Future research on news in regulation of intellect is likely to reveal other tactics that highlight deviance while simultaneously affirming journalism's allegiance to consensual belief.

Mudde characterizes populism as a "thin-centered" ideology that "considers society to be ultimately separated into two homogeneous and antagonistic groups, 'the pure people' versus 'the corrupt elite.'"[56] While populism is typically not motivated by doctrinaire thinking, it does require grounding in a medium of rationalization and mobilization to translate diffusive grievance into symbolic action. The encoding of resentment and suspicion in the news inscribes mass media as a cultural resource for the co-ordination of inchoate sentiment.

Public opinion in populist sentiment is not a matter of deliberation and compromise but expressed in the *volonté générale* (general will) of the people. Representation of the demos this way in the news animates media as a moralizing force when ideational dissent or other transgressions of cultural elites are depicted as insults to consensual belief. The coupling of populist anti-elitism with ant-rationalism in storytelling helps to explain how the social control of ideas is internalized in newswork. When journalists anticipate restive audiences in response to absolutism challenged, the imagined public compels content devices that operationalize the culturally prescribed role of social control. The interplay of anti-rationalism with populist anti-elitism is recursive at multiple levels: the psychology of news reception, routines of newswork, symbolic action extending beyond journalism, and the long-term protection of core belief.[57] At each level, a recursive regime aligns the offensive with those offended: intellect with the public. Audiences play meaningful roles that affirm their wisdom in a closed, self-referential system.

Journalists become agents and objects of social control in the linkage of anti-rationalism with populist anti-elitism. They are subdued by their own agency. When individuals conform by considering how they are perceived (the "looking-glass self"), they control themselves, and in this process writ large absolutist beliefs are rarely questioned.[58] Literature on news and deviance suggests that journalists should be quite adept at recognizing a linguistic bit as violating a core belief;[59] this violation is typically of greater news value when it is extracted from a movement or a body of work and re-contextualized to clearly convey deviance. Experimental research warrants an inferential extension of the fundamental attribution error to the evaluation of dissent. Polarization of judgment about activists is more pronounced when they are described as individuals rather than as members of a group advancing a particular cause.[60] Idea rendering in news production is consequently an overtly interventionist and ideological tactic that serves journalism's credibility at the expense of its own intellectual integrity.

The subtle nature of social control in newswork coupled with the dissonance of professional ideals juxtaposed against practice imply that journalists would deny that they participate in the quashing of intellect. On the other hand, the very existence of professional angst about working conditions signals that a corrective reflexivity endures in an era of corporate downsizing of newsrooms and tabloidization.[61] As documented in Chapter 7, journalists express ambivalence, regret, and resistance in response to pressures that compel moralistic depictions of intellectual dissent. In one form of resistance, "dangerous professors" engender reflexivity when interviewed by reporters in ways that break recursive thinking, making the news a safer space for intellect (Chapter 9).

Journalists nevertheless foreclose on their ability to deliberate by subjecting intellect to the judgment of the citizenry. Internalization of idea suppression is hinted at in the protest paradigm, where reporters describe bystanders of collective action as symbols of public reaction to protestors, similar to how a chorus performed in ancient Greek theater.[62] Bystanders appear bemused, irritated, enraged, sobbing, and mocking as protesters march by, anything but curious about the ideas that motivated protests in the first place. These depictions also condone a journalism that is likewise disinterested—if not hostile—to the ideas that fuel social movements.

Political communication in a recursive system comprises a compressed universe of legitimate and legitimating discourse. News in this habitus is self-referential,[63] justified by content that conforms to expectations of journalists[64] and audiences they imagine.[65] The enveloping nature of this dynamic—including feedback of a reified public affirming reporting tactics—helps to explain why reporters and editors fail to see their complicity (Chapter 3). The fact that public mood is imagined yet so consequential underscores the pernicious hold of recursion.

The recursive regime is purposefully schematic for the sake of theory building, to show how journalism is deployed in sustained, symbolic action. Over time, however, efficiency in idea suppression would engender a collectively internalized recursion in less need of overt retribution. The final chapter contemplates how preconditions for tyranny are eerily recursive in a media landscape that echoes incantations of demagogues. In the worst outcome, the processes and sequences depicted in Figure 5.1 collapse into a singularity. News as a technology of control transmutes into a state of mind—the authoritarian thinking that shadows redress.

6

Social Drama at Macro and Micro Levels

The Fractal Control of Dissent

A scholar of Native American studies, Ward Churchill totes an AK-47 on the jacket of *On the Justice of Roosting Chickens: Reflections on the Consequences of U.S. Imperial Arrogance and Criminality*.[1] He has been active in militant protests since the Vietnam War; his resume includes stints with the Black Panthers and the Weather Underground. More recently, he was one of the leaders of the Colorado American Indian Movement's (AIM) annual confrontation with a Columbus Day parade in Denver. He taught an unsanctioned class after University of Colorado (CU) officials seemingly banished him from the Boulder campus.

Media studies was the last thing on his mind when he sat down, within hours of the 9/11 attacks, to knock out "Some People Push Back."[2] The essay ridiculed the premise that America's presence in the world could be understood in terms of moral exceptionalism. He argued that ordinary Americans were complicit in supporting a history of militarism in the Middle East. Churchill plowed through the motives and consequences of US involvement in various regions of the globe, dismissing with contempt the notion that Americans could have been surprised by payback. In Colorado and elsewhere, news media responded with the most ferocious blowback against intellectual dissent in the post-9/11 era.

Deviance—whether behavioral or intellectual—is controlled through isolation in a setting of intense scrutiny and concern about moral contagion.[3] The Churchill case highlights the agency of proximate media in social drama, a form of media ritual that links storytelling to social action in idea suppression. Cottle writes that mediatized rituals "are those exceptional and performative media phenomena that serve to sustain and/or mobilize collective sentiments and solidarities on the basis of symbolization and a subjunctive orientation to what should or ought to be."[4] This chapter documents how social drama is embedded in the news in response to an intellectual breach. The analysis uncovers a fractal-like structure, such that ritualistic punishment as

Where Ideas Go to Die. Michael McDevitt, Oxford University Press (2020). © Oxford University Press.
DOI: 10.1093/oso/9780190869946.001.0001

a cultural response is anticipated in the first wave of news text. Exposure of the macro-micro constitution, in turn, leads to a discussion as to whether journalism's performance is best understood as culturally conscripted or opportunistic. The former is the more benign interpretation. In the latter scenario, a predatory press elevates its cultural status at intellect's expense.

Dramaturgy of Suspicion

The Norwegian playwright Henrik Ibsen depicted the complicity of a community newspaper in *An Enemy of the People*,[5] a plot that foreshadowed McCarthyism in the middle of the twentieth century. An editor in Ibsen's play conspired with the mayor to turn the people against a doctor who discovered contaminated water in the town's health baths. The American playwright Arthur Miller adapted the drama for Broadway in a production that opened in 1950. Newspaper complicity resurfaced three years later as a subtext to *The Crucible*.[6] Miller conceived the play—a dramatization of Salem witchcraft trials—as an allegory to McCarthyism.

Possibilities for stirring mistrust subsist in any culture preoccupied by subversive elements. Journalists in these circumstances write the news by telling stories that resonate in mythology of innocence and proximate danger. The cultural historian Robert Darnton recalled his experiences in writing news to account for "a way of seeing the world that somehow reached the *New York Times* from *Mother Goose*."[7] The striving of reporters for recognition in the newsroom is accompanied by an internalization of ancient ways of storytelling. The personal experience of writing the news is validated by cultural affirmation as well when the narrative produced casts the people as united in the defeat of an internal enemy. Intellectuals evoke resentment as experts (e.g., Ibsen's physician) and ideologues (e.g., McCarthy's artists and academics). Their defeat requires a mobilization of the people unified against those with superior knowledge, an alignment of populist anti-elitism with anti-rationalism.

News media are attuned to the internal enemy, a wariness that serves storytelling but also surveillance and exposure.[8] The dramaturgy of journalism in this respect helps to account for how intellectuals are invested with the power of subversion. In the case of McCarthyism, crusaders were indifferent to communism's actual power in world politics.[9] Instead, they fixated on domestic, impotent communists, taking advantage of a compliant press.

Far afield from American media, the anthropologist Victor Turner apprehended social drama while documenting the symbolism of crisis resolution in Ndembu villages of Zambia.[10] A social drama is comprised of "discernible inaugural, transitional, and terminal motifs, that is, a beginning, a middle, and an end."[11] In Turner's four "acts," the first is a rupture in relations; a *breach* makes evident a deeper division of interests and loyalties than what appears on the surface.

> Once visible, [a breach] can hardly be revoked. Whatever may be the case, a mounting crisis follows, a momentous juncture or turning point in the relations between components of a social field—at which seeming peace becomes overt conflict and covert antagonisms become visible. Sides are taken, factions are formed, and unless the conflict can be sealed off quickly within a limited area of social interaction, there is a tendency for the breach to widen and spread.[12]

In the second act, a *crisis* expands "until it coincides with some dominant cleavage in the widest set of relevant social relations."[13] Media are perhaps most consequential at this stage. Social drama is not necessarily a manifestation of moral panic, but in keeping with Cohen's conception, media mobilize and amplify collective fears and anxieties, focusing agitation against a symbolic other.[14] Journalists thereby make clear the deep division of interests and loyalties between the populace and the offending/disloyal intellectual. Subversive ideas normally repressed or ignored in the academic-media nexus tear through to the surface.

The third act is a remedy to the initial problem, or *redress* and reestablishment of social relations. Mechanisms of redress can range from interpersonal advice to informal arbitration to judicial inquiry to full-fledged performance of public ritual. "Such ritual involves a literal or moral 'sacrifice,' that is, a victim as scapegoat is offered."[15] In a Durkheimian interpretation,[16] the ultimate purpose of redress is not punishment of an offending individual; ritual reinforces social cohesiveness while situating the element in question within a stable location of deviance. Turner, however, emphasized the liminality of social drama, its betwixt-between quality and indeterminacy of outcome; the redressive phase can break down, returning to crisis. Ritual, "in its full performative flow,"[17] is also capable of creative modifications at many levels of societal change. The final act occurs as *reintegration*, return to the status quo, or *recognition of schism and separation*, an alteration in social arrangements.

The heuristic value of social drama is evident in the range of case studies to which it has been deployed: mayoral politics in Chicago;[18] the benching of an iconic quarterback;[19] conservative reaction to a Christian/feminist conference;[20] newspaper coverage of stadium construction controversies;[21] and the phenomenology of slam-dancing.[22] None of these applications address the ritualistic summoning of anti-intellectualism, but this literature does offer insights about the form and function of mediatized ritual in social control.

Ettema's review of the "Cokely affair" in Chicago represents the most explicit effort to link journalism studies with a cultural understanding of ritual in social drama. Steve Cokely, an aide to the mayor, made anti-Semitic remarks in speeches to black nationalists during the spring of 1988, triggering a press rite of discord and healing. In conceptualizing press *mediation* of social drama, Ettema refers to both *representation* and *attempted resolution*. Throughout a drama, media "provide the enactment with its particular symbolic form—its imagery and plotline—and they assemble an audience to witness, and perhaps become involved in, the performance."[23]

The Case of Ward Churchill

American journalism operated under the weight of formidable expectations in the years following September 11, tasked with protecting the national grieving process,[24] negotiating collective memory,[25] and affirming innocence within a reassuring binary of good and evil.[26] Intellectual positions deemed "'relativistic' or 'post-' of any kind were viewed as either complicitous with terrorism or as constituting a 'weak link' in the fight against it."[27] A strategic orientation in news media would likely take heed of anti-rational and absolutist rumblings in the post-9/11 climate.[28]

As discussed in Chapter 5, Tuchman's conception of news as strategic ritual fails to protect journalism in direct engagement with intellectual transgressions.[29] Vetting of dissident perspectives might signal tolerance for reviled ideas. Protocols in the objectivity paradigm—attribution, balancing of opinions, use of quotes to set off the offensive from the reasonable—might fail to sufficiently insulate the news.

Social drama provides journalism with an elaborate and sustained script in the control of intellect. Turner emphasized that social drama does not refer merely to genres of storytelling, gossip, and rumor. Social drama embodies social action, a perspective that resonates with cultural approaches to textual analysis. Culture as text itself "can have moments of 'deep play' . . . beyond the direct producers' and audiences' attentions."[30] Textual analysis for this chapter addresses the following question: In alignment with other institutions, how did the Denver press contribute to social drama in portraying Churchill's dissent as deviant, requiring some kind of intervention (i.e., redress)?

The *Rocky Mountain News* closed on February 27, 2009, but that paper (circulation 340,000) and *The Denver Post* (also 340,000) boasted the largest distributions in the Rocky Mountain region as the drama unfolded. Using Nexis Uni, I retrieved articles and commentary on Churchill, excluding items less than 100 words, from print versions of *The Denver Post* (*DP*) and *Rocky Mountain News* (*RMN*). The study period begins September 12, 2001, with the essay published online and ends July 15, 2009 with a ruling against Churchill's reinstatement following a vote of CU regents to fire him. The search yielded 413 items (news accounts, opinion columns, and editorials). Figure 6.1 maps the time span, major events, and coverage associated with breach, crisis, redress, and separation. I also draw from the event sequence chronicled more exhaustively in Appendix Table 6.1. The chronology that follows recognizes a reverberating dynamic in the representation and performance of social drama, rather than a linear progression.

Act I: Breach

Churchill was by some accounts the most frequently cited scholar of ethnic studies in the United States. Still, his broadside on motivations for 9/11 lay frozen in a far corner of the Internet until January 21, 2005, when he was scheduled to speak at Hamilton College in New York and the student newspaper published excerpts. Coverage that ensued fixated on one passage from the essay, and one analogy in particular, in which Churchill questioned the innocence of those who perished in the World Trade Center:

> If there was a better, more effective, or in fact any other way of visiting some penalty befitting their participation upon the little Eichmanns inhabiting the sterile sanctuary of the twin towers, I'd really be interested in hearing about it.[31]

Churchill hammered out the essay within hours of the 9/11 attacks. A Native American activist, he would later describe the polemic as "gut

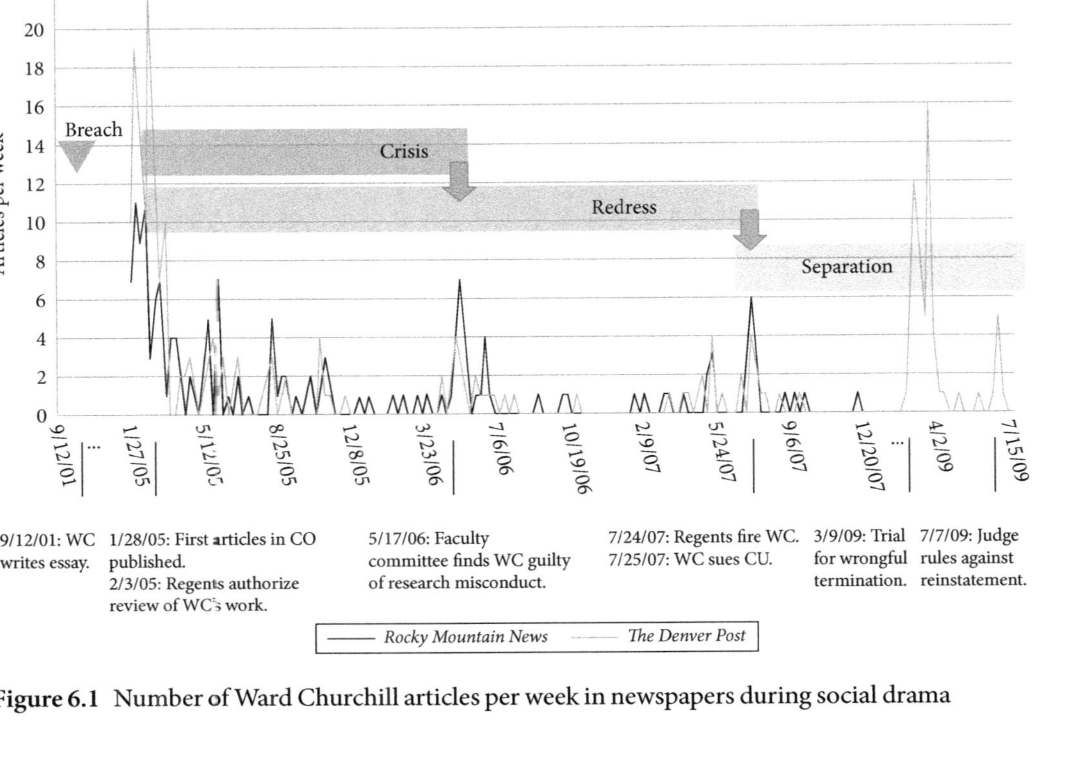

Figure 6.1 Number of Ward Churchill articles per week in newspapers during social drama

Table 6.1 Scripting of social drama in initial wave of newspaper leads

---

Italics—breach/crisis; **bold—redress/separation**

The Denver Post	Rocky Mountain News
1-28-05 Two Colorado **congressman demanded** Thursday that a University of Colorado professor **apologize** for *comparing victims of the Sept. 11 World Trade Center attack to Nazis.*	1-27-05 A University of Colorado professor has *sparked controversy* in New York over an essay he wrote that maintains that *people killed in the Sept. 11, 2001, terrorist attacks were not innocent victims.*
1-31-05 **Regents** at the University of Colorado **have called a special meeting** Thursday over concerns about a professor who *likened victims of the Sept. 11 attacks to a manager of the Nazi plan to exterminate Jews.*	1-28-05 For a man who has weathered *anonymous death threats* telephoned to his home, the latest turmoil is comparatively tame.
2-2-05 **Hamilton College** in New York **has cancelled** the panel discussion featuring University of Colorado ethnic-studies professor Ward Churchill, citing *dozens of threats* to the college and members of the panel.	1-29-05 Hamilton College will likely expand the size of next week's panel featuring *controversial* University of Colorado professor Ward Churchill, in the wake of *heavy public criticism* concerning his upcoming appearance.
2-3-05 The **Keetoowah Band of Cherokee Indians said** Wednesday that University of Colorado professor Ward **Churchill is** an associate member of the tribe but **not a full member**, which requires a person to have at least one-fourth Cherokee blood.	1-31-05 The University of Colorado **Board of Regents has called a special meeting** Thursday to discuss the views of Ward Churchill, a professor who says *people killed in the Sept. 11 terrorist attacks were not innocent victims.*
2-3-05 A University of Colorado regent says the board won't fire *controversial* ethnic studies professor Ward Churchill when it meets today, despite *urgent* **calls for his termination from lawmakers** at the Capitol **and Gov. Bill Owens.**	2-1-05 *Embattled* University of Colorado professor **Ward Churchill resigned** his chairmanship of the school's ethnic studies program Monday.
2-4-05 University of Colorado *regents on Thursday apologized to "all Americans"* for remarks an Ethnic studies professor made *comparing victims of the 9/11 attacks to a Nazi leader.*	2-2-05 Europeans stole a continent from American Indians, and they treat the rest of the world the same way. That's the theme to which University of Colorado ethnic studies professor Ward Churchill has returned repeatedly in writings over the past 25 years.
2-6-05 Top state and University of Colorado officials say more *radical comments* by professor Ward Churchill *calling for the United States to be put "out of existence" and saying that more "9/11s are necessary"* **should be included in a review of whether to fire the controversial professor.**	2-2-05 **Gov. Bill Owens called on Ward Churchill to quit** Tuesday as the *embattled* University of Colorado professor returned to the classroom for the first time since he became the center of what has become a *political firestorm.*

Table 6.1 *Continued*

Italics—breach/crisis; **bold—redress/separation**

The Denver Post	Rocky Mountain News
2-8-05 Citing *threats of violence,* University of Colorado **officials canceled a speech** scheduled for today by controversial professor Ward Churchill.	2-2-05 Will the real Ward Churchill please stand up? Almost everything about Churchill seems to be in dispute—from whether he really is an American Indian to the value of his scholarship.
2-9-05 Met by *wild* applause Tuesday night from hundreds of supporters, *controversial* University of Colorado professor Ward Churchill *strongly attacked* Gov. Bill Owens and the CU Board of Regents and said he would *never back down* from his *comparison of some 9/11 victims to Nazi Adolf Eichmann.*	2-3-05 The **United Keetoowah Band Cherokee says** University of Colorado professor Ward **Churchill is not a member** of their tribe
2-10-05 University of Colorado **officials reviewing Ward Churchill's writings** and qualifications will find questions about his scholarship and accuracy dating back at least eight years.	2-3-05 University of Colorado **regents seem united** on one thing: *They abhor* what ethnic studies professor Ward Churchill had to say about the Sept. 11 terrorist attacks.

reaction" to motives for the attack. The essay confronts the idea of American innocence while assigning collective guilt to the "technocratic corps" (stockbrokers and others) of empire, far removed from the consequences of their actions that result in the "starved and rotting flesh of infants."

King and deYoung argue that the essay's theme was not unique in claiming that the attacks were a result of US foreign policy;[32] several authors by early 2005 had challenged the frame advanced by President George W. Bush of "a monumental struggle of good versus evil."[33]

What does separate the Churchill counterframe from all others that began emerging in 2005, however, is its transgressive nature. In Churchill's narrative, it is not just U.S. political leaders and their policies, or, for that matter, the nation-state who are responsible for the September 11 attacks but all ordinary Americans who like "good Germans" gleefully "cheered" the devastating effects of those policies.[34]

Schulz and Reyes suggest that Churchill's polemic "might have encouraged reflection among its readers regarding the causes of 9/11, but instead it provoked a backlash of monumental proportions."[35] As rhetorical scholars, Schulz and Reyes argue that Churchill violated public memory in combination with a destruction of *sensus communis*. To be sure, Churchill's polemic was overtly antagonistic, but I am less satisfied with a reading confined to the essay. Journalistic rendering of Churchill's ideas helps to explain both the backlash and a disconnect between the content of the essay and content of the news controversy, suggesting a kind of gatekeeping whereby ideational substance is blocked and deviance extracted.

Churchill apparently did not breach norms in the academic culture—or in the online world of leftist activism—however incendiary the Eichmann comparison was to so many. His invective sat like a delayed explosive for more than three years, illustrating how the transgression required journalistic agency for the breach to become visible to a large audience. This is shown in Figure 6.1 with the breach phase accompanied by no news coverage.

The time lag echoes the social drama described by Hoover and Clark. Topics and themes addressed in a Christian/feminist conference "were believed, by planners and participants, to exist within a protected space."[36] Churchill may have violated an implicit rule of academe, but this norm refers to the acceptability of academic labor that could foreseeably engage mainstream media.[37] In other words, while Churchill's essay violated the core, cultural belief of American innocence, and represented a combustible polemic in mass media, it was not necessarily a breach of academic discourse.

Tuchman's construct of newsmaking as defensive ritual brings up the question whether the essay constituted a breach of journalism itself.[38] In Turner's framework, a breach signals a threat to individuals and institutions responsible for maintaining norms. In the Churchill case, the little Eichmanns trope became an opportunity for journalism to elevate its ideological status as a watchdog in patrol of the university sphere. However, the opportunity was also a threat in light of scholarship portraying a patriotic press in response to 9/11. US journalism had adopted and internalized the War on Terrorism frame propagated by the White House.[39] As a "shared organizing principle," the War on Terrorism frame was manifest in news content but also in how journalists thought and talked about post-9/11 events.[40] Consequently, while Churchill did not directly target news media in the essay, US journalism was in some respects under ideological attack vis-à-vis the meaning of 9/11.[41]

A breach against journalism adds to an already complex endeavor in theorizing about the role of media in social drama. Notice that Cokely's anti-Semitic remarks were not a breach of journalism in the sense that news media are not predisposed to protect politicians who voice ethnic slurs. By contrast, Churchill's essay transgressed the profession's understanding of the terrorist attacks.[42] Thus, to Ettema's representation and attempted resolution, I propose *predation* as a third role for journalism when social dramas defend fundamental beliefs.

Act II: Crisis

A crisis "represents a moment when a more true state of affairs is revealed, when it is least easy to don masks."[43] The Churchill case epitomizes what contemporary universities try to avoid in the academic-media nexus. As discussed in Chapter 4, risk-averse tactics represent an effort to forestall mutual hostility: intellectuals' contempt of the public, and the public's periodic desire to humiliate cultural elites.[44]

In January 2005, with Churchill scheduled to speak at Hamilton, a professor of government forwarded the essay to an editor of *The Spectator*, the student newspaper. A firestorm leapt across media venues, from an initial Associated Press (AP) story on January 26, 2005, to cable news networks, newspapers in Colorado and New York, and talk radio. The first AP article declared: "A University of Colorado professor who compared the victims of the Sept. 11 attacks on the World Trade Center to Nazis has ignited protests on a college campus where he's been invited to speak." Tumult around the Eichmann reference brought a flurry of insinuation, innuendo, and grudges that resembled, at times, a circus of political diatribe. On January 28, a *Rocky Mountain News* editorial stated flatly: "The University of Colorado employs an apologist for mass murder as a professor of ethnic studies, but we can't say we're terribly surprised."[45]

The media glare forced Churchill to issue a press release on January 31 to explain that he is not a defender of the 9/11 attacks, and that he was not characterizing children, service workers, and firemen who died as little Eichmanns. Churchill's effort to re-situate the reference in a banality-of-evil thesis appeared futile against a tide of de-contextualization.

Within days of the discovery of his essay, Churchill was elevated in the national consciousness as an iconic figure, symbolizing an imagined cadre of disloyal professors undeserving of the academic freedom they hide behind.[46] On February 1, Hamilton canceled Churchill's appearance, citing death threats. That same day, according to CU President Elizabeth Hoffman, Colorado Governor Bill Owens made "a short and threatening phone call" telling her to "fire Churchill tomorrow."[47] Two days later, CU regents authorized an examination of Churchill's writings and speeches (Figure 6.1). On February 21, CU launched a review of instructors' files to identify faculty who had not signed "loyalty oaths." Contributing to a leitmotif of crisis, the *Rocky* and *Post* produced 81 news accounts during the initial month of the frenzy. Including commentary, the papers published an average of four items per day. The volume of coverage is explained in part by a "Republic of Boulder" effect. Denver editors pounce on incidents that resonate with imagery of the campus community as notoriously liberal.[48]

Act III: Redress

Judging by the heft of news attention, the crisis dissipated soon after a faculty committee found Churchill guilty of research misconduct in May 2006.[49] Redress blended the symbolic with the pragmatics of punishment, as the governor, regents, and others manipulated "the machinery of redress."[50] In one of the incidents, Governor Owens leveraged the weight of his office to demand immediate firing of a tenured professor. After a two-year investigation, the regents would later dismiss Churchill on charges of research misconduct concerning the claim that the US government was complicit in genocide committed against Native Americans, but at the time of the phone call to CU's president, the governor's only grounds for complaint was a professor's political speech.

The Churchill case does not reveal the journalistic reflexivity observed by Ettema. In a liminal moment, Chicago "journalists spewed out all sorts of hypotheses and considered many modes of explanation that they would ordinarily exclude from political reportage."[51] By contrast, the Colorado press was unwilling to pursue redress through deliberation. Content analysis conducted for the next chapter reveals a persistent pattern of reporters extracting "little Eichmann" from its banality-of evil context. Denver newspapers did, however, appear to enter a liminal phase, as evident in the loosening of professional norms associated with a restrained objectivity. The staggering volume of coverage, rampant de-contextualization, and strident commentary reflected opportunism, if not a predatory instinct.[52] While Ettema noted that media "perhaps become involved" in performance,[53] the Churchill drama clearly shows a blending of narration with antagonism.

The *Rocky* was known as the more conservative of the Denver dailies, and it devoted more resources to the Churchill affair, publishing 56 news articles during the first month; the *Post* published 25. The attention the *Rocky* gave to the controversy at key moments suggests a de facto intervention into the academic field or at least a concentrated effort to influence how CU would proceed. An abbreviated timeline, while not suggesting causality, shows the interplay of Denver newspapers and CU in redress leading to separation:

- January 29, 2005: *DP* editorial: "If Churchill is so out of sync with the chancellor and the campus . . . why is he chairing an academic department at the University of Colorado?"
- January 31, 2005: WC resigns as chair of ethnic studies.
- February 2, 2005: *RMN* questions Churchill's ethnicity following charges that he manufactured his Native American identity to advance his career.
- February 2, 2005: *RMN* editorial calls for firing WC.
- February 5, 2005: *DP* offers legal grounds for firing.
- March 7, 2005: Hoffman announces her resignation as CU president.
- March 24, 2005: Regents approve a systemwide review of procedures for awarding and maintaining tenure.
- March 29, 2005: A CU committee receives allegations that Churchill committed research misconduct.
- June 2005: After weeks of investigative reporting, *RMN* judges WC guilty.
- June 16, 2005: *RMN* reports that CU is expanding its investigation to include allegations discussed in the paper's two-month investigation.
- August 1, 2005: Hank Brown, co-founding member of the American Council of Trustees and Alumni (ACTA), is named interim CU president. Founded in 1995 with seed money from conservative foundations, ACTA issued a report in the aftermath of 9/11: *Defending Civilization: How Our Universities Are Failing America and What Can Be Done About It.*
- July 24, 2007: Regents vote to fire WC.

Act IV: Reintegration/Separation

In my reading of the drama, the final act commences with the regents' vote. The day after Churchill sued the university for wrongful termination, CU President Brown appeared on *Fox News*, describing the professor and his lawsuit as "absolute fraud." There was a bit of drama still to unfold, however, when a jury ruled that the regents had, in fact, fired Churchill in retaliation for ideas expressed in the essay. A Denver district judge ultimately denied Churchill's request for his position back. Issued on July 7, 2009, the ruling argued that reinstatement would give the impression that CU tolerates research misconduct.

Social dramas embody social action, and in the Churchill case the modes of separation were conducted by academic and judicial institutions. Nonetheless, the symbolic structuring of crisis and redress show that news media had unambiguously classified Churchill as an enemy from within, suggesting that symbolic separation preceded—and perhaps facilitated—actual separation. On May 17, 2006, about three years prior to the court ruling, a *Rocky* editorial put CU administrators on notice: "Unless University of Colorado officials harbor a secret death wish for their institution, Ward Churchill will never teach another class in Boulder." As early as February 3, 2005, editorial cartoons marked a transfiguration of the treasonous professor into an object of mockery. The *Post* portrayed a dwarf Churchill, suspended from a playground swing, his motion propelled by tantrum; a bubble caption contains no words, but a garbage can spewing fumes. In national media four days later, *Indian Country Today* mocked Churchill's claim of Native American ancestry. A carton depicted the professor—half human, half chicken—dressing himself with accoutrements from a "Real Injun Kit!" The cartoon portrayed the scholar, his ethnic identity, and his polemic as fraudulent.

Three Scripting Elements

Up to this point, I have described media ritual primarily at the level of culture and ideology. We also want to comprehend how social drama works at an occupational level, within the logic of defensive ritual.[54] A cross-level analysis is overdue in scholarship of media ritual,[55] which tends to follow one of two tracks: strategic protocols and tactics in organizational sociology, or media performance on behalf of cultural imperatives. A cross-level approach allows for the possibility of journalism acting somewhat autonomously in policing ideational dissent, in ways that serve its strategic interests. Social drama provides journalism with a symbolic form for representing dissent without deliberating with it, distancing reporters from transgressive ideas. This cross-level heuristic, however, raises the question as to how social drama—conceived as a cultural construct—is embedded in the micro context of news production. The Churchill drama suggests three scripting elements: *projection* of ritualistic punishment, *reification* of a punitive public, and subsequent *rendering* of academic labor to clarify deviance.

Projection of Punishment

Tuchman described newsmaking as social action "cast into the future in order to accomplish acts that will have happened, should everything go as anticipated."[56] In media ritual, projection encompasses a dynamic of journalistic cue taking and cue giving. The former involves an intra-journalism norm for anticipating story arc (narrative structure) and story potential (magnitude). Cue giving refers to relationships between journalism and other actors invested in social drama. By providing ritual "its imagery and plotline,"[57] media establish a symbolic structure primed for exploitation by opportunists.

Table 6.1 illustrates the cue-taking and cue-giving dynamic in the scripting of social drama. I duplicated the initial 10 leads from both newspapers. Breach/crisis components are shown in italics; redress/separation are indicated in bold. In the *Post*'s first lead (January 28, 2005), two congressmen demanded an apology from a professor (redress) for "comparing victims . . . to Nazis" (crisis). Atmospherics of crisis are conveyed in boilerplate descriptions of Churchill as "controversial" and "embattled"; in standardized extraction of the Eichmann bit; and in references to a "firestorm" (*RMN*, February 2) and "threats of violence" (*DP*, February 8). Churchill is met by "wild" applause, declaring he would "never back down" (*DP*, February 9).

A fractal formation emerges, such that Turner's symbolic structure is already present, implicitly, in the initial wave of text. Many of the leads can be read as a microcosm of what would transpire in the years to come. Media sociology accommodates the premise that social drama can arise organically without purposeful coordination, due to journalists internalizing cultural norms for legitimate and deviant discourse.

Fractal scripting implies a narrative structure that transcends the individual intentions of reporters and editors. In some respects, the same structure is observable when zooming back, from leads to stories to aggregate patterns. The volume of coverage during key moments reflects Fürsich's observation that text "takes on a life of its own" in moments of "deep play."[58] We should look, then, for meta-textual evidence that might capture journalism's instinctual response to intellect exposed. Returning to Figure 6.1, the temporal distribution of articles resembles "news waves," signifying peaks in volume tied to important events.[59] An initial crest corresponds with commencement of crisis followed by a crest in the transition to redress; separation corresponds to a final peak associated with the trial for wrongful termination.

Reification of a Punitive Public

Reification of a punitive public aligns media with populist sentiment, distancing journalists from academic dissent while casting audiences as active participants in social drama. By representing a public unwilling to engage with ideas, yet justifiably angry, journalism legitimizes an anti-deliberative response. In the Churchill case, reification of an offended and wounded public provides a subtext for the initial wave of leads (Table 6.1). Leads that incorporate redress/separation refer to legislators demanding an apology, regents calling a special meeting, and Hamilton College cancelling a panel—actions at once redressive and non-deliberative or anti-deliberative.

This conception of reification is in some respects compatible with the protest paradigm, whereby journalists deploy micro-descriptive depictions of public opinion to convey consensus.[60] The protest paradigm, however, is not designed to explain control of intellectual deviance—that is, deviance as an abstraction—because of its reliance on portrayal of unruly behavior. From a dramaturgical perspective, depictions of the citizenry are ultimately in service to idea suppression, such that populist anti-elitism is invoked to protect belief through anti-rationalism.

Rendering Ideas to Clarify Deviance

Journalists render intellectual dissent into objects of deviance, advancing social control through symbolic action (Chapter 5). In media ritual, idea rendering isolates and magnifies deviance by tearing away the textual fabric that makes an assertion worthy of deliberation. Turner explains that rituals are "designed to influence preternatural entities or forces on behalf of the actors' goals and interests."[61] Purification of deviance thereby summons "a mobilization of energies."

As shown in Figure 6.2, journalism contributes to purification through factism and contextomy in social drama.[62] Journalists typically engage in factism by relying on official or other authoritative sources such as public opinion polling.[63] Factism is arguably more interventionist in the context of intellectual discourse. The "little Eichmann" reference is situated in an idea network, connected to Hannah Arendt's reflections on the banality of evil and willful ignorance.[64] The polemic engages a history of genocidal foreign policy (by Churchill's account) and predictable payback from those on the receiving end of violence. The Eichmann "fact" is extracted during breach/crisis and remains the most salient aspect of the essay moving toward redress and separation. The Colorado press trafficked in contextomy, which entails *de*-contextualization followed by *re*-contextualization in violation of an author/speaker's intent.[65] Contextomy is thereby functional in the control of intellect. An argument—crafted with dynamic interconnections among ideas—is rendered as an object of deviance, reconstituted for ease of packaging, and prepared for public consumption in ritualistic sacrifice.

Reporters and editors interviewed for Chapter 7 insisted that the Eichmann reference was the only newsworthy aspect of the essay. This perception could be explained as a conflation of de-contextualization with essentialism—a seemingly virtuous effort to get at the nut of a story. Almost immediately in news coverage, the essay faded from view, as if Churchill's breach was some kind of gaffe. A *Post* lead on February 4, 2005, reported that regents apologized "for remarks" made by an ethnic studies professor.

Contextomy and factism as tactics of control are reinforced by personification of ideas as dangerous. Animation of ideas emerges in a motif of fire and explosiveness, the public alarmed at a professor's incendiary intent. While Churchill's polemic sat in online obscurity for more than three years, the *Post* described him as "igniting" (editorial 2-01-05) and "setting off a firestorm" (news 2-25-05), or as someone who "has come under fire" (news 2-09-05). The *Rocky* deployed similar imagery, warning Denver readers that the nearby Boulder campus employs "an apologist for mass murder" (editorial 1-28-05).

To summarize: news and commentary follow an implicit script, projecting into the future a performance of media and non-media actors in social drama. Reification of a punitive public and rendering of ideas to clarify deviance further guide newswork in the cultural work of social control.

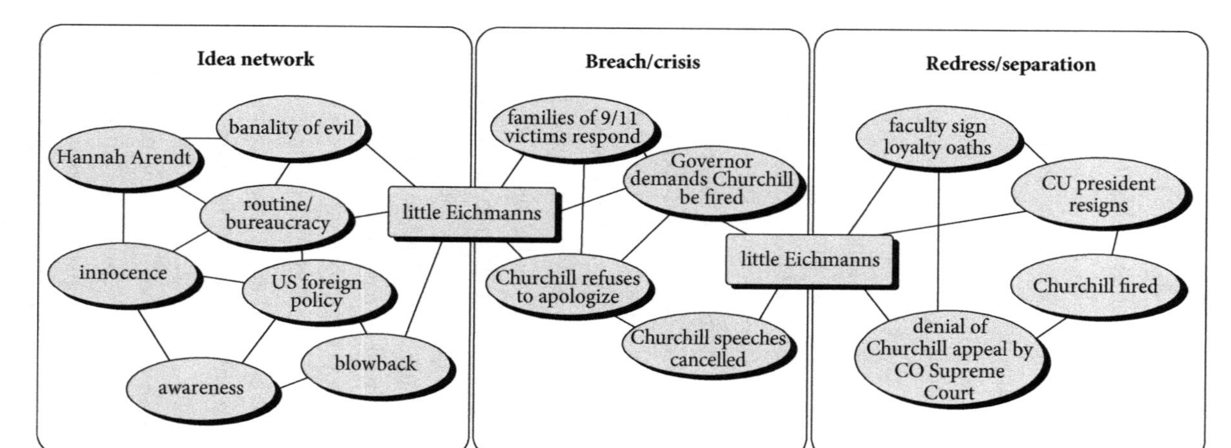

Figure 6.2 Idea rendering in symbolic action: factism, contextomy, and social drama

Media Performance: Conscripted or Opportunistic?

Liminality in the academic-media nexus can play out as a journalistic intervention. "Prompted by the appearance of a wrinkle in the cultural fabric, ritual is intended to smooth things out."[66] Turner explains that ritual reminds people that "it is good and appropriate when things adhere to their proper place and when people do what is appropriate for them to do in their stage of life and status in society."[67] In regulation of intellect, journalism's ideological agency is evident in its capacity to transform an abstract provocation into a sociocultural breach and to rapidly marshal a crisis through media ritual.

The Churchill case suggests that a crisis atmosphere justifies a journalistic intervention into university affairs as one form of redress. In the Colorado drama, Churchill was destined for separation, and I mean this literally, with his job and tenure stripped away. Journalism's hand in the resolution was evident in a narrative structure in which symbolic separation preceded the legal outcome.

Ritualistic representation of punitive populism constitutes a largely unrecognized yet formidable expression of journalism's cultural authority in the policing of ideas. The Colorado drama represents a tour de force of media prowess, but journalism is incapable of predatory ritual independent of other institutions. Churchill's essay challenged the absolutism of American innocence, and this compelled a tactical response from both news media and the academy. The academic-media nexus, consequently, is arguably unique in the way that media ritual aligns social control across domains of knowledge work.[68]

Relationships among parties change in social drama when reintegration fails; "new power will have been channeled into old and new authority."[69] In the punishment of deviance observed here, the status of the parochial press in reaffirming boundaries for tolerable discourse seems to have been raised, a reminder of what might befall dissent in the space where mainstream media and the academy meet.

Analysis of the Churchill case is confined to the interplay of legacy newspapers and critical academic discourse that challenges core, cultural beliefs. Outlets in the prestige press such as *The Nation* and *Slate* did contextualize Churchill's ideas and defended the principle of academic freedom. I should also note that many intellectuals—inside and outside of higher education—criticized Churchill's abrasive style and substantive ideas. Still, the case illustrates the alignment of newswork with the cultural imperatives of social control in response to an ideational breach.

Journalism's instinctual alignment with normative ideology is a reoccurring theme in frameworks such as news waves,[70] indexing,[71] and cultural approaches to framing.[72] Similarly, news media demonstrate ideological allegiance through ritualistic performance. This instinct takes the form of fractal alignment, such that embedded, textual scripting anticipates—and doubtlessly assists in realizing—what is projected into the future, in a full-blown performance of cultural allegiance.

Ironically, the realm of abstract ideas can be a greater threat to journalism's cultural authority than material events. Bennett argues that disturbing but spontaneous incidents elevate the critical capacity of journalism.[73] By contrast, contextualized ideas, when hosted in journalistic venues, are not entirely externalized, and therefore constitute a potential threat to the ideological legitimacy of the profession. An authentic effort at contextualism requires some kind of epistemological engagement, transparently recognized by audiences. Deliberating with contextualized ideas requires *use of the intellect by journalism itself*. Media ritual allows journalism to align itself with an aggrieved public, to forgo deliberation, and to thereby distance itself from the intellect unbound.

I am not arguing that "news as strategic ritual"—Tuchman's foundational insight—is somehow flawed or inoperative in cultural practice. Instead, this chapter identifies those practices not identified by Tuchman that arise as a response to ideational deviance. Rendering ideas to clarify deviance entails a more adversarial tactic than the protocols identified by Tuchman (e.g., balancing partisan views, relying on verifiable facts, attribution to official sources).

Fractal scripting could be viewed as *tactical* in the short term, guiding reporters and editors in the day-to-day treatment of deviant ideas, while a *strategy* becomes visible across time, in the progression of social drama. From an instrumental perspective, social drama as strategic ritual crystallized a rational response to risks and rewards presented by Churchill.

The first scripting element, projection of punishment, constitutes a dynamic of cue taking within journalism—and cue giving to other actors—such that plotlines, themes, and events are aligned in internal coherence. Reification portrays the demos as spontaneously engaged, while idea rendering ensures an impression of the public justifiably outraged. Projection, reification, and rendering guide journalism in a culturally conscripted performance, such that the logic of newswork conforms to the logic of social control.

Tuchman's strategic ritual and Turner's social drama describe one and the same process in the Churchill affair, albeit from distinct perspectives. I would not advocate a blending, rather retaining a productive tension across levels of analysis. This allows for a dialectic consideration of the extent to which journalism is an autonomous agent of idea suppression within a larger, cultural context. For example, one might propose that marginalization of dissent in strategic ritual requires an organizational, journalism-centric perspective, even as social drama provides a symbolic structure for exploitation by non-media actors in recognizing a breach, amplifying crisis, and pursuing forms of redress and separation. Media ritual protects, and might enhance, the ideological status of journalism within a larger, cultural dynamic of mobilized sentiment and symbolization.[74]

In this view, journalism provides added impetus to idea suppression beyond cultural expectations for that function. If so, parochial media are not simply *conscripted* but *opportunistic*. Journalism in social drama would then act as a regressive, anti-intellectual force against a culture's capacity for tolerating dissent.

7

Deviant in Residence

Idea Rendering and Repair in the Parochial Press

In response to suicidal/homicidal attacks of September 11, 2001, US news media became fiercely protective of American innocence and public memory of the trauma.[1] Parochial media practice "guard dog journalism" with particular zeal in this type of climate. As Donohue, Tichenor, and Olien observe, "The guard dog media are conditioned to be suspicious of all potential intruders."[2] This instinct is attuned to internal threats as well—traitors, agitators, dissidents—including the disloyal intellectual, a source of subversion subject to surveillance and attack.[3]

If local journalism is acutely attuned to ideational deviance, we should expect reporting tactics that discriminate among shades of transgression.[4] For instance, while blowback circulated as a controversial interpretation of 9/11 terrorism, that theme was not as incendiary as Professor Churchill's portrayal of attackers as rational. Proximity and deviance as core news values are fluid concepts in that the closeness of an action, event, or idea to the public depends on how the community is imagined and portrayed.[5] Constraining the diffusion of deviance is paramount, and thus the object of concern must be clearly identified.[6] Local journalists' dependence on elite sources and identification with communities served diminish tolerance for conflict.[7] In a study of community newspapers, Bunton concluded that reporters failed to offer "comprehensive, contextual coverage" of local controversies.[8] Depending on the ideological context, a failure to contextualize could be viewed in a more proactive sense, as the shedding of nuance to clearly mark deviance in a community where dissent is expressed.

When intellectual discourse confronts absolutist belief in areas such as religion and sanctity, authority, social order, and national identity, regional news outlets might shift in orientation from secular and cultivated to parochial and oppressive.[9] These spatial dynamics come into play when the academic-media nexus fails to prevent an intellectual breach (Chapter 4). From a temporal perspective, the immediate containment of discourse degrades ideas

Where Ideas Go to Die. Michael McDevitt, Oxford University Press (2020). © Oxford University Press.
DOI: 10.1093/oso/9780190869946.001.0001

available to negotiate collective memory when the same topics return to news salience (Chapter 5).

While the Colorado social drama could be viewed as a paradigmatic assertion of media power in punishment of dissent,[10] this case also provides an opportunity to explore journalistic and audience resistance at the epicenter of crisis and redress. The Churchill drama illustrates *idea rendering* and *repair* as a dynamic in which newswork prompts a corrective response. Content analysis in this chapter focuses on de-contextualization as the rendering practice. We then consider repair—how contributors to the opinion pages strived to retain context and otherwise engage with ideas in the Churchill polemic. Journalists, for their part, are not simply enlisted in the suppression of transgressive discourse, even in ideological climates unfriendly to dissent. The chapter documents reflexivity as revealed in interviews of reporters and editors who participated in the media frenzy. I confronted Colorado editors and reporters with the same evidence of de-contextualization presented here. They responded in a range of perceptions loosely characterized as denial, ambivalence, regret, and resistance. The chapter concludes with a discussion of news media's role in the control of ideas across time and place.

Idea Rendering

Idea rendering hinges on journalistic recognition of an ideologically charged excerpt within a body of discourse, and selective exclusion of context that, if preserved, might facilitate the exchange of ideas. Intellectual dissent consequently requires precision in conveying an ideological breach without actual engagement with offending ideas. Operational measures of de-contextualization should capture journalistic sensitivity based on two factors: proximity to the source, and the degree to which a specific idea offends absolutist sentiment.

Systemic de-contextualization should constrain journalism itself when events offer opportunities to reconsider the same ideas. Following a peak of coverage in 2005, the Churchill saga included a faculty committee finding the professor guilty of research misconduct on May 17, 2006; regents firing him on July 24, 2007; and Churchill suing the University of Colorado the next day, alleging wrongful termination. Intrigued by the long-term implications of idea rendering, I established a sizeable gap between the initial content analysis in early 2005 (T1) and a second timeframe (T2). The second period is bounded by denial of Churchill's appeal by the Colorado Supreme Court on July 15, 2009, and a final denial by the US Supreme Court on April 1, 2013. I extended the period to April 10, 2013, to pick up news features that would take some time to produce. Newsworthy events in the legal drama at T2 might prompt journalists to consider the ideas that prompted the controversy in the first place.

As chronicled in Chapter 6, a media firestorm ignited with an Associated Press article published on January 26, 2005, when Churchill was scheduled to speak at Hamilton College in New York. "A University of Colorado professor who compared the victims of the Sept. 11 attacks on the World Trade Center to Nazis has ignited protests on a college campus where he's been invited to speak." The initial period for content analysis—January 25, 2005, to February 25, 2005—represented an opportunity for journalists to engage the polemic motives and perspectives of the essay's author. I considered a longer time frame, but several sub-controversies erupted after the initial weeks of coverage, and the substance of Churchill's arguments about US innocence were arguably less relevant. For example, journalists wrote about allegations of Churchill fabricating his Native American ethnicity.

I obtained articles for content analysis from Colorado and non-Colorado news organizations. Five Colorado newspapers contributed to the sample: *The Denver Post, Rocky Mountain News, Longmont Daily Times-Call, Boulder Daily Camera,* and the *Colorado Daily*. With the *Post* and *Rocky* part of a joint operating agreement (JOA), editors celebrated what they considered a competitive relationship between the news divisions. The newsrooms were located in downtown Denver, approximately 25 miles from the CU campus. Circulation for both hovered around 340,000 at T1. The *Boulder Daily Camera* (circulation 33,000) and the *Colorado Daily* (18,000) are located in the foothills college town of Boulder. *Camera* reporters cover the city along with CU; the *Colorado Daily* focuses on campus life and the university. The *Longmont Daily Times-Call* is the only other daily with a Boulder County readership; its circulation of 21,600 is concentrated in a suburb northwest of Denver. I acquired non-Colorado articles from two sources: major newspapers (as classified by Nexis Uni), and Associated Press stories with datelines outside the state.

The T1 sample included 200 articles—166 published in Colorado and 34 in non-Colorado papers. The Appendix provides details on sources and selection criteria. Using the same procedures, the T2 sample includes 37 articles, albeit none from the *Rocky*, which closed in February 2009.

In manifest news content, de-contextualization is operationalized with respect to crucial perspective, intent, and justification systematically excluded in portrayal of dissent. Measurement consequently requires a preliminary qualitative analysis to identify the context from which a bit is extracted. Churchill's polemic is structured by three interconnected themes: a history of genocidal foreign policy (about 40% of the essay) is perpetuated by willful ignorance of the citizenry, akin to the banality of evil of "good Germans" (about 25 percent), resulting in the normal response of payback by those on the receiving end of massive violence (about 25%).

Coders determined whether an article (1) described *any essay content* beyond the Eichmann/Nazi trope; (2) conveyed the blowback/payback perspective; (3) referenced US historic or ongoing foreign policy; (4) referenced civilian deaths as a result of US interventions in the Middle East; (5) conveyed a view of Americans in denial about interventions; and (6) expressed the view that 9/11 attackers were rational. The subversive meaning of the essay is most apparent as items become pointed and confrontational to mainstream beliefs about American innocence and foreign policy.

Sensitivity to Deviance

The six measures allow us to detect with some precision how sensitive news media were in response to distinct elements from the essay. Journalism is consequential in political discourse in the classification of discourse into spheres of full legitimacy, partial legitimacy, implicit deviance, or explicit deviance.[11] The exact sorting of ideas is open to interpretation, and I consequently organize essay components into Hallin's more basic distinction between legitimate and deviant ideas.[12]

Table 7.1 places the first three content measures under *legitimate debate* and the second three under *deviance*. The table reports percentages for the outcomes in Colorado and non-Colorado media in 2005. The first measure determined whether a story described the essay beyond a boilerplate statement that Churchill compared World Trade victims to Eichmann. Of the 200 articles from both categories, only 93 (47%) mentioned *anything* about the essay beyond the Nazi reference; 71 articles (36%) conveyed the blowback perspective; 52 stories (26%) referenced foreign policy; 29 articles (15%) referred to civilian deaths; 17 articles (9%) conveyed the view of US citizens in denial; and 15 articles (8%) expressed the view of attackers as rational.

Table 7.1 De-contextualization in Colorado and non-Colorado newspaper articles

	Sphere of legitimate debate			Sphere of deviance		
	Does article describe essay beyond Eichmann?	Does article convey blowback perspective?	Does article reference US foreign policy?	Does article refer to civilian deaths caused by US?	Does article refer to US citizens in denial?	Does article express view of attackers as rational?
Colorado $n = 166$	66 (39.8%)	53 (31.9%)	37 (22.3%)	17 (10.2%)	8 (4.8%)	8 (4.8%)
Non-Colorado $n = 34$	27 (79.4%) $\chi^2 = 17.836$, $df = 1, p < .001$	18 (52.9%) $\chi^2 = 5.442$, $df = 1, p < .05$	15 (44.1%) $\chi^2 = 6.989$, $df = 1, p < .01$	12 (35.3%) $\chi^2 = 14.287$, $df = 1, p < .001$	9 (26.5%) $\chi^2 = 17.009$, $df = 1, p < .001$	7 (20.6%) $\chi^2 = 10.115$, $df = 1, p < .01$
Total $N = 200$	93 (46.5%)	71 (35.5%)	52 (26.0%)	29 (14.5%)	17 (8.5%)	15 (7.5%)

The findings confirm that Colorado newspapers were more likely to practice de-contextualization: 40% of in-state articles described essay content beyond the Nazi reference, compared with 79% of non-Colorado articles. (Percentage breakdowns for each variable across the five Colorado newspapers and the two national categories are provided in Appendix Table 7.1.) About 32% of Colorado articles referenced blowback, compared with 53% of non-Colorado articles. Approximately 22% of in-state articles made any reference to foreign policy, compared with 44% for out-of-state articles; 10% of local articles referred to civilian deaths compared with 35% of non-Colorado stories. About 5% of Colorado articles conveyed the view of US citizens in denial, compared with 27% of non-Colorado media. Finally, 5% of Colorado articles expressed the view of attackers as rational, compared with 21% of non-Colorado articles. All of these differences are statistically significant.

Given the lack of prior research on how news media directly confront subversive ideas, a supplemental analysis identifies elements of news production that accompany or counteract proximity in idea suppression (Appendix Table 7.2). Types of sources, for example, might reflect journalistic tolerance for essay ideas. I determined whether articles included views of politicians, members of the general public, and individuals who lost family members on 9/11—all non-academic sources that could serve a latent purpose in portraying public outrage.[13] Multivariate analysis confirmed that the proximity effect is distinct from—rather than a proxy for—other content attributes such as sources, article length, and publication date.

The results reveal a more aggressive impulse toward de-contextualization in Colorado, along with a pronounced pattern of exclusion of the most transgressive elements.[14] Still, in comparing Colorado to non-Colorado news, I did not anticipate such a close matching in sensitivity across the six items, such that essay components with the most infrequent appearances in news coverage are presumably the most transgressive ideas. In a type of correlation that assesses similarity of rankings, sensitivity to degree of offense was nearly identical: r_s = .985.[15] A perfect correspondence would equal 1.0. Rankings are identical with the exception that in Colorado news, the view of citizens in denial and attackers as rational share fifth place for frequency of appearance, and in non-Colorado news these items rank fifth and sixth.[16]

Journalists de-contextualize in a nuanced fashion, making distinctions among provocative, highly charged, and incendiary assertions. For example, the citizens-in-denial assertion alludes to Hannah Arendt's banality of evil and represents the only measure that captures Churchill's direct attack on citizens.[17] I doubt that there are many newsroom conversations about sensitivity to ideational deviance even as the craft of de-contextualization is practiced at such a high level of precision.

With protection of public memory at stake, I expected that Colorado newspapers were more likely than the non-Colorado press to de-contextualize Churchill's ideas in 2009–2013. The results, I have to say, are humbling for me as a predictor. Ideational elements *never appeared* at T2. No variance occurred as all 222 decisions (37 articles x 6 measures) produced 0 for the coding value. The results reveal a rigid adherence to ideational gatekeeping—at local and national levels—when journalists returned to the Churchill affair. From a cultural perspective, the finding/non-finding illustrates the power of news media in "collective forgetting."[18] I should note that essay ideas remained potentially newsworthy; Churchill's backers emphasized implications of his firing for academic freedom in expressing unpopular views.

Idea Repair

News commentators are in some respects members of the same interpretative community as journalists, united by "shared discourse and collective interpretations of key public events."[19] Shared discourse might imply an over-reliance on news content, but also the possibility for reflexivity in critique of the news as a basis for negotiating the meaning of 9/11 in public memory. The question, then, arises as to the survival of Churchill's ideas on the opinion pages. At issue is the extent to which editorialists, columnists, and letter writers grappled with the raw material of the essay, rather than commodified text served up in the news.

As discussed in Chapter 3, recent research describes an increasing willingness of journalists to self-criticize in response to troubling developments that threaten the profession's credibility, a practice known as "paradigm repair."[20] Unusual circumstances also offer opportunities for readers invested in the news to think critically about reporting and editing. Idea rendering originates from the juxtaposition of discursive norms in journalism and academia, providing a basis for comparison.

While journalists recognized some assertions as more offensive than others, idea rendering can be viewed as a fairly blunt instrument in a binary logic of inclusion/exclusion, lending itself to nominal measurement. Textual analysis affords more flexibility to document how commentators in Colorado might restore the contextual basis for Churchill's ideas. The sample is comprised of 181 items: 21 editorials, 24 op-ed columns, and 122 letters to the editor at T1; 3 editorials, 4 op-eds, and 7 letters at T2.

I identified two forms of repair: direct engagement with Churchill's ideas, largely bypassing reporters, and reflexivity toward reception of news. In a letter to the *Post*, Nancy McGuire invited readers to read the essay, asserting that it was less shocking than portrayed by reporters: "The saddening effects of the sanctions on the children of Iraq have been discussed for years" (T1: February 14, 2005). *Rocky* columnist Stuart Steers addressed the ethical ambiguity of blaming a people for the actions of their government, disagreeing with Churchill, but he nonetheless showed a willingness to consider the banality-of-evil theme (February 5).

A notable divergence from news content was the effort of letter writers at T1 to *summarize* Churchill's perspectives rather than to *excerpt*. Bill Murray cautioned: "Let us not look only at headlines for the basis of our thinking" (*Rocky*, February 5). Donald Heinkel admonished: "Instead of focusing on an unfortunate metaphor, the controversy and discussion should be on the main thrust of Ward Churchill's essay—namely, that US foreign policy plays a major role in fomenting terrorism" (*Rocky*, February 9). This non-professional commentary rejects the essentialist notion of an extract representing an argument, working instead to repair the context and the writer's intended meaning. Julian Friedland challenged Churchill to "unambiguously state whether he supports violently 'pushing back' against institutional oppression" (*Daily Camera*, February 13).

The desire to circumvent reporters suggests reflexivity in news reception as a related form of idea repair. Reflexivity occurs when an agent turns back on itself, an act of self-reference that encompasses expression as well as its reception.[21] Ann Little, a professor of history at Colorado State University, contrasted journalistic to academic styles of argument in a letter to the *Post*:

Your story suggests that because not everyone in University of Colorado professor Ward Churchill's field agrees with him, this somehow casts doubt on the quality or validity of his scholarship. This is wrong, and I believe that most academic faculty would take issue with the notion that professional disagreement means that one side of a scholarly argument must "win," and the other side be totally discredited. (February 14)

John Stevenson, a CU professor, came closest to an idea rendering critique in a *Camera* column. Churchill's arguments

> are not simple, but neither are they subtle, and like many provocative arguments, they are susceptible to reduction. The gap between what he said and what has been generally reported in the press is wide. (February 3)

The two academics are not merely seeking a fair hearing for Churchill's views, but inviting news consumers to reflect on journalistic practice in the portrayal of ideas that originate in scholarship.

Notwithstanding evidence of corrective effort, commentary generally adopted the problem definition and moral evaluation made salient in news framing. Churchill's understanding of US foreign policy as *the* problem in a polemic text was eclipsed nearly completely by commentators' perception that the problem amounted to viable punishment. *Rocky* columnist Paul Campos described the professor as "our burden, our shame" (February 5). In an act of redemption, Colorado media would presumably carry the burden of protecting transcendent values by containing the deviance locally. The *Post* editorialized:

> The Sept. 11 essay may be the tip of some iceberg. The regents are elected officials, and the world is watching. (February 9)

The volume of coverage prompted reflexivity in both editorials and letters, but in oppositional perspectives with regard to whether newspapers should provide a forum for Churchill's ideas. None of the editorials joined letters in criticizing news fixation on the Eichmann trope. Instead, the concern was granting Churchill a media foothold. The *Rocky* acknowledged that "several pundits have suggested that Churchill's most vociferous critics have played into his hands by turning an obscure academic into a national celebrity" (February 16).

Impatience in holding Churchill accountable appeared contagious in news and commentary. From a speech in Boulder, waiting for Churchill to take the podium, a *Rocky* reporter observed, "it was clear the crowd wasn't going to punish him for the delay" (February 9).

In anticipation of (non-deliberative) redress, mobilization of populist sentiment took on a liminal dynamic, empowering ordinary citizens to guard community values by summoning suspicion against a local professor.

Rocky letters invoked imagery of the intellectual as an internal enemy, as treasonous,

> I do not want Churchill to be my neighbor or my co-worker. I do not even want to meet him casually in a mall or in a restaurant. He is certainly not my friend or my fellow American. (Robert Wesley, February 2)

and subversive,

> If Churchill wants to expound on his inflammatory view, fine. However, he must not be allowed to do so to a captive student audience. (Jo Priest, February 12)

At T2, with Churchill banned from CU, the limited editorial comment expressed frustration with court delays. "If it seems as though the Ward Churchill saga has dragged on for eons, that's because it has" (*Post*, September 12, 2012). The editorial board seemed anxious to nail down the meaning of the essay and its attack on memory of 9/11. "With any luck, the [U.S. Supreme Court] ... will decline to hear the case and Colorado can relegate the Churchill matter to the history books." The *Post* assured readers that the essay was an "intellectually vapid piece," a reasonable view perhaps for editorialists who relied on prior news content to recall the essay. Picking up the boilerplate from 2005, the *Post* reduced the essay to Churchill "comparing victims of the World Trade Center terrorist attacks to Adolf Eichmann, a Nazi war criminal."

Commentary was not entirely devoid of ideational engagement despite results from the content analysis of news at T2. CU sociology professor Tom Mayer rejected the extractive approach of editorials, stating that the purpose of his letter was to ground an "audacious public voice" in the larger perspective of scholarly reputation. Mayer argued that CU "lost a scholar who pioneered new interpretations of Native American history and its relationship to other indigenous struggles" (*Colorado Daily*, September 13, 2012). Another reoccurring theme was the effort of citizen commentary to assert views independent of professional newswork. In a guest opinion, Cindy Bedell bypassed media content to emphasize what she recalled from a public lecture:

> What I heard him say is that U.S. foreign policy is a metaphysical boomerang. People want to hurt you when you cause harm to their children. (*Camera*, September 6, 2012)

Reflexivity in Newswork

Idea rendering illustrates the cultural contradiction of American journalism—the tension between its commitment to a marketplace of ideas and its agency in the foreclosing of deliberation. This section conveys responses of Colorado journalists when confronted with the same content analysis presented above. The sociologist Brian Klocke and I interviewed a broad sample of Colorado journalists who contributed to coverage during the first month of the controversy, when prominent news frames rapidly crystallized.[22] We interviewed 40% of the available journalists who wrote about Churchill for newspapers and wire services in the Boulder/Denver metro area ($n = 12$).[23]

Textual analysis of interview transcripts and reporters' bylined articles ($n = 64$) allowed us to compare output with claims about work.[24] Interviews explored how journalists evaluated the Churchill coverage and accounted for their participation. Perceptions of complicity in de-contextualization ranged from denial to not merely acknowledgment but resistance against overeager editors.[25]

Denial

Several journalists seemed to deny Colorado media's contribution to stigmatization of Churchill's ideas. They emphasized that while Churchill's essay was volatile and unusual in its confrontational tone coming from an academic, the journalism in response was routine, objective and fair.

> I: What journalistic values were at play in coverage of Churchill?
>
> J: *We approached this the same way we approach any story, so it would be hard, actually I can't really identify anything that we did differently than we would do in any case. And that is, we just tried to stay out of it and be fair and be as thorough as we can.* (Denver reporter)

Reporters and editors saw their concentrated attention to the Eichmann analogy as a "natural thing" for them "to pick up on" (Denver reporter). They viewed their professional role as remaining impartial, as simply reporting the facts, denying their own agency in contributions to public reasoning or lack thereof.

I think it's the job of the press to raise these issues and let people decide for themselves . . . You should see here's a fact, here's another fact, here's a fact and I will decide for myself whether I want to take Churchill's class, whether I want him in the university. (Boulder reporter)

Reporters' denial of de-contextualization was usually not explicit but emerged in contradictions between interview statements and articles. Another Denver reporter observed:

Ward Churchill didn't say the 9/11 hijackers were great guys and let's mobilize everybody and do the same thing: kill more people . . . He really wasn't comparing people to Nazi war criminals directly. It was a little more nuanced point.

Yet in his first two articles (February 3, 2005 and February 9, 2005), leads indicated that Churchill compared "victims to a Nazi war criminal."

Everyone interviewed claimed that their newspaper or news wire fairly portrayed Churchill's ideas. A Denver editor told us: "The journalistic principles of fairness and accuracy were extremely important." However, his newspaper had the highest (worst) levels of de-contextualization from the content analysis. He disagreed that his paper in any way amplified public backlash:

I: If you accept that there's some degree of truth to the statement that the local press contributed to public outrage—

J: *—My response would be instant: contribute to? Or chronicle. I think we chronicled public response to Churchill.*

The terse response highlights a strategic defense evident in both news and interviews: an objectification of deviance established by de-contextualization, inevitability of massive coverage, and unified public hostility to Churchill. This interpretation echoes Glasser's explanation that "news is viewed as something that journalists are compelled to report, not something they are responsible for creating."[26]

All but three reporters and editors claimed the idea of blowback (the main argument of Churchill's essay) was not "newsworthy" even though they did not find the idea offensive; most saw a blowback perspective as valid or even expressed agreement with it. Reporters and editors seemed to make an implicit distinction between deliberation and newsworthiness. Blowback had already been said by others; it wasn't anything new or "headline-grabbing" (Boulder reporter), "other than the Nazi" reference (Denver reporter), which was seen as "the magic phrase" (another Denver reporter) presumed to be "highly offensive" and "that's why it was newsworthy" (yet another Denver reporter).

I: In 2005, would it have been problematic for reporters to talk about blowback?

J: *If I wanted to write an article on Ward Churchill's thoughts on the war, and we said . . . that it was about "little Eichmanns," then it would be inaccurate reporting. That's not what we're reporting. We were reporting the fallout from his use of language . . . The "little Eichmanns" remark is what brought the news, is what created the news. And we're reporting news.* (Denver reporter)

This notion of newsworthiness puts Churchill in a bind, and by extension, any public intellectual addressing core beliefs with provocative language. Contextualized "thoughts on the war" are not worthy of news attention. An extracted "remark" is passable through the news gate because of its effect on public emotion.

A prominent theme in interviews and news articles is the portrayal of a wounded public. Outrage precluded substantive deliberation of the ideas that undergird the essay. A Boulder reporter put it succinctly, "that one line was really enough to get them going and get them on fire."

I think what happened is that the "little Eichmanns" reference was so shocking it kind of just overwhelmed that nuanced discussion of the political system or whatever. And it kind of, it was like the shock or the outrage, whatever, kind of overwhelmed whatever discussion might have taken place about it. (Denver reporter)

Crisis after crisis has buffeted the University of Colorado over the past year . . . but nothing has incited more passion and outrage than Ward Churchill, an ethnic studies professor whose comparison of World Trade Center victims to a notorious Nazi has led to death threats, arrests and condemnations by two governors. (Denver news, February 8, 2005)

Journalists presented the controversy as beyond the bounds of normal partisan discord. People who normally disagree were depicted as united in outrage.

Ambivalence

Other reporters were more ambivalent—expressing mixed or unclear evaluations—when reflecting on journalists' role in de-contextualizing Churchill's ideas.

> I: Another finding is that 9% of articles mentioned a prominent theme of the essay—that Americans are in denial about consequences of US foreign policy. How would you explain why reporters generally avoided that piece of the essay?
>
> J: *I don't know that is an "oh wow" figure . . . I can't really say definitively, and I won't sit here and argue with you that it is a good number . . . So I don't know if 9% is the right figure, if it's too low or too high, I have no way to judge it. I don't even know if I'm surprised by it.* (Denver reporter)

Another Denver reporter did indicate the importance of exploring Churchill's ideas:

> *I personally, in this case, thought it was important as a reporter to explain not only what was said, but dig a little bit deeper and look at what was meant as well as what was said . . . At the core, what's he really saying. If you took the sensational nature of the words away, what's the meaning?*

Indeed, in one article he provided a deeper explanation.

> The essay said some of the trade center victims were "little Eichmanns," a reference intended to suggest that white-collar "technocrats" who died that day were no better than Holocaust organizer Adolf Eichmann because they are furthering U.S. policies harmful to Arabs and indigenous people. (February 11, 2005)

In his other articles, however, the boilerplate Nazi reference appeared often.

Regret

Other reporters and editors, when provided with results from the content analysis, expressed disappointment:

> *Any story that mentioned the phrase "little Eichmanns" also needed to have the context in which it was written in his essay, and I'm disappointed to hear that only 9% of all those articles contained some context for what his point was.* (Denver editor)

A Boulder editorial writer suggested that a news article about blowback would have been appropriate:

> *But if you read the actual essay, when you get into the stage where you've written your 15th story and you're down to short-handing it, you might not just say, "Churchill called them Nazis." You might write an essay about blowback.*

He insisted that news media should be more tolerant of dissent and should do "a better job of reporting public discourse generally." He mourned the "character of the debate" in reaction to Churchill, adding that newspapers should have shown "that he's trying to make an argument" and "he's not just out there throwing Molotov cocktails at people who were murdered." Nevertheless, this regret contradicted his published commentary:

> Phil DiStefano, CU's Boulder campus chancellor, announced Thursday that Churchill, probably CU's only al-Qaida apologist, will be investigated by a faculty committee for alleged "research misconduct" and for possibly exploiting a false ethnic identity. At the same time, he announced that Churchill will face no repercussions for his odious political statements. (March 25, 2005)

Resistance

During the peak of coverage, a student intern at *The Denver Post* mentioned to me that someone had anonymously posted a flyer on a newsroom bulletin board: "Had enough Churchill?" Subsequent interviews confirmed that while reporters were not comfortable with directly advocating restraint, they found ways to push back against editors. A few reporters not only expressed regret but also showed effort in their writing to resist what they described in interviews as "fanning the flames" (Boulder reporter); a "media circus" (Denver and Boulder reporters); and a "media frenzy" (Denver reporter).

An article by a Boulder reporter focused on newspapers' role in de-contextualizing Churchill's ideas with a "type of pack journalism." The story quoted two journalism professors critical of the coverage, indicating that the press was "making this event more dramatic" and creating "dueling sound bites." This reporting matched the journalist's concern expressed when interviewed:

> *I think that's where the coverage was lacking overall, was the perspective and the bigger picture. It was very, very focused on the most incendiary thing that could be gleaned from the essay.*

Two other Denver reporters acknowledged newsroom dissent.

> *At least two of us felt that we really need to start winding this down, particularly since the university was looking into the allegations of academic misconduct and we should give it a rest for a while. But of course they [the editors] went just the opposite way . . . I'm sure me and this other guy weren't the only ones; it's just that I didn't hear it from anyone else. But I'm sure the others felt the same way at that point. After a while as a reporter you feel like you're plowing the same ground over and over again.*

The same reporter emphasized that the rift between reporters and editors could not be acknowledged openly:

> *There's definitely a prohibition on open discussion. You don't tell the editor that they're wrong. You tell them they're wrong and you're dead . . . I think there's a top-down attitude; people are expected to do what they're told.*

Another reporter expressed a similar frustration, coupled with resignation:

> *You know, again with the understanding that my comments are not going to be attributed to me by name . . . I think any . . . reporter from this paper who is honest about it would say that there was not much opportunity for*

pushback, particularly with that weeklong series . . . an editor sat us down and said, "This is what we're going to do. This is what we need to do, and this is how we're going to do it." There was an understanding, and there is an understanding, that if an editor lays it out that way, that's what's going to happen.

The reporter emphasized that Churchill, contrary to what other journalists and his paper's editorials expressed, was not advocating violence and "is not crazy . . . and has a perspective that . . . many Americans share on some level." This reporter pursued an interview with Churchill, writing an article that quoted him liberally, offering fuller explanations of his ideas, and providing some academic legitimacy by reporting that the book version of the essay was nominated for an award for advancing human rights and naming two academics who published books with similar theses. When interviewed, the Denver reporter validated Churchill's ideas and acknowledged the newspaper distorted them.

> I: Would you agree with the perspective that his ideas were de-contextualized and that had an impact on the university?
>
> J: *The ideas were completely de-contextualized . . . That's absolutely true.*

This sentiment seems congruent with subtle approaches to his news writing:

> So, people are mad at Ward Churchill. What else is new? . . . In an essay written the day after the attacks, Some People Push Back: On the Justice Of Roosting Chickens, he said America was merely reaping what it had sown through a long history of violent domination and assault upon indigenous people. (January 28, 2005)

The article, unlike most within the first month of the controversy, does not use the Eichmann trope and gives the context of blowback. Other early articles by the reporter also provided some discussion of themes from the essay. However, later articles questioned Churchill's Native American status (February 11, 2005; February 12, 2005; February 17, 2005), his process of acquiring tenure (February 16, 2005), his treatment of a former wife (February 17, 2005), and implied an association with terrorists (February 11, 2005).

Rendering, Repair, and Realism

Journalists interviewed expressed unanimity on newsworthiness of "little Eichmanns" rather than the essay's substance, despite most saying they agreed with the blowback perspective or viewed the interpretation as worthy of debate. De-contextualization was facilitated in news output by depicting Churchill's words as so gratuitously transgressive that they ignited outrage from citizens from both sides of the political aisle and precluded deliberation.

When confronted with evidence of de-contextualization, editors and reporters responded with perceptions that range from denial and ambivalence to regret and resistance. Some journalists appeared to internalize a hegemonic orientation, a few were equivocal, and still others resisted their paper's approach, but in subtle ways that would not risk their employment or image of themselves as impartial and autonomous. Most of the journalists we interviewed asked to remain anonymous, and several were afraid of commenting on Churchill's essay and sought permission from editors to participate. One journalist who declined an interview expressed fear of "a lynching." She recalled that when she told colleagues that she intended to interview Churchill, they responded with: "You're going to give it to him, aren't you?" and "Why would you even want to give that man a forum?"

Despite idea repair practiced by readers, the Colorado press did not subject its frenzied coverage to front-stage criticism. On the other hand, a foreclosing of deliberation in news practice was not accompanied by an unqualified foreclosing of reflexivity in backstage interviews. The tactical nature of news construction suggests that professional craft is, at its core, a matter of negotiation and ambivalence in ideologically charged climates.[27] The type of reflexivity observed here brings us back to *professional realism*, introduced in Chapter 3. This defensive stance overlaps with paradigm maintenance in news practice and a constrained backstage paradigm repair when challenged by academic researchers. Professional realism infuses the news with an instrumental calculus and results in an externalization of ideological agency, while retaining professional autonomy and a strategic defense against critics. It departs from paradigm repair in its emphasis on scaling back professional expectations rather than front-stage acknowledgment of a practice in need of repair. In paradigm repair, journalists establish the "boundaries of the permissible."[28] Professional realism is less about repair of normative journalism than a reification of organizational and professional constraints and, ultimately, a denial of agency in the reification and affirmation of a punitive populism.

A discourse of professional realism downplays the potential for news as a venue for provocative ideas. "We don't train reporters to cover ideas," a Boulder editor politely informed me, adding, "No offense to you as a journalistic educator, but we're not conditioning them in the newsroom." Many reporters challenged the implicit idealism of the interview script with a "let's be real" attitude, offering insider truth claims about how the world of professional journalism works.

To be sure, resistance against editors supports an interpretation of reporters not fully internalizing an intolerance of dissent in the 9/11 era. Ultimately compliance, with some accommodation for regret and resistance, reflects professional realism. Assumptions about shared professionalism, however, might overestimate collegial sentiment in reporter/editor interaction. Future research should consider possibilities of newsroom coercion. This inquiry could link Warren Breed's seminal "Social Control in the Newsroom,"[29] published in 1955, to self-censorship induced by broader climates of opinion, as in Noelle-Neumann's spiral of silence.[30]

An overt episode of idea suppression should trigger the corrective response of idea repair beyond news organizations, particularly in an ecosystem of digital media, where activists and intellectuals possess amply opportunities to resist. Shared discourse of news and commentary engenders possibilities for reflexivity that arise from the juxtaposition of journalistic and non-journalistic orientations to ideational dissent. This chapter does not provide direct evidence of citizen repair prompting journalistic resistance, but another look at the content analysis hints at *Rocky Mountain News* reporters echoing letters to the editor. At the more editorially conservative paper in a JOA, reporters produced 56 articles during the initial month of the Churchill coverage, compared with 25 at *The Denver Post*. Yet de-contextualization was more extreme at the *Post* for all six measures (Appendix Table 7.1). Working in a newsroom with seemingly insatiable editors, *Rocky* reporters may have pushed back with effort to contextualize Churchill's ideas.

Resistance in one form or another is vital if journalism is to avoid complicity in the suppression of intellectual dissent.[31] To the extent that idea rendering aligns news media with absolutist beliefs, the channeling of a punitive populism enhances the profession's cultural authority. In this view, journalism accrues cultural capital by mining intellectual discourse for extracts that, once exploited, can be used to mobilize collective solidarities. Suspicion of intellect is thereby condoned in technique as much as ideology. My hope is that this book will prompt recognition of idea repair as a viable response of audiences to journalistic excess. Corrective action should, in turn, empower resistance in newsrooms along with reporter/scholar alliances that seed tolerance for intellectual dissent in newswork (Chapter 9).[32]

Social Control in Time and Place

Cultural studies has analyzed how knowledge is constructed in part through its absence.[33] The same approach is necessary in journalism studies to comprehend how the news functions as a medium for the control of ideas. The tracking of idea rendering and repair requires a rethinking of methods for documenting symbolic action, and this must include a direct comparison of ideas before and after they are translated. Theory on journalism and deviance, however, lacks a corresponding method that documents how ideas are transfigured in newswork and how the content produced is used in symbolic action to protect core belief. Idea rendering represents a bridging construct, linking newswork with cultural perspectives on the policing of dissent. I propose a four-stage method for documenting rendering and repair.

1. Deploy textual analysis to establish themes with newsworthy relevance in a discursive context, such as a book or blog, an academic symposium, or online activism hospitable to intellectual debate. In this pre-rendering phase, the analysis is sensitive to how the conceptual building blocks of contextualized arguments are *potentially* engaged in the news.

2. Next, develop content analysis measures for documenting decontextualization of intellectual discourse in news production. Conceptual network analysis represents a promising supplemental approach in its ability to compare the semantic relations of key concepts in an original text to those of news content.

3. Returning to textual analysis, identify how extracts are used in symbolic action, in processes such as the building of frame repositories in public memory and the stirring of populist mistrust of intellect in social drama and moral panic.

4. Finally, document resistance and reflexivity of journalists and non-journalists in efforts to repair ideas.

In the current study, newspapers operated as provincial media in protecting collective memory and core beliefs about American innocence (Table 7.1).[34] Viewed from the perspective of time and place, de-contextualization reveals the formidable agency of local media in social control. Journalism should be particularly vulnerable to idea rendering given circumstances in which proximity amplifies perceptions of deviance and danger.[35] The proximate response, in turn, constitutes an intervention in intellectual discourse that constrains journalism itself as an interpretive community in future engagement with the offending ideas.[36]

Sensitivity to shades of deviance appears to apply across media categories. Findings from content analysis suggest that journalists handle subversive discourse with dexterity. De-contextualization is not simply the blunt instrument of clumsy or lazy journalists. News media appeared to calibrate how much offense readers would tolerate—based to a large extent on proximity—but inside and outside of Colorado, journalists shared the same ideological nervous system in sensitivity to degree of deviance.

I expected at least some engagement with Churchill's ideas in the 2009–2013 sample. The stark result implies that de-contextualization in 2005 had drastically reduced the resolution of the essay in news memory, and therefore the capacity to negotiate alternative meanings of 9/11 when future circumstances might otherwise offer interpretive flexibility. As anticipated in the modeling of a recursive regime (Chapter 5), the journalistic response to an intellectual breach is consequential long after redress.

From a spatial perspective, journalists render deviant ideas so that they become suitable for sanction in the community-bounded system in which proximate media operate. Offending ideas that transcend community sentiment—such as challenges to core, cultural belief—might compel most forcefully a response by media within the community system. In other words, when media isolate a proximate threat, local news and commentary are most immediately tasked with the burden of social control. Local media can most effectively juxtapose normative social distance and physical proximity of a subversive intellectual or institution. Shifting to a temporal perspective, the combination of immediacy and proximity would fade as factors in social control, but increased tolerance becomes irrelevant if substantive ideas are obliterated from news memory.

PART III
EDUCATION AND REFORM

8

Closing of the Journalism Mind

Anti-intellectualism among College Students

Walter Lippmann argued that stereotypes offer readers a foothold into news stories.[1] The "most influential journalist" of the 20th century was, if anything, realistic about the intellectual aspirations of newspapers and their readers.[2] Still, the wielding of stereotypes is a guilty pleasure, as any egghead should know. Some stock imagery seems inevitable when anticipating the intellectual development of college students depending on major. This chapter measures anti-intellectual dispositions of journalism and communication students for the first time, and with no prior theorizing on the topic, we have to begin somewhere. The first stereotype that comes to mind is Will Ferrell's news anchor ("You stay classy San Diego"). If Ron Burgundy haunts the data, broadcast students will score higher on anti-intellectualism indices compared with news-editorial (i.e., text-based) students.

Prior chapters examined how anti-intellectualism is condoned in professional ideology, epistemology, and practice. In an optimistic scenario, journalism education would inoculate undergraduates as they begin to identify with the craft and comprehend the intellectual contributions of best practices. On the other hand, the recursive activation of anti-intellectualism in and through the news is likely to leave a mark on professional enculturation (Chapter 5). A perspective on journalism as cultural practice implies that the news articulates and reinforces attitudes toward intellect, experts, and expertise. Not surprisingly, as Claussen notes, journalists and journalism educators are less than proactive in acknowledging the profession's contributions to resentment of intellect.[3]

This cultural backdrop is hardly front and center in the textbooks that students read. Journalism educators, for their part, have not had a chance to look at evidence of anti-intellectual sentiment among students, or how their students compare with those in other programs. I recognize that evidence must precede reform, and to that end, this chapter documents levels of anti-intellectualism among students in journalism and communication. Findings

Where Ideas Go to Die. Michael McDevitt, Oxford University Press (2020). © Oxford University Press.
DOI: 10.1093/oso/9780190869946.001.0001

establish a benchmark for future survey research, allowing for comparisons across time and college major. I am ultimately interested in developmental processes, however, and hope to identify educational experiences and perspectives that protect undergraduates against the incursion of anti-intellectualism into professional norms.

Anti-intellectualism in Professional Development

With anti-intellectualism intertwined in US cultural history, media contributions are relatively benign if engagement with ideas is of little interest to most audiences. If, however, students predisposed toward resentment of intellect find justification in journalistic practices, media education might make a distinct contribution to anti-intellectualism. The premise that students act as agents of cultural hegemony in control of ideas is unlikely to sit well with educators. The 2016 election and the rise of neo-populism globally nevertheless highlight a need to think broadly about how attitudes toward intellect influence young adults as producers and consumers of the news.[4] The purpose of this chapter is not to propose a pedagogical remedy or to contemplate the failure of professional education, but to explore how support for journalistic anti-intellectualism is shaped in a sample of media-literate students.

Hofstadter and Rigney understood anti-intellectualism as a style of thought expressed in contexts such as populist politics, practical-minded business, and evangelical religion.[5] Perrin, Roos, and Gauchat characterize the sentiment as "an individual disposition or set of attitudes that is deeply intertwined with specific social locations, networks, and institutions."[6] I consequently distinguish anti-rationalism and anti-elitism as *cultural* dispositions from *journalistic* attitudes as they would crystallize in the emerging adult years, in experiences associated with college life and professional training.

Among other measures, I use the student anti-intellectualism scale (SAIS) introduced by Eigenberger and Sealander with survey respondents from the general liberal arts, philosophy, and education.[7] SAIS measures unreflective instrumentalism in attitudes about course content, pedagogy, and professors. This version of instrumentalism embodies the presumption of consumer entitlement, the notion that students are buying goods and services that should include, for example, entertaining instructors.[8] Anti-intellectual students are prone to boredom;[9] score low on academic self-efficacy;[10] and prefer professional majors such as business administration over more theoretically oriented disciplines such as sociology.[11] SAIS scores correlate with political and economic conservatism and religiosity.[12]

Critical and literary traditions in the American press still attract at least some of the best and the brightest, but scholars describe journalism education as sensitive to cultural factors that impinge on professional training.[13] In the recursive regime explicated in Chapter 5, news functions as a medium for the expression of resentment and suspicion. Beyond major or course of study, students are subject to expectations for how news should negotiate boundaries between legitimate and deviant ideas. As Hallin writes, the cultural work of journalism includes "exposing, condemning, or excluding from the public agenda those who violate or challenge the political consensus."[14]

A latent mistrust of intellectuals should influence judgment when reporting situations—or survey interview cues—involve intellect in contentious scenarios. In a study of journalism students in the United States and six other countries, Mellado et al. found that college students identify with a citizen role conception, to "develop the intellectual and cultural interests of the public," but they also support a loyalty role, to "cultivate nationalism/patriotism."[15] Cultural anti-elitism could surface as journalistic anti-elitism when intellectuals challenge core values and beliefs, prompting journalistic identification with perceived public mood and the loyalty role. Cultural anti-rationalism could likewise compel journalistic anti-rationalism when transgressive ideas warrant news attention.

I assess three dimensions of anti-intellectualism as cultural sentiment (albeit measured at the individual level)—SAIS, anti-rationalism, and anti-elitism—along with two measures of professional sentiment: journalistic anti-rationalism and anti-elitism. All but SAIS are used for the first time here, and I consequently devoted substantial time to pilot testing questionnaire items with students on my campus (University of Colorado). These measures all ask students to estimate how much they agree with evaluative statements using a 1-to-7 response scale.

Eigenberger and Sealander devised SAIS to assess instrumentalism in the context of college instruction. Students express level of agreement to statements such as "I prefer courses offering practical skills over 'liberal arts' kinds of courses."[16]

Items for anti-rationalism focus on the value of religion and other non-rational guides to life and making decisions. For example, "Creationism is as valid an explanation for the universe as any," and "Sometimes the way I feel about a subject overrides cold hard facts." Statements for anti-elitism reference professors—a social category respondents would possess opinions about—although the emphasis is on populist resentment toward intellectuals rather than preference for instrumental instruction. For example, "A lot of professors think they're better than everyone."

Generally speaking, these broad attitudes toward intellect should precede and predict journalistic manifestations. Survey items for journalistic anti-intellectualism involve assertions about what journalists should do in reporting scenarios. Statements force students to consider whether news media should be aligned with public sentiment or open to ideas that irritate audiences. Threats to binding beliefs activate through journalism the loyalty/betrayal dimension as described in moral foundation theory.[17] Reasoning in this framework is servant to moral emotion, departing from rationalist approaches to human development pioneered by Piaget and Kohlberg.[18]

Items that measure support for journalistic anti-rationalism reference balance as a guide for covering controversies that pit religion against science. For example, journalists "should include religious beliefs as much as science in debates about public policy." Items for journalistic anti-elitism ask students to respond to statements in which news affirms equality of citizen participation or casts suspicion on professors as subversive and disloyal. For instance, journalists should "expose professors who undermine American values."

Role Identity, Major, and Reflexivity

Students' identification with critical-minded roles in journalism and an appreciation for reflexivity offer two mechanisms that might counteract anti-intellectualism. Research on role identity of US journalists spans 50 years, much of it anchored by a series of national probability samples directed by David Weaver at Indiana University. Johnstone, Slawski, and Bowman documented support for three roles in 1976—interpretive, disseminator, watchdog—and Weaver et al. subsequently provided evidence for a fourth role: populist mobilizer.[19] I used the Weaver et al. measures for the student questionnaire. To assess support for interpretive journalism, students were asked, "How important is it for journalists to provide analysis and interpretation of complex problems?"

Weaver et al. report that only 16.8% of professional respondents who rate the interpretive role as "very important" (the top quartile of each scale) also rate the disseminator role as very important. The latter is operationalized as "How important is it for journalists to concentrate on news that's of interest to the widest possible audience?" The deployment of these role identities as predictors of journalistic anti-intellectualism appears intuitive. I expect support for the interpretive function to correlate negatively with support for journalistic anti-rationalism and anti-elitism, while support for the disseminator role—a populist orientation—should correlate positively with these two orientations to newswork. Interpretive reporting favors quality over audience reach. By contrast, support for widespread distribution resonates with the "passion for equality" that Hofstadter described as endemic in America.[20] The disseminator role and journalistic anti-elitism are aligned in commercialization of news—in mass production of pre-digested content.[21] In factor analysis of role identities among college students, Mellado et al. found that items traditionally deployed to measure the disseminator conception cohere under the heading "consumer oriented."[22]

The adversarial function is probably the least intuitive role in its orientation to intellect. Does the watchdog role extend to policing ideas? Respondents are asked, "How important is it for journalists to be an adversary of public officials by being constantly skeptical of their actions?" Skepticism of authority is baked into professional education, captured in the bromide: "If your mother says she loves you, check it out." Still, the survey item articulates the watchdog *in relation to officials* rather than skepticism toward fundamentalist belief. Support for adversarial reporting could, consequently, justify distrust of cultural elites. Recent research on political disaffection of college students shows that cynicism toward leaders is negatively related to dispositions such as interest in public affairs and information seeking.[23] Consequently, identification with the adversarial role might correlate positively with journalistic anti-elitism in a sample of young adults. On the other hand, an adversarial stance motivated by critical thinking should align with an aversion to the populist penchant for simple solutions.

To assess support for the populist mobilizer role, respondents are asked, "How important is it to give ordinary people a chance to express their views on public affairs?" I anticipate that support for giving "ordinary people" a voice will correlate positively with journalistic anti-elitism. The final item in this battery is the loyalty role, an identity Mellado et al. documented in their student sample: "How important is it for journalism to cultivate patriotism?" In the current study, support for loyalty should predict journalistic anti-rationalism. Intellect is most subversive, as per Hofstadter, when it challenges the core beliefs that underlie collective identity.

Attitudes about intellect that students bring to college are likely associated with self-selection to major. Survey data for this chapter are cross-sectional rather than longitudinal, making it difficult to tease out predispositions that students bring to college from feelings toward intellect shaped by a particular course sequence. The response of professional education to converging technologies may have blurred in students' minds distinctions between print and broadcast journalism that were once meaningful to their instructors.[24] Even so, students confident in their ability to convey nuance and to engage ideas are likely to identify with traditions in the American press such as literary, analytical, and explanatory journalism. In the present sample, news-editorial represents the major most aligned with these genres. News as hedonistic distraction, by contrast, is arguably most evident in televised content, and the implications for self-selection would seem to underscore perceptions of broadcast students as too often attracted to news as infotainment.[25] This is where Will Ferrell peaks behind the curtain.

Surveys of US journalists reveal a pluralism of values that underlie role conceptions in print, broadcast, and digital media.[26] Weaver et al. explain that journalists' "perceptions of their roles are not one-dimensional, but tend to be composed of several roles at the same time."[27] However, the premise that anti-elitism and anti-rationalism seep into professional socialization implies base levels of resentment and suspicion. To the extent that professionalism engenders homogeneity in education, we could see a narrow band of scores for journalistic anti-intellectualism among news majors. Glasser argues: "Whereas the goal of diversity is to foster an appreciation for differences in experience and therefore differences in knowledge, the goal of a professional education is—in effect and usually by design—to unify knowledge by glossing over differences in experience."[28]

As discussed in previous chapters, studies on newswork increasingly highlight reflexivity to account for critical thinking in service to transparency.[29] From a normative perspective, journalists hold themselves accountable in transparency of method and motive. The democratic rationale is articulated in communitarianism and civic/public journalism.[30] Transparency is operationalized here with prescriptive statements about how journalists should acknowledge the values and methods that shape coverage.

Sensitivity to reception of news, however, helps to explain media in cultural hegemony, in the circulation of narratives that engender consent for dominant ideology.[31] A willingness to deliberate with ideas requires some degree of intellectual autonomy among journalists themselves. An audience-facing transparency, by contrast, could lend itself to journalistic anti-rationalism. Tactical or defensive transparency embodies a form of accountability that is more strategic than the reason-based accountability associated with Habermas's public sphere.[32] Transparency would justify journalistic anti-elitism when motivated by a perceived need to answer to the public, particularly when activists with provocative ideas become targets of suspicion.

Study Design and Findings

I worked with a research team to conduct a purposive sample of undergraduate students at four public universities and one private liberal arts college ($N = 1,472$). All five campuses offer comprehensive programs in journalism and mass communication (JMC). We set out to capture educational experiences that span 10 majors along with socio-demographic diversity with respect to gender, ethnicity, strength of religious identity, and political ideology.

We recruited students from the College of Media, Communication and Information at CU Boulder ($n = 288$); the School of Journalism and Mass Communication at the University of Wisconsin, Madison ($n = 242$); the College of Communication Arts and Sciences at Michigan State ($n = 423$); the Grady College of Journalism and Mass Communication at the University of Georgia ($n = 274$); and the School of Communication and the Arts at Marist College, ($n = 245$), a campus on the Hudson River known for its use of technology in professional curricula. The field sites for college instruction and media markets encompass the Rocky Mountain West, Southeast, Midwest, and Northeast. Journalism students major in news-editorial, broadcast news, and broadcast production. The sample includes majors in visual communication/design, liberal arts, media studies and information, pre-professional (non-media careers), public relations, communication, and advertising. We began data collection on October 8, 2015, and closed the survey on December 23. The Appendix provides details on recruitment, response rates, and sample demographics.[33]

With data in hand, I was curious, first of all, about how respondents in this sample compare with majors outside JMC on the SAIS, in disciplines as diverse as psychology, accounting, nursing, and criminal justice. The Appendix includes item wording for all measures and reliability scores for the multi-item scales. As shown in Table 8.1, JMC majors fare well when ranked with students at three accredited business schools[34] and a four-year, state-funded university.[35] Eight of the ten majors in the current sample represent JMC

Table 8.1 Mean scores for student anti-intellectualism scale by undergraduate major

Economics	2.76
Visual communication/design	3.25
Liberal arts	3.28
Psychology	3.30
News-editorial	3.31
Media studies and information	3.44
Management and information systems	3.62
Pre-professional (non-media careers)	3.64
Public relations	3.65
Communication	3.66
Education	3.71
Broadcast production	3.73
Nursing	3.74
General business	3.75
Finance	3.80
Multimedia design	3.82
Advertising	3.82
Broadcast news	3.83
Business administration	3.83
Accounting	3.84
Management	3.84
Marketing	3.85
Criminal justice	3.90
Biology	3.91

Note: The table ranks majors from the current study, students at three accredited business schools (Rafik Z. Elias, "Anti-Intellectualism Attitudes and Academic Self-Efficacy among Business Students," *Journal of Education for Business* 84, no. 2 (2008): 110–16), and students from Cameron University (Antonio Laverghetta and J. Kathleen Nash, "Student Anti-intellectualism and College Major," *College Student Journal* 44, no. 2 (2010): 528–32). Majors interviewed for this chapter appear in shaded rows; journalism majors are in boldface. The range for possible mean scores on SAIS is 1–7.

disciplines; all eight score lower on SAIS than students in biology, a core discipline in the sciences and humanities. Students in visual communication and news-editorial score lower on SAIS than students in all of the business majors: management and information systems, general business, finance, business administration, accounting, management, and marketing. On the other hand, journalism majors are assessed higher on SAIS compared with students in economics and psychology.

The remaining analyses are confined to students recruited for the current study. Prior to accounting for the strength of predictors, I examined whether the three news majors generate notable differences among themselves for mean scores on cultural and journalistic anti-intellectualism. News-editorial majors score significantly lower on SAIS (M = 3.31) compared with broadcast news (M = 3.83) and broadcast production students (M = 3.73). News-editorial majors score lowest on anti-rationalism (M = 3.23), anti-elitism (M = 3.85), journalistic anti-rationalism (M = 3.09), and journalistic anti-elitism (M = 3.94).

The results so far conform to the stereotype of writing/text-based journalists more cerebral than peers in broadcast media. Still, with socio-demographics and other education experiences as controls, we will see more clearly whether majoring in news-editorial stands out as a negative predictor of journalistic anti-intellectualism. The analytical model (specified more completely in the Appendix) stipulates support for anti-rationalism and anti-elitism as correlates of support for the corresponding journalistic practices. This scheme allows us to isolate major, role identities, support for transparency, and other factors that might guard against a cultural milieu conducive to journalistic anti-intellectualism. Model specification is based on the assumption that influence from anti-intellectualism at the cultural level precedes student experiences and attitude crystallization within a college setting. I also presume that role identity and audience-facing reflexivity (transparency) contribute to students' evaluative orientations toward the news as it confronts intellect and intellectuals in contentious scenarios.

Table 8.2 highlights only two predictors that generate significant and negative coefficients: grade point average and support for the watchdog role. Nearly all of the educational experiences are either inconsequential or positive correlates of journalistic anti-intellectualism. (Appendix Table 8.2 accounts for influences on journalistic anti-rationalism and anti-elitism in more detail.) Student support for anti-rationalism and anti-elitism are robust predictors of the matching journalistic orientations.

Table 8.2 Predictors of college student support for journalistic anti-intellectualism

	Journalistic anti-rationalism	*Journalistic anti-elitism*
Predictors		
Support for anti-intellectualism at cultural level		
Anti-rationalism	.48***	.16***
Anti-elitism		.23***
Socio-demographics		
Ethnicity		
Gender		
Strength of religious identity	.20***	
Ideological identity		
Educational experience		
Grade level		
Grade point average		−.06*
News-editorial major		
Broadcast news major		
Broadcast production major		
Support for journalistic roles		
Interpreter		
Disseminator		.19***
Adversary/watchdog		−.05*
Populist mobilizer		.07**
Loyalty	.09**	.17***
Support for transparency	.12**	.24***

Note: $N = 1{,}472$ students recruited for interviews at five colleges: University of Colorado Boulder; University of Wisconsin, Madison; Michigan State; University of Georgia; and Marist College.

Cell entries report coefficients that reach statistical significance in the final model of hierarchical multiple regression. $*p < .05$, $**p < .01$, $***p < .001$.

Data are weighted to account for unequal sampling probabilities for majors.

Strength of religious identity correlates with journalistic anti-rationalism. This result supports construct validity; from the perspective of moral development, fundamentalist faith should be leery of intellect.[36] Higher grade level fails to inoculate students, but grade point average nets a negative coefficient in protection against journalistic anti-elitism. The non-finding for grade level implies that JMC education lacks the kind of rigor needed to mollify suspicion of intellect. Meanwhile, the three news majors fall flat as predictors.

Critical and analytical orientations to role identity would brighten the picture for those who view journalism education as an intellectual enterprise. The interpretive role, however, fails to pull weight as a negative correlate of journalistic anti-rationalism and anti-elitism. I expected this identity would welcome news that engages with challenging or provocative ideas. In retrospect, support for interpretive reporting might overlap with a diffusive distrust of expert authority. The good news here is that the interpretive role does not correlate positively with journalistic anti-intellectualism. "Critical" thinking directed against intellect would constitute a perverse outcome of college instruction. This possibility is not farfetched in light of recent research showing that people with the most extreme and confident views on genetically modified food know the least about the applicable science.[37] Also, somewhat reassuring, is that student support for the adversary/watchdog function is aversive to journalistic anti-elitism. The other role identities conform to expectations. The disseminator and populist mobilizer roles predict support for journalistic anti-elitism, and the loyalty role correlates with both dimensions of journalistic anti-intellectualism.

Finally, I anticipated that affinity for audience-facing reflexivity would be compatible with journalistic anti-intellectualism. Endorsement of transparency is operationalized with survey items such as "Journalists must ultimately answer to the public when questions arise about reporting methods." Unfortunately for the many advocates of communitarian journalism,[38] support for transparency among digital natives generates significant and positive coefficients for both journalistic anti-rationalism and anti-elitism. These results echo back to Chapter 3 on the eclipse of reflexivity in populist climates. Reporters and editors exercise disciplinary power over themselves by imagining anti-intellectual audiences. Findings from this chapter suggest that an inclination to please the public is already internalized before students leave classrooms for newsrooms.

A Hidden Curriculum

Several generations of journalism educators have sought to elevate the intellectual status of the profession in higher education, contending that their programs fit comfortably within the liberal arts.[39] One of the more disconcerting findings, consequently, is the failure of grade level to negatively predict support for journalistic anti-intellectualism. The results imply that freshmen and seniors hold similar attitudes when intellect is aligned against public sentiment in the news. If expectations for journalism are internalized as cultural practice, *any* student with propensities toward anti-rationalism and anti-elitism would prefer that media support those sentiments. Recent strands of political sociology are skeptical about efforts to inculcate deliberative dispositions in higher education, as research on human development accommodates the darker dimensions of youth politicization.[40] Frustrations with complexity of governance; disdain for compromise; discomfort with political discussion; and preference for simplistic solutions are rooted at least partially in the unreflective hedonism of youth culture.[41]

Resentment of intellect is a persistent feature of American society, as is, apparently, expectation for a moralistic press. Educators might highlight reflexivity as a corrective, but student support for transparency predicts journalistic anti-rationalism and anti-elitism.

A comparison of news majors with students in other fields and colleges offers a more hopeful view. News-editorial students score lower on the SAIS than majors in education, perhaps the best comparison possible from Table 8.1. Education like journalism integrates theory and practice; both identify with the university mission of cultivating informed citizenship.

In another comparative study with implications for critical thinking, Coleman and Wilkins reported mean scores for moral development, placing professional journalists below seminarians/philosophers, medical students, and practicing physicians, but above dental students, nurses, graduate students, undergraduate students, orthopedic surgeons, and business professionals.[42] (Prison inmates escaped from last place by beating out junior high school students.) To the extent that moral development demands postconventional thinking,[43] journalism students and professionals are likely to resist anti-intellectualism.

Still, majoring in journalism does not guard against support for journalistic anti-rationalism and anti-elitism. Anti-intellectualism as cultural sentiment appears to filter into training without much resistance. The student sample is not representative of undergraduates nationally,[44] but JMC majors presumably think more about normative media practices than other students. A connection between the commercial pressures on media professions and a populist disregard for cultural elites suggests that broadcast news majors should score similarly to advertising majors on anti-elitism. On the 1-to-7 scale, means are nearly identical: 4.22 for broadcast news, 4.11 for advertising. Students following these tracks are likely to internalize the temporal imperative of capturing audiences in broad appeals.

In this first documentation of anti-intellectualism in a JMC sample, the results suggest that journalism anti-elitism ($M = 4.19$) is a larger concern than journalism anti-rationalism ($M = 3.44$). Persons attract more news attention than abstractions, generally speaking.[45] A plausible corollary is that intellectuals—more so than their ideas—are perceived with suspicion by news majors and other students. To the extent that students harbor resentments toward faculty, those attitudes might shape their perceptions of public intellectuals.

Support for role identities is not uniformly aligned with anti-intellectualism, although the primary push is toward a legitimation of journalistic anti-elitism. The disseminator and populist mobilizer roles appear to justify journalistic anti-elitism in commercial and civic terms, respectively. The scale for journalistic anti-elitism includes items such as "Journalists should focus on stories that average citizens care about." An egalitarian ethos comports with the view that media should disseminate news as widely as possible. The commercial and populist mobilizer rationales for a marketplace of ideas are thereby justified—perhaps paradoxically—in suspicion of intellect among emerging adults. Pending replication, the findings imply a cultural contradiction in US journalism rooted deeper than boundaries of the profession itself, in the attitudes and expectations of media consumers. As I discuss in the final chapter, the *marketplace* of ideas is incoherent as a metaphor for journalism in service to informed citizenship. To the extent that expressions of anti-intellectualism become more sophisticated and persuasive in post-truth politics, students must recognize that the resonance of familiar ideas is a product of recursive communication (Chapter 5), not intellectual rigor.

The interpretive and adversarial roles fall short as robust, negative predictors of professional anti-intellectualism (Appendix Table 8.2), but they should be conducive to critical thinking, at least in some respects. News majors are more supportive of the interpretive role than other students ($M_{\mathrm{diff.}} = .18$) as well as more committed to the watchdog role ($M_{\mathrm{diff.}} = .24$). And news majors are much less likely to endorse a patriotic press in the loyalty role ($M_{\text{diff.}}$ = .37). These differences are all statistically significant.

Reflexivity refocuses the lens from latent influence of cultural anti-intellectualism to awareness associated with transparency. A public-oriented reflexivity is central to communicative ethics, a prescriptive that "expects from journalists a commitment to respond, openly and candidly, to any serious question about what they do and why they do it."[46] Support for transparency by news majors suggests a commitment to accountability (M = 5.32, range 1–7), even as this form of accountability appears to condone journalistic anti-intellectualism. Future research should develop additional measures of reflexivity for student and professional samples. For example, *peer-oriented reflexivity* in classrooms and newsrooms could anchor intellectual autonomy against populist and nativist currents.

This chapter has been interested in cultural influences rather than effects of pedagogical practices, textbook content, or learning styles. That said, with baseline findings established here, future research could explore connections between curricular components and support for—or aversion to—journalistic anti-intellectualism. In media ethics textbooks, for example, accountability in Kant's moral system establishes a rationale for transparency while respecting the dignity and reasoning capacity of individuals processing the news.[47] An authentic application of Kantian principles would cultivate commitment to transparency that is also supportive of intellectual journalism.

A hidden curriculum nevertheless connects student enculturation with how professionals imagine a judgmental public as documented in Chapter 3. Students unsure of themselves are unlikely to adopt story themes that challenge orthodoxies of the public or journalism itself.[48] Their instructors assign textbooks that valorize the press as tribune of the people.[49] They learn that journalism is the "handmaiden of the citizen."[50] Efforts to democratize and de-professionalize journalism education imagine rampant elitism in US journalism, *a problem that does not exist*.[51] The news paradigm, if anything, enforces the learned helplessness I describe in Chapter 1: a practice of bad faith in which journalists demonstrate objectivity by letting prominent sources dictate the news.[52] As I argued in Chapter 2, academic anti-elitism as cultural critique further repudiates journalistic authority in ways that undermine intellectual aspirations.[53]

My view is that student support for transparency represents a negotiation between the need for accountability and internalization of cultural hegemony. This interpretation is consistent with the form of reflexivity described earlier as professional realism. When confronted by intellectual discourse that challenges core beliefs, journalists lower expectations for themselves and audiences. Young journalists would ideally feel compelled to engage boldly with ideational dissent. Media education's contribution to anti-intellectualism is ironic at several levels, to say the least. A civic-minded journalism is subverted when practitioners view themselves as loyal to binding belief rather than protective of conditions that foster public deliberation. Reflexivity as transparency—the awareness and adjustment that should ensure accountability—appears to condone rather than correct problematic practice.

Cultural expectations for news media are likely to confound a healthy distrust of power with mistrust of intellect when the latter's degree of autonomy from entrenched interests is not considered. As Schudson writes, citizens "do not have to like the authority of experts," but they should support "good use of expertise in making policy."[54] Many students are drawn to journalism—as a profession and as a field of study—because of its populist mythos. Especially with this tradition and this student inclination in mind, educators should emphasize a critical autonomy that makes room for transparency but does not succumb to climates of opinion.

9

In My Buggy

How Dangerous Professors Seed Intellect in a Hybrid Field

Intellect does not perform well as journalism's mule. Neither does it thrive in academia when corralled into narrow pens of expertise. Even as ideas born in critical thinking migrate in search of validation, many go to die in the space where journalism confronts intellect. A sphere of knowledge work beset by contradiction, the academic-media nexus is nevertheless attractive to professors and reporters seeking to overcome limitations of their respective fields.[1]

Journalists for the most part retain the power of selection, context, and framing when scholars consent to interviews.[2] Intellect in this exchange finds itself subservient to common sense. As shown in social drama (Chapter 6), journalism's acute sensitivity to violations of binding beliefs allows it to periodically exploit academic labor by distilling discourse into deviance.[3]

The nexus of academia and media, consequently, can seem like a kaleidoscopic space where public intellectuals experience reversals of hierarchy, where perceived rules of engagement are, at best, implicit and contingent. In an analysis of how ideas circulate in social movements, Gamson and Wolsfeld characterize journalist/activist interactions as a "dialogue of the deaf."[4] Neither reporters nor activists "make an effort to understand how the other views their relationship or, better yet, the complex nature of these transactions." Mutual miscomprehension is accompanied by derision born out of mutual dependency.[5] Digital platforms allow activist scholars to bypass news media in emerging forms of public scholarship, but social movements rely on a mainstream presence for mobilization, validation, and enlargement of the scope of conflict.[6]

Exchanges of critical scholarship with popular media today are more fraught with uncertainty than the interactions described by Gamson and Wolsfeld in the 1990s. Looming in the background of civil interactions between reporters and professors is an "organized outrage machine"[7] dedicated

Where Ideas Go to Die. Michael McDevitt, Oxford University Press (2020). © Oxford University Press.
DOI: 10.1093/oso/9780190869946.001.0001

to surveillance of academic discourse in its many forms: news commentary and blogs,[8] social media,[9] conferences,[10] commencement speeches,[11] and peer-reviewed work.[12] Surveillance extends to lectures and even classroom skits, with university administrators spooked by provocations that might attract a spotlight. Worried about perception of sexual harassment on my campus (University of Colorado), a provost intervened in a sociology of deviance course that cast teaching assistants as prostitutes.[13] And then there are the student informants in the back row with mobile recording devices.[14]

This chapter explores motivations of faculty targeted by vigilante groups. Interviews of 25 "dangerous professors" probe their tactical experiences in the academic-media nexus, a field defined by contradiction, doubt, and status inversion (Chapter 4). A multiplicity of epistemic communities interacting with journalism implies a faint centrifugal coherence, but conflict and disorientation could induce a productive reflexivity. Interviews with faculty from the life sciences, social sciences, medicine, law, and the humanities focus on how targeted scholars pioneer practices that allow them to navigate uncertainty and populist blowback. Over time, risk-tolerant and conflict-seeking activists should become sensitive to constraints of news production on the free play of intellect. One way or another, they must rework relationships with reporters to confront the news as a paradigm of conventional wisdom. For a reporter, rapport in interviews sometimes requires the acknowledgment of a scholar's critique of the news. The disorientation of a hybrid field is consequently generative of shared reflexivity in efforts to reconcile intellect with journalism. If intellect juxtaposed with mass media embodies the contradiction of deliberative democracy, these interviews in microcosm suggest openings to reconcile.

A Field of Fields

The academic-media nexus could be viewed as a field of fields in the sense that journalism relies on knowledge from disciplines across the scholarly landscape. This interpretation is compatible with Bourdieu's understanding of fields of knowledge work as heteronomous; they bump and blur into one another.[15] The forms of capital exchanged within and across fields "create friction, and thus excite action."[16] Actors in a social field acquire a practical sense of the game, a habitus shaped by implicit rules and sensibilities that impose order while allowing discretion and the capacity to resist countervailing forces.

Cultural capital in journalism can range from the technical (how to write a lead) to the sacerdotal (telling stories that resonate with binding beliefs) to the theatrical (how to provoke the president in the Rose Garden). For public scholars, the overlap of news media and academia is beset by ambiguous rules of the game and uncertainty about strategies effectively deployed. Levels of risk are unclear depending on contingencies such as the news pegs that trigger interviews, interview tactics of reporters, ideological climate, and how professors will be perceived by colleagues once they go public.

Dissident academics often identify with the traditional role of the public intellectual, compelling some kind of presence in mass communication. Townsley writes that formulations of the truly intellectual—"the transcendent, the pure, the free, the critical"—are juxtaposed against "the technical, the narrow, the applied, i.e., the historically determined or class-bound."[17] Intellectuals would become apologists for power in the cultural studies critique that Liu refers to as "academic antielitism" (Chapter 2),[18] but the traditional role of the public intellectual is still endorsed by activist scholars in an aspirational sense. Public scholars strive to overcome both the narrowness of academic disciplines and the instrumental uses of their labor by journalists who say they "love the experts."[19] In preserving a voice against orthodoxy, scholars must work out relationships with reporters in which the appropriate capital is exchanged.[20]

Public scholars are predisposed to think of media as liminal space that brings risk but also opportunities to trigger reflexivity. Oliver Wendell Holmes comes to mind: "Every idea is an incitement. It offers itself for belief and if believed it is acted on unless some other belief outweighs it or some failure of energy stifles the movement at birth."[21] Most ideas never reach the threshold of incitement, but Holmes captures a pragmatic faith in creative dissonance. For reporters, reflexivity in exchanges with scholars might activate resistance to those elements of news incompatible with intellect. In interviews with beat reporters covering a Midwestern farm crisis, Meyers confirmed earlier research on how the craft of *authoritative writing* can produce "oppositional news."[22] Her observations echoed Stark's 1962 finding "that 'the most intangible way' for reporters to subvert management policy is in their writing, which is 'almost impossible for management to combat.'"[23] Editors can still spike stories, but reporters motivated to challenge conventional narratives invite a natural alliance with critical scholars. The success of academics in conveying dissident views might depend on backstage negotiations with reporters that precede editing.

These dynamics assume base levels of goodwill. Political science and media sociology, however, have criticized journalists as lapdogs for centrist ideology since at least the Vietnam era.[24] As a test for goodwill, I will examine whether contrarian professors perceive media contagion from two vigilante initiatives. These watchlists affirm populist suspicion in an expanding network of right-wing media.[25] Interviews of professors targeted by the watchlists should offer insight as to whether they perceive quality news media as safe or weaponized space.

Textual Analysis and Interviews

Media sociology on reporter-source relations generally adopts the perspective of journalists, an orientation that began with newsroom ethnographies of the 1970s.[26] Science communication, by contrast, is attentive to strategies of expert sources in shaping public policy. While news as a foil of scientists is a recurrent theme,[27] *targeted* academics—those potentially most critical of media—are interviewed for the first time in this chapter. I recruited faculty with recent appearances in *The New York Times* (*NYT*). A prominent newspaper of record, the *NYT* constitutes "a critical space where different intellectuals gather to compete over definitions of legitimate intellectual practice, and it represents an important general public sphere."[28] An appearance in the *NYT* provides a reference point in interviews to make salient how provocative ideas are potentially engaged by the quality press.

The sample frame is defined by two criteria. First, professors with university appointments or retired faculty profiled in David Horowitz's *The Professors: The 101 Most Dangerous Academics in America*[29] and/or those named in Professor Watchlist (*N* = 251), a website launched by Turning Point USA (TPUSA) on November 21, 2016, shortly after the Trump election. Second, the professors must have appeared in the *NYT* within a two-year period prior to recruitment for interviews, which began March 23, 2017. Faculty must have published an op-ed column/letter to the editor, contributed as a source, or appeared in some other role in a news article. The resulting sample includes 17 scholars from Professor Watchlist and 25 from Horowitz (*N* = 42). The higher number from *The Professors*, published in 2006, reflects the effort of Horowitz to expose faculty at the "forefront of their professions,"[30] which translates in part to a presence in elite media.

Unveiled a decade apart, the lists share a perception of higher education polluted by leftist indoctrination. "Under the influence of tenured radicals," as Horowitz's puts it, "American liberal arts faculties have become more narrow-minded and intellectually repressive than at any time in the last hundred years."[31] Professor Watchlist (PWL) declares: "TPUSA will continue to fight for free speech and the right for professors to say whatever they wish; however students, parents, and alumni deserve to know the specific incidents and names of professors that advance a radical agenda in lecture halls."[32] Both projects emphasize the factual basis of their portraits. Horowitz describes his documentation as scholarly in establishing patterns of conduct. PWL relies on conservative media:

> This watchlist is an aggregated list of pre-existing news stories that were published by a variety of news organizations. While we accept tips for new additions on our website, we only publish profiles on incidents that have already been reported by a credible source.[33]

Apart from the gluttony of de-contextualization practiced by Horowitz and PWL, reputable scholars have investigated whether the academy has become a liberal hegemony.[34] Openly conservative faculty are certainly subject to ideological climate and surveillance, but a well-publicized list of offending scholars from the right is not yet part of the vigilante apparatus in academia.[35]

Prior to recruitment of targeted scholars for interviews, I conducted a textual analysis to document the deviance tropes that circulate in the two watchlists. This allowed me to ask professors to comment on whether they observe migration of the depictions to news about their scholarship and activism. A "playing field of tropes" provides action repertoires (codes, frames, narratives) in particular modalities and mediated contexts.[36] The public intellectual trope in US political discourse is contested and multifaceted. The next section documents whether activist scholars perceive that tropes of deviant professors infect the news.

I initially contacted Horowitz's "dangerous academics" and PWL professors through email and emphasized that the preferred interview mode was video chat using Skype, but other options included phone or follow-up email. This recruitment delivered 25 completed interviews, which began March 24, 2017 and ended September 10, 2017.[37] I did not offer, and the professors did not request, anonymity. Horowitz features 11 of the professors and PWL profiles 10. Four appear on both lists.

My approach was largely inductive in textual analysis of the transcripts, while sensitive to field-spanning ideologies that might explain strategies of targeted scholars. Ideas as action-guiding thoughts are prescriptive *within* well-established fields; I did not expect a coherent ideology in the coordination of scholarship, activism, and journalism.[38] I did presume, however, that activist academics align their belief systems with those action-guiding ideas of newswork receptive to reflexivity. This follows from the premise that success of scholar activists is accompanied by cultivation of critical thinking in journalism.

The first analysis ventures into the vigilante mind by identifying tropes that circulate in the watchlists. These depictions, in conjunction with interview transcripts, will identify risks inherent in the expression of ideas that disturb orthodoxy. With these field conditions surveyed, we then focus on the more intimate setting of the professor/reporter relationship as a resource for seeding of intellect in journalism.

Shades of Deviance

Most of the Horowitz profiles run three to four pages, while PWL provides one to several sentences per professors with links to news stories. Prior research has not inventoried these expressions of deviance, and the number of distinct tropes is not presented here as definitive. A reading of the portrayals does suggest an implicit structure based on level of threat to social order, from annoyance to absurdity to actionable offense. Preferred redress can vary from pressure on universities to fire faculty, to dirty tricks (described below), to death threats. Table 9.1 identifies the 25 professors interviewed vis-à-vis watchlist appearance, university affiliation, and discipline. They are organized into a sequence of increasing deviance, from *divisive* to *disloyal*, *subversive*, *unhinged*, and *dangerous*. Horowitz (DH) and PWL both used all five tropes.

The watchlists portray five of the professors as divisive, and in each case the theme is operationalized by supposed racial incitement. PWL quotes the historian Gerald Horne saying that the Pledge of Allegiance is the "glue" that binds a "former slaveholders' republic." Professors are deemed disloyal based on their affiliations or purported views on foreign policy, terrorism, and immigration. Growing up a red-diaper baby warrants some suspicion (PWL), and in the case of Bettina Aptheker, the women's history scholar is by proud admission "both a Communist and a self-described 'lesbian activist'"

Table 9.1 Interviewed professors by watchlist and deviance trope

Professor	Watchlist	Deviance Trope
		Divisive
Gary Gutting, philosophy, Notre Dame [emeritus]	PWL	"Dr. Gutting claims that 'permissive gun laws are a manifestation of racism.' He believes that the mostly white gun lobby is forcing black people to live in fear."
Gerald Horne, history, Univ. of Houston	PWL	"The professor of history and African American studies says that the Pledge is the post-Civil War 'glue' that binds together this 'artificially-constructed former slaveholders' republic.'"
Mary Frances Berry, history, Univ. of Pennsylvania	DH	"In Professor Berry's radical perspective, white racism is an intractable and pervasive crisis in America fifty years after the civil rights revolution."
Kathleen Cleaver, law, Emory	DH	"According to Cleaver, the 'inability to treat Black people in a humane fashion' has 'become part of the identity of the United States.'"
Joe Feagin, sociology, Texas A&M	DH	"In Feagin's view, whites who cannot see the logic and the justice of reparations are suffering from a psychological malady he calls 'slavery denial.'"
		Disloyal
Bettina Aptheker, feminist studies, UC Santa Cruz	PWL DH	PWL "Aptheker was raised by well-known members of the Communist party, and then continued membership into her adult life, including being a leader of Leftist groups at her college as a student in the 1960s." DH "Professor Aptheker is by her own proud admission both a Communist and a self-described 'lesbian activist.'"
Arthur Caplan, bioethics, NY Univ.	PWL	"Caplan argued that Trump's immigration plan 'should be viewed in the repugnant tradition of Hitler.'"
Bruce Cumings, history, Univ. of Chicago	PWL	"Dr. Cumings placed most of the blame of North Korea's problems on the United States, while also whitewashing problems in Korea."
Mark Ensalaco, political science, Univ. of Dayton	DH	"Professor Ensalaco regards the United States as responsible for the 9/11 attacks on itself."
Matthew Evangelista, history, Cornell	DH	"That same month, during a discussion of Iraq with Cornell faculty members, Professor Evangelista declared that the planned American bombing attacks would make American forces look like 'war criminals.'"
		Subversive
Juan Cole, history, Univ. of Michigan	PWL DH	PWL "He believes right-wing Jews and an 'Islamophobic network' were 'a key influence' to the shooting that killed nine people at Emanuel African Methodist Episcopal Church in Charleston, S.C." DH "His recurrent theme is that a nebulous 'pro-Likud' cabal controls the American government from a small number of key positions in the Executive Branch."

Table 9.1 Continued

Professor	Watchlist	Deviance Trope
David Barash, psychology, Univ. of Washington	DH	"A brief section of *Peace and Conflict Studies* is devoted to the 9/11 terrorist attacks on the United States. It provides troubling insight into the impact courses like this may be having on American college students as their country faces the terrorist threat."
Michael Bérubé, literature, Pennsylvania State	DH	"That Professor Berube's class promoted his anti-religious prejudices under the guise of 'postmodern theory' and did so at the expense of the literature he had been hired to teach, did not trouble him."
Richard Falk, law, Princeton [emeritus]	DH	"He alleges that terror warnings and threat assessments are tools used by the government to frighten and thereby control the American people, observing that the 'periodic alarmist warnings of mega-terrorist imminent attacks' have not yet been followed by any actual attacks."
Jerry Lembcke, sociology, Holy Cross [emeritus]	DH	"In the same article, Professor Lembcke darkly warned that 'reclaiming our memory of the Vietnam era entails a struggle against very powerful institutional forces that toy with our imaginings of the war for reasons of monetary, political, or professional gain.'"
Victor Navasky, journalism, Columbia [emeritus]	DH	"From the platform that his academic employment provides, Professor Navasky has labored to disseminate *The Nation*'s far-left agendas throughout the American education system."
		Unhinged
Robert Jensen, journalism, Univ. of Texas Austin	PWL DH	PWL "Jensen also attacked a major anti-sexual assault group for blaming the perpetrators for rape, instead of focusing on the patriarchal culture as the main cause." DH "He has urged that 'God condemn America, so that the world might live,' though there is little evidence that he is a believer in anything but Marxism."
Ellen Lewin, anthropology, Univ. of Iowa	PWL	"Dr. Lewin recently came under fire for her passionate response to a campus-wide email sent by the College Republicans. The email was an advertisement for 'Conservative Coming Out Week!' Lewin, in a fit of rage, replied, 'F@#$ YOU, REPUBLICANS.'"
Dale Maharidge, journalism, Columbia	PWL	"After finding out he was under investigation on Project Veritas' 'To Catch A Journalist' he reacted with a series of explicit and sophomoric rants on social media."

Continued

Table 9.1 Continued

Professor	Watchlist	Deviance Trope
Darry Sragow, political science, USC	PWL	"Darry Sragow, a professor at the University of Southern California, attacked Republicans during a political science class. He angrily called them old, white, racist, 'losers' and encouraged illegally suppressing Republican votes."
Charles Strozier, history, CUNY	PWL	"Dr. Strozier argues law-abiding citizens become Taliban terrorist extremists due to climate-change."
Dangerous		
Bill Ayers, education, Univ. of Illinois at Chicago [retired]	PWL DH	PWL "Ayers was the leader of the 'Weather Underground' group responsible for setting off bombs that destroyed government property and infrastructure." DH "Ayers summed up the nihilism of Weathermen's ideology as follows: 'Kill all the rich people.'"
George Ciccariello-Maher, global studies, Drexel [resigned][a]	PWL	"Ciccariello-Maher tweeted on Christmas Day 2016 that he wanted 'white genocide' for Christmas, and later tweeted, 'To clarify: when the whites were massacre [*sic*] during the Haitian revolution, that was a good thing indeed.'"
Greg Hampikian, biological sciences, Boise State	PWL	"In his editorial entitled 'When May I Shoot a Student?', Hampikian writes about how the library would make a good shooting range, and asks when he can fire a warning shot in class when students try to correct his equation."
Paul Ehrlich, biology, Stanford	DH	"He suggested adding 'temporary sterilants' to the water supply but thought 'society would probably dissolve' before the government could do that."

Sources: PWL: Professor Watchlist, Turning Point USA, launched in 2016. All depictions retrieved from http://www.professorwatchlist.org/. DH: David Horowitz, *The Professors: The 101 Most Dangerous Academics in America*. Washington, DC: Regnery, 2006.

[a] Ciccariello-Maher held this position when interviewed.

(DH).[39] Unpatriotic faculty become more than just an annoyance when they act as agents of subversion. Misuse of intellect presents as the ability to disorient in six cases. Horowitz writes, for example: "Professor [Jerry] Lembcke darkly warned that 'reclaiming our memory of the Vietnam era entails a struggle against very powerful institutional forces that toy with our imaginings of the war.'"[40] Subversive faculty should instead face up to external enemies (such as terrorists) or internal threats (such as postmodernism).

I situate "unhinged" as a transitional identity between the first three orientations and the truly dangerous. In three of five profiles, a premise is stated in such stark terms as to startle readers with the intellect unbound. For instance, "Dr. [Charles] Strozier argues law-abiding citizens become Taliban terrorist extremists due to climate-change" (PWL). Faculty are exposed as emotionally unstable. Anthropology professor Ellen Lewin is quoted responding to an email of College Republicans: "F@#$ YOU, REPUBLICANS" (PWL). De-contextualization portrays four of the professors as dangerous. A statement extracted from its polemic or satirical context is insensible (to some) unless taken on its face. With dangerous professors capable of obfuscation, extraction pins intellect so that it cannot wiggle away. Thus, when George Ciccariello-Maher tweeted on Christmas Eve 2016: "All I Want for Christmas is White Genocide" (Figure 9.1), PWL presented the post as self-evident, as if context would dilute evidence. The politics and global studies scholar later explained that white genocide "is a figment of the racist imagination, it should be mocked, and I'm glad to have mocked it."[41]

Goodwill between public scholars and journalists would take a hit if tropes from the watchlists act as news subsidies. Interview transcripts reveal that none of the 25 professors perceived uptake of tropes in quality journalism. Lembcke recalled how reporters signaled to him that they recognize the Horowitz book as a hack job. An interview might end with: "Oh, by the way, congratulations. I see you're on the Horowitz list."

Michael Bérubé, professor of literature at Penn State, took notice when Horowitz was making friends in the Pennsylvania General Assembly.

> Horowitz succeeded in getting a House subcommittee appointed to investigate liberal bias in Pennsylvania public universities. He didn't get that in any other state. He was zero for 28 nationwide.

Figure 9.1 Tweet from a Drexel professor

A DH target, Bérubé was quick to add, "I had taunted him on my blog for quite some time that year, and it was great fun." In response to Horowitz's inroads with legislators, the *Pittsburgh Post-Gazette* published a sympathetic profile of Bérubé: "The professor the right loves to hate." Beyond the *Post-Gazette*, an alternative weekly, did regional news depict faculty as biased and worthy of inspection?

> There was no real firestorm of press outrage about this. If anything, the reporters I dealt with were looking at this with a sort of raised eyebrow, like "This is weird."

Targeted scholars did observe, however, that while deviant-professor tropes do not influence how they are portrayed in the quality press, university administrators implicitly trade in this imagery when a campus is besieged by blowback. When Ciccariello-Maher posted what he wanted for Christmas, the intent was to mock a white supremacist fiction, "to show how ridiculous it was." While some in the social media mob might have taken the tweet literally, campus leaders knew better, of course, but declined an opportunity to engage the satire, even in a critical response. An immediate release from Drexel was "clearly written" by university communications, not by an academic official, Ciccariello-Maher told me. A subsequent statement signed by the president and provost "claimed it was satire, when of course, they could have very simply said that it was satire."

> They could have said it's a satirical critique of Nazi discourse. Of this thing that's very present in our culture at the present. And they missed that opportunity as a university to very un-controversially re-contextualize . . . they say one of the big concerns is what the students think, how does it make them feel? And my response to them on multiple occasions was, "You told them how to feel when you said it was reprehensible."

A public scholar should not assume faculty colleagues will have her back. She should expect chancellors and provosts to cower from populist blowback, according to Robert Jensen, a journalism professor painted by both watchlists as unhinged.

> I did a lot of TV after 9/11 because cable TV news shows needed people who could come on and articulate an anti-war perspective. And so, people

would say, "I saw you on TV last night," but they never want to talk about the actual ideas. And that's been my experience with academics . . . in large part the modern academy is pretty cowardly.

Bioethicist Arthur Caplan described departments as resentful when they see their disciplines degraded in the news. Presumably his colleagues in philosophy possess free will to talk with reporters, but those who decline, by Caplan's account, are often those most critical of scholars who do take risks in the public sphere.

Activist scholars are hardly representative of faculty in their disciplines. Risk tolerant, they seek trusting relationships in media where they can find them. The next section explores the professor/reporter relationship in the brokering of unpopular ideas.

The Professor and the Reporter Backstage

Interview transcripts reveal four critiques of the news as a paradigm of conventional wisdom. The first two—favoring expertise over intellect and sourcing patterns that uphold static binaries—reference everyday newswork. The third and fourth critiques adopt a cultural perspective on journalism as a guardian of centrist ideology and a trustee of collective memory. Scholars find ways to rework relationships in their favor as they enlist reporters in critical thinking despite these limitations.

Favoring expertise over intellect. Public scholars perform tactically in front-stage interactions with reporters. Bérubé was president of the Modern Language Association at the peak of media attention to the serial sexual abuse of Jerry Sandusky at his campus. He recalled an initial interaction with MSNBC.

"Can you be down on the lawn in a half an hour?" And guess what, they're in with a microphone in front of my face, a three-minute interview.

The Modern Language Association consultants subsequently brought him in for training.

I found to my dismay that on TV when I'm asked a hard question, I roll my eyes for a minute, and I'm thinking, but it looks like I'm signaling that this is the stupidest question I've ever heard.

Strategic communication of this sort is incompatible with intellect in dialectic mode. Seeding of critical dispositions becomes more plausible when scholars act as mentors for reporters in backstage interactions. Aptheker, the feminist studies scholar on both watchlists, described a tradeoff between working with open-minded, young reporters with little background knowledge and veteran reporters, more well read, but more likely to cherry-pick quotes to fit predetermined frames.

> I'm interviewed by a journalist about violence against women for example, like violence against women on campus for example, which tends to be a younger person and usually a woman . . . And if you try to introduce a concept, for example, of what we mean in feminist studies when we talk about a rape culture, they're very interested in that concept.

The biologist Greg Hampikean stressed the obligation of faculty to engage citizens beyond the classroom.

> I've spoken to nursing homes; I speak to preschools; I've spoken to church groups. I love to talk to anybody about my field, especially those who know nothing about it because that's the biggest differential. That's where you get the largest transfer of knowledge.

He strives for dialogue rather than projecting expertise. Similarly, the scholar/activist Bill Ayers rejects the notion that faculty should speak to the public only as experts.

> Imagine the brave new world we would have if we allowed only experts to speak; only nuclear physicists can speak on nuclear power or weapons; only criminologists can speak on prisons.

Sourcing patterns that uphold static binaries. Professors observed how journalism funnels discourse into a bipolar arrangement that is at once familiar to audiences and dysfunctional to public comprehension. Bruce Cumings, a scholar of modern Korean history, acknowledged that the media landscape accommodates many voices. When a crisis develops on the peninsula,

> all sorts of people appear on TV, in print, and on the Internet whom I've never heard of, but you still have only a handful who get things right. Most of the time you get the same story 100 times over.

While professors appear wistful in wanting to extend a classroom-style dialectic to mass media, blog space is increasingly shared by public scholars and elite journalists. The historian Juan Cole attributes his prominence in foreign policy debate to a blog that pokes at cranky ideas.

> You can understand from a journalist's point of view, you call one of these right-wing foundations, you know exactly what you're gonna get . . . you call a university professor, they're often hard to get a hold of and then you don't know what damn thing they're gonna say. So with me, what counteracted this tendency to be cut out in favor of the think tanks was 9/11 and the Iraq War, about neither of which it was fairly obvious anybody in Washington had a clue. And whatever the think tanks were telling the journalists struck the journalists, often, as highly implausible. And they would start calling me to, as a B team basically, to check out whether I thought what they were being told in Washington was very likely.

Mark Ensalaco, a scholar of human rights, views his encounters with reporters as an opportunity to disorient.

> I'm a Catholic so I'm a nomad. I don't belong anywhere . . . I take positions that Marx would find radical when it comes to the economy, but I'm quoting the Pope.

Guardian of centrist ideology. The gatekeeping and rendering of ideas in journalism is conducted against the backdrop of perceived public mood, particularly in nationalistic and populist climates (Chapters 5–7). Professor Horne, portrayed by PWL as divisive, experiences latitude to express radical views with reporters based on his identity as an African American historian.

> I try to ground myself in the black community and the US ruling elite is still a little nervous about the Negroes. Negroes have a tendency to explode.

Horne brings to interviews deep knowledge of subjects such as white supremacy and the roots of slavery in seventeenth-century capitalism. He relies on the "protective shield" of the black community, as he puts it, in tactical encounters with the press. "My joke is that *The New York Times* and *The Washington Post*, if I were on fire, as the saying goes, they wouldn't urinate on me." A reporter is likely to chuckle at these remarks rather than express offense. She might confirm with Horne what is "on the record." If the reporter is to retain credibility with the historian, she must go *off the matrix*, so to speak, of centrist ideology on race. She must triangulate what is discussed about race in her subfield of journalism; the perceived tolerance of audiences (including the community that Horne makes salient); and a scholar's understanding.

The sociologist Joe Feagin recounted interviews with writers curious about his assertion that reparations are owed to descendants of slaves.

> That's happened to me numerous times where I spent hours talking to a young journalist for a magazine or a newspaper. And then I get an email couple of weeks later saying, "Well, the editor didn't like it." And they profusely apologize for wasting my time.

Reporters can lose battles back in the newsroom, but Feagin and Horne invite them to turn their backs on a reified, judgmental audience. The authority of public scholars reorients journalistic accountability from the imagined public to the epistemic fields from which knowledge is obtained, a theme we return to in the final chapter.

Trustee of collective memory. Activist academics in areas such as sociology and anthropology introduce dissonant narratives when incidents or anniversaries enlist journalism as a trustee of collective memory. In *The Spitting Image*, Lembcke demonstrates that there is no credible evidence of antiwar protestors spitting on vets returning from Vietnam.[42] The myth resonates with betrayal of war stories that go back to German soldiers after World War I and French soldiers returning from Indochina. Here we do see overlap between watchlists and news media vis-à-vis public memory. Lembcke referenced recent retellings of the spitting myth in *The New York Times*, *The Washington Post*, and *Associated Press*. While journalists describe their work as "the first draft of history," they insist on the final draft when it comes to collective memory tied to national identity.

The cultural role of journalism in affirming collective memory is typically not subject to reflexivity,[43] but awareness of the problem is more likely when reporters seek credibility with historians and sociologists. Lembcke explains:

> Journalists want to stay at the empirical level. Did it or did it not happen? They don't want to go where you're wondering if they go, to the issue of collective memory, social memory [laughter]. But I'm conscious all the time that they're riding in my buggy.

With reporters along for the ride, they still want to know, in Lembcke words: "So why would he say this happened if it didn't happen?"

Ah, that's my cue then to go into the construction of memory part of it, and there I can go off their script and talk about memory and maybe even talk about the psychological rifts in these stories.

Brokering Ideas

Rowe writes that reporters seek a "sprinkling of water" to sanctify news content in their interactions with scholars.[44] Exchange of capital often accrues to journalism at the expense of other knowledge disciplines. In the social control of ideas, sanctified knowledge possesses gravitas (that which is inaccessible) even as it is rendered not to disturb core beliefs. This conflict of epistemology is innate in the orientation of academia to news media.

A further complication is sociological—the scaffolding of a vigilante mindset. A Bentham-like panopticon stretches from classrooms to cable news to watchlists in targeted harassment. Interviewed professors described an assortment of dirty tricks: hacked payroll accounts; filing of false tax-refund requests; sting operations in which informants impersonate students; filing discrimination complaints by students who have never taken a professor's course; voicemail and email threats; and websites that focus on one professor at a time to solicit spy reports.

PWL and Horowitz's list adopt trappings of journalism: extracted quotes, a terse writing style in which bare facts tell the story, and a populist instinct to expose cultural elites.[45] Depictions resonate with archetypical narratives of eggheads and internal enemies roaming the hallways of academia.[46] Yet these codes and templates have not infected the quality press, according to the same scholars depicted as disloyal, divisive, subversive, unhinged, and dangerous in the watchlists. Generally speaking, professors interviewed express more admiration for reporters than what would be predicted from much of the literature in media studies, political science, and sociology.[47] Reporters, like left academics, are regular recipients of flak from the hard right, suggesting a shared pride in withstanding the assaults. Mutual respect is vital in light of deviance tropes that circulate in the organized outrage machine.

Watchlist-targeted professors are obviously not representative of faculty in their disciplines. This outlier status helps to explain why they are so attuned to varying incentives on campuses for speaking out on sensitive topics. Chancellors and provosts are oddly complicit with watchlists in *purposefully* avoiding any contextual consideration of ideas that might offend regents, parents, alumni, and legislators. Faculty, for the most part, are similarly aversive when controversy ensnares a campus. Professor Cole characterized his Michigan colleagues as "Amish."

Yet interviewed scholars sense a receptivity to intellect in newswork and some autonomy in journalism to question orthodoxy. Their relationships with reporters, for the most part, reflect not a grudging willingness to engage but a genuine admiration. The psychology professor David Barash conveyed his view of reporters as overworked following "the great newspaper die-off." Reporters are "not only quick studies, but quite interested in ideas." Even after witnessing feverish attention to the Sandusky scandal at Penn State, Bérubé insisted that he engages with reporters "who are nothing but impressive, and nothing but thorough." Activist academics express goodwill earned not in their role *as sources* but *in relationships* with reporters.

Not surprisingly, public scholars possess high levels of media literacy, but this chapter reveals how and why they intervene in newswork. Their goals for any given encounter could be viewed as instrumental in advancing a particular perspective, but over time the seeding of intellect in journalism appears plausible. The successful brokering of ideas depends in part on professors and reporters jointly recognizing the constraints of newswork. For their part, public scholars are reflexive in observation of the academic-media nexus as a field of fields. They delight in tracking how disciplines are portrayed. The following mapping of the journalistic imagination is a composite from multiple transcripts, with Professor Cumings providing several contributions.

Journalists are impressed by neuroscience. They enjoy knowing that neuron #6743 fires when you drink a certain vintage of cabernet. They welcome the cold sensibility of economics and political science in portrayal of behavior as rational when individuals pursue their own interests (even if the behavior is morally suspect.) Closer to home, the political economy of news media is off limits in areas such as the manufacturing of consent. Journalists seem tickled by sociobiological explanations for gendered behavior. They like to read about baboons with briefcases and female primates who "aunt" infants to death.[48] History is a list of names and a series of facts: "history just as it was." Beyond an affinity for objective history, journalists become more critical when reading the softer sciences. Postmodernism and post-structuralist theories are nearly always ripe for ridicule in *The New York Times Book Review*. Marxist and neo-Marxist perspectives are not so much ridiculed as boycotted. Much of the humanities is mired in hyper-intellectualism. And philosophy is populated by eccentrics. "Can you believe he cooks his own pancakes every day?"

The mishmash is derived from equal parts whimsy and frustration, but meta-field perspectives evoke intuition in exchanges with reporters. For professors with ideas designed to disorient, relationships with reporters are experienced as a microcosm within the macrocosm of hegemonic communication. When Lembcke takes pride in steering interviews so that a reporter ends up in his buggy, he recognizes that a shared reflexivity is experienced at multiple levels. For a scholar, critiques of newswork in particular outcomes—such as a reporter preferring expertise over intellect during an interview—should lead inductively to recognition of journalism's cultural role as guardian of centrist ideology and trustee of collective memory. Reporters in backstage interactions might find themselves defending their craft by rethinking boundaries of acceptable discourse. Striking gold in interviews could depend on a reporter acknowledging a scholar's critique of the news. If reporters model these dialectic, reflective exchanges in blogs or newsroom conversations, they would support each other when drawn to provocative ideas.[49]

Ryfe explains that social fields inflate in response to countervailing forces, bringing to mind the bending of tent poles.[50] "Like tents, social fields come into being when properties (such as values, norms, beliefs, identities, practices, and so on) interact *relationally*."[51] If we consider all possible matchings of journalistic and scholarly expertise in the universe of knowledge work defined as such, a gravitational force does emerge: shared dissatisfaction with working conditions in one domain or the other. The disorientation of a hybrid field is consequently generative of corresponding reflexivity in emerging rules of engagement that reconcile intellect with journalism. While paradigm shifts sometimes require a generational die-off of scientists,[52] we can expect epistemological conflict as a regular occurrence in the nexus of media and academia.

10

What Intellectual Journalism Would Look Like

A popular press with popular information and the increasing means to circulate it, is but a prologue to a farce, or a tragedy, or both.

—James Madison, reimagined

The political scientist Michael Crozier calls attention to a lithograph by Dutch artist M. C. Escher to illustrate pathologies in advanced democracies when an open circulatory system becomes too self-referential.[1] Hooded monks in an unknown sect march on stairs that seemingly ascend and descend simultaneously. The viewer is challenged to sort out reality from illusion; a purposeful exercise is perceived at another level as a strange loop.[2] Recursion arises in the repeated application of rules or procedures to successive results.

Could everyday politics become absorbed in a never-ending mimetic round of fickle citizen sentiment and political choreography? To varying degrees, these types of scenarios are already part of political realities in Western democracies. Much of the critical analysis of this type of phenomenon describes it as a pauperization of political life, as a decline into a tabloid world in which politics is hawked like soapsuds.[3]

In *On Tyranny*, Timothy Snyder's preconditions for tyranny are eerily recursive.[4] He warns against shamanistic incantations of demagogues and mindless repetition of catchphrases. Americans convinced themselves of a politics of inevitability following the defeat of fascism in World War II. "The politics of inevitability is a self-induced intellectual coma."[5] The danger we now face is more like hypnosis, a politics of eternity. "We stare at the spinning vortex of cyclical myth until we fall into a trance—and then we do something shocking at someone else's orders."[6]

Where Ideas Go to Die. Michael McDevitt, Oxford University Press (2020). © Oxford University Press.
DOI: 10.1093/oso/9780190869946.001.0001

The uptake of authoritarian thinking is not easily reversed in political communication as a self-reinforcing system. For realists, truth is obtained in a correspondence between statements and facts. In recursion, truth is experienced as reassurance in a compressed universe of legitimate and legitimating discourse. Hooded monks are themselves not suffering from disorientation.

Journalism, for its part, is not simply a stir stick in recursive communication. Chapters 2 and 3 portray news media as vulnerable to incursion of mobilized irrationalism but also opportunistic in enhancing their cultural authority by condoning anti-elitist anger. Scores of journalists in the elite press and elsewhere were undoubtedly repulsed by Trump in the 2016 campaign. The "earned media" he benefited from nevertheless suggests that reporters and editors were fascinated by the emotive mainsprings of populist support.[7] This indulgence implies more than intellectual lazines or an elitist voyeurism of agitated, downscale Americans. Election coverage appeared to validate the Katz and Liebes premise of news media and anti-establishment agents operating as co-producers in a crisis of democracy.[8]

I began the book with the premise that anti-intellectualism operates something like dark matter, an unseen, controlling force not subject to reflexivity even as US news media have embraced transparency. Journalism becomes an object of its own agency in the social control of intellect. The book concludes with a discussion of how intellectual journalism would forge a healthier relationship with the public by overcoming recursion. Insights from prior chapters suggest that intellectual journalism emerges in a shift from public to craft accountability; the wisdom to reject misguided reform; reporter-scholar alliances in the academic-media nexus; and playful forms of resistance.

A Shift from Public to Craft Accountability

Pedagogy of journalism should account for dispositions that students bring to newsrooms and classrooms, including fear of reprisal for voicing unpopular views. As part of a larger "deliberative turn" in social science, scholars of political socialization stress "positive youth development," "civic learning," and "youth civic engagement."[9] Political enculturation nonetheless encompasses compliance with authority and sensitivity to climates of opinion.[10]

I initially thought about the developmental roots of anti-intellectualism when interviewing Colorado journalists about their contributions to news coverage on Ward Churchill. Content analysis findings presented to reporters and editors showed how their work failed to engage with Churchill's ideas despite waves of news copy flooding the Front Range. I recall a testy exchange in a Boulder coffee shop. While interviewing a veteran reporter from the *Rocky Mountain News*, I suggested a thought experiment: Imagine that college students were asked to read and summarize Churchill's essay on causes of the 9/11 attacks.

> I: If I asked students to summarize the essay, and they said it was about American denial, I would say yes. If they summarized as Churchill called victims "little Eichmanns," I'd say no that's wrong, that's not the theme. But the news coverage used the Eichmann reference as a proxy for what the essay was about.
>
> J: *No it wasn't a proxy for describing what the essay was about . . . Look, it's not different from what happens when a politician or anyone else makes a comment in the course of a speech that gets everyone's attention, makes a good sound bite, and it sets everyone off and everyone forgets the rest of the speech.*

I would reformulate the sequence: a speaker or writer presents ideas tightly bound in thematic connections. The "comment in the course of a speech" is noted by journalists sensitive to a bit that could be rendered deviant if extracted. The speech "gets everyone's attention" due to the journalistic extraction, and "makes a good sound bite" as an outcome of a *journalistic intervention*. The speech "sets everyone off" in the journalistic imagination before actual public sentiment has a chance to crystallize. "Everyone forgets the speech" is nonsensical because the speech was never conveyed to a journalistic audience. Substantive content never has a chance to register in collective memory.

The journalistic formulation happens in an instant, a full-blown social drama imagined before it occurs, before the fractal encoding of initial news content provides a script for social action (Chapter 6). Newswork inculcates a submission to ideological convention in the way that reporters and editors imagine audiences. The extraction/creation of deviance from a larger body of discourse is elemental to journalism, a tribal, protective impulse rather than a learned skill. Anticipated symbolic action is likely already internalized by journalism students, and perhaps by anyone asked to play the role of a journalist.

The thought experiment with the *Rocky* reporter did not go over well: a CU researcher playing the role of stuffy professor challenging the professional competence of a Denver reporter. Insistent—or stubborn, I suppose—I revised the thought experiment as a writing exercise for two reporting courses in the fall of 2014. I asked twenty four undergraduates to read the Eichmann paragraph with these instructions:

> The following excerpt comes from Prof. Ward Churchill's essay, *Some People Push Back: On the Justice of Roosting Chickens*. The essay was published online the day after the terrorist attacks of September 11, 2001. In this paragraph, Churchill questions the innocence of those who perished in the World Trade Center

Students responded to two prompts:

- What would you say is the theme of this paragraph?
- Imagine that you are asked to write a newspaper story about this essay and you want to focus on this paragraph. Write a one- or two-sentence lead for the article. The assignment calls for a news article, not commentary.

Themes and leads produced by students are assembled in Appendix Table 10.1, and I will summarize some of the patterns here.

None of the themes but 10 of the 24 leads labeled the essay as "controversial," "shocking," or "scathing." None of the themes but six of the leads referenced "little Eichmanns" or "Nazis." None of the themes and six of the leads described public sentiment in response to the essay. Themes convey a matter-of-fact tone. The following is typical: "The theme is that those working in the twin towers were not innocent, but deserving of what happened on September 11." By contrast, leads exhibit a liminal quality: elements of factism and convention (who, what, when, where, how) combined with an uninhibited signaling of deviance. "Little Eichmanns" is an undisputed component of the essay, a *fact* that appears to justify a paradoxical release from the objectivity paradigm. One student deployed quotation marks to mock Churchill: "According to the CU professor Ward Churchill those who got killed, overall Americans in the global financial empire, 'deserved it.'" Another student felt a need to misconstrue the essay: the 9/11 victims "may as well be more murderous than the terrorists who crashed the planes."

Objectivity as strategic ritual presumably applies to any person[11]—professional, student, or otherwise—asked to report to a community that a core belief has been violated.[12] The act of signifying a breach demands an allegiance to community and a distancing from the offending ideas. Hofstadter characterized anti-intellectualism as "resentment and suspicion of the life of the mind and of those who are considered to represent it."[13] Much of the evidence assembled for this book shows a retributive orientation toward intellect, a collective desire to punish and to humiliate that goes beyond resentment or suspicion.

Distrust of intellect is both endemic to the role of public communication and internalized in journalism, evident in classrooms before students file their first stories. The problem defies any glib suggestion for reform. A fate more promising for intellect will require a shift in thinking about accountability, from public to craft-oriented reflexivity. Much of the literature on news media and accountability can be organized in terms of *public* and *craft reflexivity*. In any system of signification, reflexivity occurs when an agent turns back on itself, creating an identity of subject and object.[14] In front-stage, public reflexivity, journalists hold themselves accountable in transparency of method and motive. The democratic rationale is articulated in communitarianism,[15] civic/public journalism,[16] and most recently in a critique of professional ethics to favor a more inclusive and relational ethics.[17]

In craft reflexivity, journalists take responsibility for their work by exercising judgment that arises from professional acumen and *the creative process itself.* Journalists reject a naïve empiricism and recognize that the news is what they produce; news is a product of the decisions they make. News received well by the public is not by itself a reason for satisfaction or pride.

In supplemental analysis for Chapter 8 on student anti-intellectualism, I narrowed the operationalization of craft reflexivity to contextualism, a principle that calls for journalists to actively construct a comprehensive view of events in a meaningful context. I simply asked students whether they agree that "facts speak for themselves" without any reference to the public. Absence of this cue is essential. The intent is to evoke critical thinking as the basis for reporting rather than evaluation tied to public approval. A rejection of the bromide "facts speak for themselves" indicates an awareness of the principle that comprehension is tied to a journalism of synthesis and interpretation. My hypothesis was that direction of reflexivity—toward the public or craft— would predict whether students supported journalistic anti-intellectualism. As reported in Chapter 8, student affinity for transparency lends itself to professional anti-rationalism, a reporting leery of direct engagement with intellect when ideas are deemed subversive. A tactical transparency is also conducive to journalistic anti-elitism when targets of suspicion include intellectuals as a social class.

The supplemental analysis revealed a series of statistically significant correlations. Support for transparency and contextualism associate negatively, suggesting distinct forms of reflexivity. Contextualism also correlates negatively with journalistic anti-elitism and the student anti-intellectualism scale (SAIS), which measures an instrumental attitude toward the purpose of college courses.

Heralded in normative theory as a form of public justification that promotes accountability, transparency appears to condone intolerance of intellect and intellectuals.[18] Conversely, craft reflexivity recognizes limitations of relying on isolated facts and would welcome engagement with intellect as a tool of comprehension. Over time, a dedication to craft in day-to-day reporting might induce a second-level reflexivity that recognizes and seeks to overcome recursion. Access to this level of abstraction might seem unrealistic for working journalists, but intellect is relentless and self-perpetuating in the asking of inconvenient questions. Once seeded, intellect will not die without a fight. It resonates too strongly with autonomy as an aspirational value in newswork.[19]

The Wisdom to Reject Misguided Reform

The news as public discourse, with all its flaws, provides the "oxygen of publicity" to ideas and social movements,[20] motivating incursion from the academy into newsrooms. In the opposite direction, media foundations stage interventions into the lecture halls and computer labs where reporting is taught.[21] At some point journalism begins to resemble the Eurasian plain of knowledge professions, periodically invaded by proximate forces.

Vulnerability is explained, in part, by journalism's vexed relationship with intellect. As described in Chapter 1, newswork is at once passive and deferential, dismissive, impatient, suspicious, and exploitive in the way it engages intellect. These contradictions leave journalism susceptible as a semi-autonomous field of knowledge work. Loss and casualization of labor is evident in robots and amateurs joining the workforce, supplemented by the regular flow of unpaid college interns. Threats to autonomy arise in unreflective exploitation of digital affordances: forays such as native advertising and use of news metrics to guide reporting and editing.[22] Overlaid on these material conditions is browbeating from scholars who insist that journalists must overcome an elitist detachment from the public.[23] Journalists should be content with modeling responsible practice and should give up trying to define who is, and is not, a member of the profession in a democratized mediascape.[24]

A prevailing view in normative theory depicts autonomy as overriding accountability. Glasser and Gunther contend that journalists "measure themselves and their independence against the Kantian ideal of wholly autonomous agents whose legitimacy and authority require complete isolation . . . from any pressure or influence that might compromise the presumably 'pure' judgments they can and should make."[25] Journalists do indeed value autonomy and will, at times, fiercely defend it. In the spring of 2018, for example, a *Denver Post* editorial described its hedge fund owners as "vulture capitalists" in an extraordinary act of defiance.[26]

Sociologists define professional autonomy as wide latitude of judgment in carrying out occupational duties.[27] Autonomy fosters professional identity, boosts morale during periods of structural change, and creates space for critical reflection.[28] Intellectual autonomy elevates the concept into a moral dimension when journalists take ownership of the reasons for their decisions rather than simply asserting their First Amendment freedom or "the public's right to know."[29]

As a former reporter, I believe that the dissonance in how journalists and scholars value autonomy is explained in part by the nature of newswork. Threats to autonomy that arise internally from profit-maximizing management and externally from hostile audiences engender a tacit understanding of how to proceed, a subjectivity not easily captured by theorists. Would the same scholars who are skeptical of journalistic autonomy be willing to relinquish tenure to better serve the role of public intellectual? Would these scholars concede that some of their frustration with journalistic autonomy is due to this disposition manifesting in rejection of their critiques?

This section embarks on a tour of four traps in the reform of professional education and practice. Intellectual journalism would recognize these rationales as temptations draped in democratic populism.

Trap 1: Affective Representation

In *American Idyll*, Catherine Liu traces the origins of cultural populism to criticism of Hofstadter's *Anti-intellectualism in American Life*.[30] Academic anti-elitism viewed the postwar defense of intellect as exclusionary and hegemonic. Liu contends this ethos "has been content to celebrate an affective, personalist irrationalism: its ingrained antielitism does irreparable damage to the role that theory, reason, and history have to play in establishing authentic forms of solidarity between popular discontent and the life of the mind."[31]

The academics and journalists interviewed for Chapter 3 overlapped in criticism of the press as elitist. Both groups advocate misguided reform when they perceive the problem of 2016 as a failure of the press to affirm public frustration. Intellect will thrive in news media only if we accept journalism's limitations by recognizing that its duty to represent diverse communities is primarily *epistemological* rather than *affective*. This obligation is compromised when news media represent public mood in a plebiscitary sense. Intellectual journalism becomes more plausible when democrats, following Lippmann, circumscribe their expectations. In a study of journalism in "post-truth Russia," Roudakova illustrates how a free and responsible press is more directly linked with truth-seeking than democracy per se.[32] A unified field of journalism in the Soviet era survived despite censorship by preserving the value of truth-seeking. In its initial encounters with capitalism in the 1990s, the profession caved to authoritarian thinking as "merchants of pathos," attuned to the increasing cynicism of audiences.

Prior to the diffusion of digital technology, the press might have carried the burden of affective representation in mass communication. This role calls to mind Roman Hruska, the senator representing Nebraska who reminded colleagues that even mediocre people "are entitled to a little representation." Today, a do-it-yourself populism is aligned ideologically with cable news and mobilized through social media. Anti-intellectualism draws emotive power from many sources, and while it fluctuates in strength, it will persist without the help of journalism. Affordances of an inclusive media system create opportunities to promote idea-centered journalism.

Mass media, the blogosphere, and social media mobilize collective sentiment and solidarities. Journalism should chronicle the political ferment. Journalism's epistemological capacity is nevertheless constrained when the profession conflates representing social action in a descriptive mode with representing the populace in a political mode. Journalists should not see it as their duty to represent the public against a cultural elite. At the very least, they should look with skepticism at normative literature that promotes the "populist mobilizer" role without contemplating contradictions with the more firmly established "interpretive role" in professional identity.[33] Another celebrated role—the watchdog—should be trained not just against government corruption but also against transgressions of grassroots populism.

Political scientists recognize that news media are miscast in campaign communication, incapable of organizing elections in a coherent fashion in a system characterized by weak parties and entrepreneurial candidates.[34] Journalism is also miscast when it sees itself as an organ of direct democracy. A journalism that views itself this way risks collusion with irrationalism. In *The Open Society and Its Enemies*, Karl Popper observed: "The irrationalist insists that emotions and passions rather than reason are the mainsprings of human action."[35] The purpose of news reporting, in a deliberative democracy, is not to channel and coordinate public mood but to engage ideas in their generative movement toward policy coherence.

Trap 2: Total Transparency

Clarity resonates with transparency as core values of newswork. The role of public trustee was yoked to clarity early in the history of professional education, reflected in the Journalism Creed of Walter Williams (quoted in Chapter 2). Ideas should have nothing to hide in this doctrine: journalists must ensure that statements of experts are easily comprehensible to mass audiences. Clarity is less innocent than it seems, however. Ironically, clarity can hide the contradiction in which reporting renders knowledge without comprehending substance or appreciating nuance.

More pernicious still is the seepage of authoritarian thinking into a language that echoes Orwell's "Newspeak."[36] MacGregor argues that journalists conduct "critical distortions through a mythologizing process of 'clarity.'"[37] A doctrine of simplicity, "with its engaging ideal of demotic language, goes hand in hand with a puritanically anti-intellectual trend . . . Anti-intellectualism becomes a fellow traveler within this linguistic purging sentiment."[38]

Laclau explains that totalitarianism relies on absolute transparency in social organizations and in language.[39] Totalitarianism seeks uncontaminated purity, a sentiment advanced in the name of democratic values.[40] Journalists should be careful to not vivify "plain language" in ways suitable to the social control of dissent. In social drama, for example, idea rendering isolates and magnifies deviance by tearing away the textual fabric that makes an assertion worthy of deliberation (Chapter 6).

Interviews of Colorado journalists following the Churchill affair (Chapter 7) along with interviews of activist academics (Chapter 9) reveal the importance of backstage conversations. These interactions occur in newsrooms and between reporters and sources prior to publication. Backstage, newspaper journalists feel more comfortable about criticizing readers.[41] The profession should reflect on its historical connections with journal writing, a discipline in which readers are less immediate and salient, yet the task remains the chronicling of daily, noteworthy events.[42]

Trap 3: Unreflective Instrumentalism

In the mythology of information technology, makeover of the "the electronic sublime" into the "the digital sublime" signals a shift from confidence to contemptuous dismissal of skeptics. Clay Shirky of New York University exemplifies the adolescent swagger.

> When someone demands to know how we are going to replace newspapers, they are really demanding to be told that we are not living through a revolution. They are demanding to be told that old systems will not break before new systems are in place.[43]

As for the loss of news people? "The old stuff gets broken faster than the new stuff is put in its place."

The digital sublime in journalism reform is grounded in American cultural history in ways that conflate information with critical thinking. In a broad sense, critical thinking is an ability to apply and synthesize knowledge, and to reflect on the process of inquiry itself. The critical thinking of instrumentalism is something narrower, involving the kind of calculations that can solve practical problems in innovative ways, with immediate payoffs. In this view, communication scholarship is not merely a waste of time (and time is precious when technology leaps at blinding speed). For the instrumentalist, theory in journalism education detracts; it fogs the vision of innovation.

The impulse to disrupt or destroy requires religious fundamentalism, libertarian populism, or some other discourse of validation. Writing about creationism in the 1980s, the biologist John Baker noted that irrational thinking is a response of people "who have come to believe that they no longer control their own destiny."[44] A similar stance of the Tea Party emerged following

Barack Obama's first inauguration in 2009. Among the movement's 15 non-negotiable beliefs: "Intrusive government must be stopped." Interventions of some sort are necessary to overcome the pathology of government and its byzantine policies and processes. The analogy in higher education is the stagnant theorizing, self-indulgent scholarship, and pointless obscurities of faculty.

Unreflective instrumentalism might appear less damaging than other strains of anti-intellectualism documented by Hofstadter, Rigney, and Claussen.[45] Instrumentalism lacks the fervor of religious anti-rationalism and the democratic vocabulary of anti-elitism. In the context of communication technology, it is equated with progress yet has nothing of substance to say about what journalism should value in contemplating its future and its purpose.[46]

Trap 4: Deinstitutionalization

Markham describes a tendency of academia to romanticize the creative chaos of spontaneous activism.[47] A de-professionalized, deinstitutionalized journalism is imagined to be purer, more truthful in comprehending the restive forces of rise up, act up, and occupy movements. In reality, dissensus requires *sustained* and *organized* disagreement over conditions of understanding in knowledge fields. This is not to dismiss the value of alternative journalism[48] and agonistic pluralism[49] in looking past the outward trimmings of liberal democracy to promote inclusiveness. Still, if the goal is to empower critical citizens, institutional support for dissensus implies a defense of journalistic authority and the capacity to engage with other ways of knowing, as when reporters seek alliances with activist academics.

Respect for professions in the civil sphere acts as a ballast against mobilized irrationalism. Snyder, a holocaust historian, expresses a fondness for the press. "Choose an institution you care about, a court, a newspaper, a law, a labor union—and take its side."[50] "When political leaders set a negative example, professional commitments to just practice become more important."[51] Authoritarians depend on "obedient civil servants, and concentration camp directors seek businessmen interested in cheap labor." When professions "confuse their specific ethics with the emotions of the moment," they risk saying and doing things that they "previously have thought unimaginable."[52] Professional associations do not always operate in the public interest, but they command attention through codes of ethics, collective voices, and best practices. "Professions can create forms of ethical conversations that are impossible between a lonely individual and a distant government."[53]

The quality press and news-oriented blogs are increasingly populated with public scholars as sources and contributors,[54] allowing for cross-discipline reflexivity in detection of authoritarian inclinations that percolate through media. The news ecosystem constitutes a complex field of fields that challenges organizational routines.[55] The labor of journalists is, however, increasingly precarious, casual, and immaterial.[56] The transformation of journalism theorized by Deuze and Witschge portrays a post-industrial configuration of patchwork careers, editorial collectives, and shifting coalitions.[57] A positive development in this upheaval is the tendency of practitioners to view themselves as colleagues across organizations, "huddled together for warmth."[58]

Upheaval represents an opportunity to rethink the profession's institutional framework apart from media ownership. Journalism lacks a tradition of collective action,[59] and while professional associations proliferate, they often fail to collaborate in defense of working conditions that would allow intellect to thrive. We should take note of the exceptions. Borden recalls a scenario from the trauma of September 11, 2001, that illustrates a coordinated defense of autonomy in a nationalistic climate.[60] Trade publications echoed the Society of Professional Journalists when warning that flag displays on lapels are a bad idea for anchors and reporters.

More recently, about 350 newspapers participated in a national campaign to denounce Trump's attacks on the press (August 14, 2018). The purpose of anti-media populists is to undermine faith in journalism and other institutions. As media scholar Bernat Ivancsics observes, speakers for "the majority" claim to redeem participatory qualities of democracy, a move "that flouts the technical-bureaucratic operation of the constitutionality of democratic societies."[61] When politicians crusade against the press, editors and reporters must overcome the isolation and passive neutrality that has made them so vulnerable to recursive communication. Authoritarian movements adopt the logic of mass politics. This requires of journalism an organized defense—an assertion of autonomy at the level of profession rather than individual professionals.

Journalism schools should promote truth-seeking, science literacy, and responsible commentary as principles of the civil sphere that transcend news media. That said, they should reconsider the rationale to democratize professional training. As Petre and Besbris warn, this strategy gives "non-journalists who are already dubious of the profession's boundaries . . . more reason to doubt schooling as a necessary component of the profession's future."[62] While intellect resists containment, it requires support in secure institutions. Democracy in the advent of post-truth politics still needs institutions to give force to the force of the better argument.[63]

Alliances in the Academic-Media Nexus

Metaphors enable but also constrain experience.[64] Journalists should rethink their allegiance to a marketplace of ideas, a notion that too easily justifies a commodification of ideas as inevitable if not always desirable. Every distinct idea in the public realm potentially associates with other ideas, seeking and rejecting connections in building a framework for alternative discourses in policy, governance, and social movements. When this generative and synthesizing dynamic is disrupted, compartmentalized, and reduced into reassuring, partisan binaries, the rendered material validates the market metaphor. A better metaphor is the free play of ideas, a prescription that becomes more realistic with innovation in the academic-media nexus. Challenges to the long-standing narrative of the public intellectual in decline gain traction in digital media, where curated spaces allow the curious to approach ideas on their own terms rather than as pre-digested bits.

Recent innovations such as academic journalism[65] and knowledge-based journalism[66] provide a rationale for fortifying explanatory reporting with applied scholarship. The Conversation, a global nonprofit in which editors envision the university as a giant newsroom, is probably the best illustration of how journalists imagine possibilities for collaboration.[67] At issue here, however, is not expertise so much as a quality of thinking that develops organically in exchanges between scholars and reporters. Norms emergent in these one-on-one interactions deserve scrutiny; rejection of civic/public journalism by many news outlets in the 1990s suggest that formal initiatives pushed by academics are easily dismissed as elitist.[68]

To be sure, news media are already admiring of intelligence when applied to immediate and practical ends. Hofstadter's distinction between intelligence and intellect clarifies the shift required to seed intellect: "Intelligence will seize the immediate in a situation and evaluate it. Intellect evaluates evaluations, and looks for the meanings of situations as a whole."[69]

Hofstadter bracketed an idealized intellect from more pedestrian uses of the mind. Distinguishing intellect from instrumental reason raises the question about how intellect negotiates spaces where autonomy is not respected or protected. Intellect is, in fact, a subversive quality of the mind; it is vulnerable to depictions of its reasoning as unhinged and its motives as divisive.

Dangerous professors, of all people, make media safer for intellect in the dissonance they bring to interviews when contacted by reporters. The authority of activist scholars reorients journalistic accountability from the imagined public to the epistemic fields from which knowledge is obtained. This interpretation is supported by research dating back to 1959 in Pool and Shulman's "Newsmen's Fantasies, Audiences, and Newswriting." Imaginary interlocutors "enter the author's flow of associations at the time of composition," engendering affection for reference groups (such as academic sources) but also hostility toward obstinate audiences.[70]

Evidence for Chapter 9 is limited to perceptions of a peculiar group of professors. Still, I can point to the success of New York University's Arthur Caplan in pioneering bioethics as a new field through media.

> Early on in my career ... ethical issues in healthcare were so new that no one knew what [the field] was. And if you wanted to talk to patients rather than academics, or maybe academic doctors who worked in medical centers, you needed to find the route to do that and I realized that that was probably going to be through the media.

He began to write op-ed articles, teach ethics to journalism students, and follow the careers of former students.

> In the olden days I was doing more outreach to a group of people who didn't really understand what the topic area was. Now, I get swarmed with media inquiries. I probably get a couple a day.

Trusting relationships in the academic-media nexus represent a tangible investment for public scholars and a source of intellectual autonomy for reporters. Rowe observes that the rise of user-generated content in social media coincides with the decline of newspapers. This configuration has resulted in "a more intimate and volatile relationship between universities and the media/public sphere."[71] A sector of journalism friendly to intellect is vital space—and should be increasingly recognized as such—when so much of the mediascape is saturated in memetic ideas.

Playful Forms of Resistance

The Churchill social drama represented a watershed moment in US journalism's strained relationship with intellectual dissent, exposing pathologies of newswork in a populist mindset. Clashes of intellect with mainstream media are inevitable, although they might become more infrequent as public scholars, provosts, and chancellors take stock of the ritualistic humiliations that await the intellect unbound. When social control of dissent fails in the academic-media nexus (Chapter 4), the recursive regime modeled in Chapter 5 recognizes the unique contribution of journalism to the construction of intellectual deviance. Newswork renders ideas to distill deviance in ways that advance social control through symbolic action. Practices such as contextomy[72] and personification of ideas as dangerous[73] isolate intellect as an object of public attention, juxtaposing dissent with moral consensus. In idea rendering, the ideological agency of journalism is evident not in the selection of topics from a menu of possible items, as in agenda setting. Nor is its potency directly captured by framing theory, whereby journalists transmit (and preserve), reify, and naturalize elite-sponsored frames.[74] To the extent that journalism is subservient, idea rendering emphasizes a hegemonic logic in service to populist sentiment rather than elite strategy and manipulation.[75]

Idea rendering nevertheless triggers idea repair, a discursive practice that seeks to reestablish internal coherence by correcting prevailing depictions of a speaker/author's intentions (Chapter 7). A dialectic of rendering and repair should engender creative turbulence in digital spaces. The norms of news media—the epistemology and ethical ideologies that guide practice—are subject to reform as journalists and public intellectuals learn from mistakes and work out more stable rules of the game.

I have described anti-intellectualism as typically latent in newswork. The flip side is to explore how intellectual autonomy constitutes an underlying commitment in news reporting. The key, I think, is to look for subtle strategies that subvert the objectivity paradigm. Irreverence could signal a rejection of the bad faith that I describe in Chapter 1: insincerity and learned helplessness clothed in objectivity. Creative resistance is evident in a narrative technique used by reporters to distance themselves from tabloid coverage and other genres of tainted stories. By *disdaining the news*, journalists seek to resolve the dilemma created by a personal desire to not report when competitive pressures induce a need to join the fray.[76]

Evidence of *disdaining the publisher* goes back to the dawn of media sociology with Warren Breed's "Social Control in the Newsroom."[77]

> The reporters had fashioned a kind of underground and subversive pattern of ironic mocking of Hearst policy. Patriotic events would have speakers "proclaiming," and doing it "boldly"—not just "saying"—or "proudly clasping a flag to his heart." Nouns, adjectives, adverbs and verbs were selectively exaggerated or understated to follow, while mimicking, policy positions. Or we would omit something that would have glorified a policy favorite, or use empty generalities to weaken the image of a publisher's ally.[78]

In interviews with Colorado journalists, I sensed that reporters were eager to convey to academics that they were more tolerant of Churchill's dissent than their editors. Evidence of *disdaining the editors* emerged in an interview with a former student of mine who covered higher education for one of the Denver dailies. We sat on a park bench outside the newsroom.

> I: Was there a difference between how editors and reporters felt about the story?
>
> J: *There's a cumulative effect of having people tell you that this is a ridiculous story or what you're doing is bad, and you're kind of like uh, today I really don't feel like dealing with that . . . But yes, I think there's a piece where you're kind of giving a nod to the reader, and just saying all right, we see that you're sick of this . . . we get it and here's a quote and an acknowledgment . . . even media types make fun of media circuses . . . it's sort of a nod to like, hey, if I wasn't in the middle of this I would see how absurd it is.*

The reporter's resistance to editors, while subtle, arose in an article headlined "Frankly, I'm Sick of It." He quoted CU Boulder students saying they were tired of the affair and that the coverage was "overblown." In my interview with him outside the newsroom, the young reporter expressed anxiety over the loss of autonomy that comes from being caught in the middle of a controversy, trying to satisfy zealous editors while listening to an inner professional voice saying enough is enough.

Disdaining the public is also plausibly interpreted as an assertion of intellectual autonomy. Literature in political communication has investigated journalistic autonomy—or lack thereof—in relationship to elite actors, in frameworks such as propaganda,[79] indexing,[80] and cascading activation.[81] We know less about how journalists distance themselves from popular sentiment. "Ironic mocking" of a publisher in Breed's research from the 1950s also targets the pomposity of a flag-waving public. In contemporary news, journalists appear more willing to recognize a crude populism in campaign strategy than to acknowledge anti-intellectualism in the public itself. As discussed in Chapter 3, this pattern might be changing as reporters, editors, and bloggers observe the reality of grassroots populism in electoral politics.

I have written in the past that media scholars tend to exaggerate journalists' allegiance to the objectivity paradigm.[82] In its various forms, disdaining the news is a clear example of how reporters—in deliberate and self-conscious fashion—break from routines to protect something more important to them as professionals: their autonomy. Disdaining the news, however, is not proactive in service to deliberative democracy. These practices defend professional reputation more than they protect the integrity of ideas.

Ettema and Glasser identified an intriguing method in which reporters repurpose objectivity even as they use objective style to invest a story with moral significance. Irony in the news juxtaposes readily available facts with pronouncements of politicians. In the "peculiar language game known as journalism," journalists transfigure objective language into a moralistic vocabulary for condemnation of officials who betray the public's trust.[83] "Irony and objectivity do not merely coexist; irony exploits objectivity to work its effect."[84] As with disdaining the news, irony is only possible given the moral authority that originates from intellectual autonomy.

At the very least, we can say that intellect is an adaptive and creative phenomenon within US journalism, seeking autonomy where it can find it. Intellectual autonomy is evident in suspicion of nativists and demagogues and asserted against a public hungry for tainted news. Intellect resists control in news as a recursive regime. It is at play in the news. This inclination gives us something to build on, theoretically, and as a basis for authentic reform.

Appendix

The Appendix provides additional detail on methods and supplemental findings for chapters that incorporate textual analysis, content analysis, semi-structured interviews, and survey analysis.

6 Social Drama at Macro and Micro Levels: The Fractal Control of Dissent

Appendix Table 6.1 Event sequence in Ward Churchill social drama

Italics—breach/crisis; **bold—redress/separation**	
9-12-01	*Ward Churchill (WC) writes op-ed piece published online by Dark Night Field Notes, giving a "gut reaction" to possible causes of the Sept. 11 attacks.*
9-18-03	*Essay expanded into book length and published by AK Press: On the Justice of Roosting Chickens: Reflections on the Consequences of U.S. Imperial Arrogance and Criminality.*
Dec. 2004	On the Justice of Roosting Chickens receives honorable mention from the Gustavus Myers Center for the Study of Bigotry and Human Rights.
12-14-04	*Professor of Government Theodore Eismeier emails Hamilton College administration officials with copies of WC's writings, urging them to cancel a scheduled speech.*
1-21-05	*Ian Mandel, a junior at Hamilton College majoring in government and editor-in-chief of The Spectator, writes "Controversial speaker to visit Hill."*
1-26-05	*First Associated Press (AP) article, "Choice of speaker ignites protests again at Hamilton College," appears, identifying the little Eichmanns quote and citing a history of radicalism at Hamilton.*
1-27-05	*First Rocky Mountain News (RMN) article published.*
1-27-05	*CU Interim Chancellor Phil DiStefano calls Churchill's remarks "offensive" and "repugnant" and unrepresentative of CU.*
1-28-05	*Bill O'Reilly reports on Churchill's remarks on Fox, calling him "insane" and* **advocating that he should be arrested for "sedition."**
1-28-05	*First Denver Post (DP) article published.*
1-28-05	*First RMN editorial appears, describing Churchill as "an apologist for mass murder."*
1-28-05	*Wall Street Journal editorial calls Churchill a "fraud," a "Marxist," and a "radical," and warns that indoctrination occurs at "campuses everywhere."* **The editorial urges alumni to "push back" by withholding contributions to Hamilton.**
1-29-05	*First DP editorial appears, calling Churchill's comments "indefensible and reprehensible."*

Continued

Appendix Table 6.1 Continued

1-31-05	*New York Governor George Pataki refers to Churchill as "a bigoted terrorist supporter."*
1-31-05	Churchill issues press release, stating that he is not a defender of the 9/11 attacks, that he was not characterizing children, service workers, and firemen who died as little Eichmanns. He argues that the "only way to prevent 9-11-style attacks on the U.S. is for American citizens to compel their government to comply with the rule of law."
2-01-05	**Churchill resigns as chair of ethnic studies at the University of Colorado;** *he reports receiving death threats and a swastika painted on his truck.*
2-01-05	**Colorado Governor Bill Owens calls for Churchill to resign and phones CU President Elizabeth Hoffman, asking her to fire him.**
2-01-05	**Hamilton cancels Churchill's appearance,** *citing death threats.*
2-02-05	RMN questions Churchill's ethnicity following charges that he manufactured his Native American identity to advance his career.
2-02-05	*Colorado House condemns Churchill, saying his essay "strikes an evil and inflammatory blow against America's healing process."* **Republican lawmakers threaten to cut Churchill's salary from CU's budget.**
2-03-05	**CU Regents hold a special meeting, authorizing an examination of Churchill's writings, speeches, and tape recordings.** *They apologize "to all Americans."*
2-03-05	**Colorado Senate passes the House joint resolution with one dissenting vote.**
2-03-05	**Wheaton College cancels WC's appearance.**
2-04-05	**Eastern Washington University cancels another scheduled appearance.**
2-05-05	For the fourth consecutive day, an *RMN* article focuses on Churchill's ethnicity.
2-07-05	**Governor Owens appears on Fox with O'Reilly, calling for Churchill to be fired.**
2-07-05	**CU cancels Churchill's scheduled speech.**
2-08-05	CU administration backtracks; allows the speech to continue.
2-11-05	*RMN reports allegations that WC committed plagiarism.*
2-11-05	**Antioch College cancels Churchill as commencement speaker.**
2-11-05	**Director of a Hamilton program that originally invited WC to speak resigns under duress.**
3-07-05	**CU President Elizabeth Hoffman announces her resignation.**
3-24-05	**CU Regents approve "a system-wide review of the processes for awarding and maintaining tenure, including the processes for awarding tenure at the time of initial appointment and after a probationary period as well as the processes for post-tenure review."**
3-29-05	*Interim Chancellor Phil DiStefano submits allegations to the CU Standing Committee on Research Misconduct.*

Appendix Table 6.1 Continued

5-27-05	DP reports: "Asked to nominate their favorite professor, students at the University of Colorado at Boulder overwhelmingly picked Ward Churchill. Yet *the controversial figure's award is being withheld,* in part, *due to his tendency to 'antagonize and create enemies,' the head of the CU alumni association said."*
June 2005	*Following weeks of investigative reporting, RMN runs a multi-week, multi-page series giving its conclusions on charges pending before the Standing Committee.*
8-01-05	Hank Brown, co-founding member of the American Council of Trustees and Alumni (ACTA), is named interim CU President. Founded in 1995 with seed money from conservative foundations, ACTA issued a report in the aftermath of 9/11: Defending Civilization: How Our Universities Are Failing America and What Can Be Done About It.
Feb. 2006	*David Horowitz releases The Professors: The 101 Most Dangerous Academics in America (Regnery). Horowitz portrays WC as representative of the professorate.*
4-04-06	Regents announce that Brown is the sole finalist for the new president of CU.
5-17-06	**The Standing Committee releases a report finding WC guilty of research misconduct.**
May 2006	*ACTA releases How Many Ward Churchills? The report states that the "extremist rhetoric and tendentious opinion for which Churchill is infamous" is "quite common" as well as "enthusiastically embraced" and "rewarded" by academe. "Ward Churchill is everywhere." The report calls for more "intellectual diversity."*
6-27-06	**CU announces intent to dismiss WC, citing evidence of plagiarism and fabrication.**
6-29-06	Churchill files appeal with Privilege and Tenure Committee.
6-09-07	Privilege and Tenure Committee report submitted to CU President Brown.
6-25-07	**President Brown recommends firing Churchill.**
7-24-07	**Board of Regents fire him.**
7-25-07	Churchill sues CU for wrongful termination.
7-26-07	Brown appears on Fox, describing Churchill and his lawsuit as an "absolute fraud." *Sean Hannity argues that the "little Eichmanns" quote in itself is a firing offense.*
1-31-08	Regents name ACTA member Bruce Benson sole finalist for new president of CU.
2-21-08	Regents appoint Benson president on a 6-3 party line vote after Faculty Assembly voted against him 40 to 4. Benson, lacking a graduate degree, had been criticized for efforts to weaken tenure at Metropolitan State College (Denver) when he chaired its Board of Trustees.
3-09-09	**WC's civil lawsuit for wrongful termination begins in Denver District Court.**
7-07-09	**Denver district judge rules against WC's request for reinstatement.**
7-15-09	**Denial of Churchill's appeal by the Colorado Supreme Court.**
4-01-13	**Final denial by the US Supreme Court.**

7 Deviant in Residence: Idea Rendering and Repair in the Parochial Press

Sampling for Content Analysis

I worked with a research team to obtain a purposive sample for the content analysis at T1, defined as newspaper articles with substantial attention to Churchill, from January 25, 2005, to February 25, 2005. To be included, at least 50% of an article's content had to be about the controversy surrounding Churchill and the essay, and in the case of news briefs, the length at least 50 words. These criteria ensured that the sample was made up of articles largely focused on the essay, with sufficient length to potentially convey substantive ideas, at least in summary form. We used LexisNexis Academic to obtain articles from "major papers" outside Colorado, along with wire service articles with datelines outside the state. All wire stories were from the Associated Press.

The breakdown is as follows: *The Denver Post* (25), *Rocky Mountain News* (56), *Daily Camera* (42), *Longmont Daily Times-Call* (22), *Colorado Daily* (21), AP outside Colorado (16), and major papers outside the state (18). We coded as Colorado content any AP story published with an in-state dateline; in every case the datelines were Denver or Boulder. The AP produces copy for subscribing media across the nation, although in most cases these stories would be of greatest relevance to local publications. Thus, social control dynamics in the parochial press should apply to Colorado-based AP reporters, at least to some extent.

Circulation for papers outside the state ranged from 75,052 (*The Christian Science Monitor*) to 1,865,000 (*The New York Times*). For AP articles, we recorded circulation size for the newspapers where the articles were published. Outside of Colorado, AP datelines generally appeared in New York—site of the World Trade Center terrorism—and states where Churchill was scheduled to speak. The chapter reports what the circulation figures were in Colorado during the initial timeframe (January/February 2005).

Using the same selection criteria, the breakdown at T2 is as follows: *The Denver Post* (5), *Daily Camera* (11), *Longmont Daily Times-Call* (8), *Colorado Daily* (3), AP outside Colorado (5), and major papers outside the state (5).

Coding and Reliability

We developed six indicators to assess the extent to which news articles reported the substance of Churchill's ideas. The items are roughly sequenced from general to specific, but all measures were coded 0/1 such that the absence of content indicates idea rendering.

For the third item, "US foreign policy" meant historic or ongoing *policies* involving the United States and other countries, beyond the immediate response or context of 9/11. Foreign policy references could include such topics as the first Gulf War, historical efforts to broker a Middle East peace, US nuclear proliferation policies, relations with Saudi Arabia, Israel, Pakistan, or other countries, etc.

Seven graduate students participated as coders following training sessions, preliminary reading and discussion of content, and pilot testing. Two additional coders assessed a random sample of 10% of the articles to ensure reliability. We calculated intercoder reliability using Scott's *pi* to correct for agreement by chance for the nominal measures. Scott's *pi* ranged from .70 for reference to foreign policy to .90 for blowback, with an average reliability of 81. To test reliability for the additional nominal measures in Appendix Table 7.2, two other coders assessed a random sample of 10% of the articles. Scott's *pi* ranged from .70 (students as source and reference to scholarship) to 1.0 (talk radio), with an average of .81.

De-contextualization in Content Analysis

I expected de-contextualization to be pronounced in local news. Comparisons of Colorado vs. non-Colorado content bring up a concern whether differences are merely an artifact of stories tending to be lengthier in one category or the other. However, the mean word count in Colorado (654) is not significantly different from the mean outside the state (589). We account for article length in Appendix Table 7.2 when exploring content attributes that accompany idea rendering.

I also considered whether frequency of news articles should predispose one or the other category to substantively convey Churchill's ideas. At issue is whether content differences are due to volume of coverage as opposed to the local press more strongly enacting idea rendering. Front Range papers were far more interested in the Churchill saga than news outlets outside of Colorado, reflecting how the news value of ideological conflict is magnified when proximity is a salient factor in professional judgment. Saturation coverage itself suggests a social control response.

The primary purpose of the content analysis, however, is to document the likelihood of an article containing manifest content. One might argue that local papers would be more likely to at least occasionally describe, analyze, or otherwise address the substantive ideas of the essay; the frenzied coverage would allow ample opportunities to delve into Churchill's ideas. Out-of-state journalists would have less opportunity to cover this aspect of the controversy. During the first month of the controversy, a local reporter or editor might decide that the next article represents an opportune time to examine the essay contents. But if this intent is carried out, descriptions of essay content could be diluted by the overall magnitude of coverage. On the other hand, there should be many opportunities for local reporters to explore the essay's contents as various pro and anti-Churchill sources weighed in on the controversy. With respect to non-Colorado media, one could argue that descriptions of the essay contents should be less frequent because a reporter or editor would have fewer occasions to consider a particular story element as newsworthy. That said, the relatively infrequent coverage might predispose a non-local reporter to be more comprehensive in covering various dimensions of the controversy, including Churchill's ideas. I describe these various scenarios only to suggest that the volume of coverage does not elicit an obvious answer whether the conventions of newsworthiness predispose one or the other media category to convey Churchill's ideas.

Percentage breakdowns for each content measure across the five Colorado newspapers and the two national categories are reported in Appendix Table 7.1.

Appendix Table 7.1 Descriptive statistics for de-contextualization in Colorado and non-Colorado newspaper articles in 2005

	Does article describe essay beyond Eichmann?	Does article convey blowback perspective?	Does article reference foreign policy?	Does article reference civilian deaths?	Does article refer to US citizens in denial?	Does article express view of attackers as rational?
Colorado						
Denver Post ($n = 25$)	6 (24.0%)	4 (16.0%)	0 (0.0%)	3 (12%)	1 (4.0%)	0 (0.0%)
Rocky Mountain News ($n = 56$)	20 (35.7%)	19 (33.9%)	13 (23.2%)	6 (10.7%)	3 (5.4%)	1 (1.8%)
Boulder Daily Camera ($n = 42$)	21 (50.0%)	22 (52.4%)	13 (31.0%)	4 (9.5%)	4 (9.5%)	1 (2.4%)
Colorado Daily ($n = 21$)	7 (33.3%)	4 (19.0%)	4 (19.0%)	1 (4.8%)	0 (0.0%)	3 (14.3%)
Longmont Daily T-C ($n = 22$)	12 (54.5%)	4 (18.2%)	7 (31.8%)	3 (13.6%)	0 (0.0%)	3 (13.6%)
Non-Colorado						
Major papers ($n = 18$)	15 (83.3%)	11 (61.1%)	8 (44.4%)	9 (50.0%)	7 (38.9%)	2 (11.1%)
Associated Press ($n = 16$)	12 (75.0%)	7 (43.8%)	7 (43.8%)	3 (18.8%)	2 (12.5%)	5 (31.3%)

Appendix Table 7.2 Logistic regression predicting probability of essay elements referenced in news articles

	Does article describe essay beyond Eichmann? *Exp(B)*	Does article convey blowback perspective? *Exp(B)*	Does article reference foreign policy? *Exp(B)*	Does article reference civilian deaths? *Exp(B)*	Does article refer to US citizens in denial? *Exp(B)*	Does article express view of attackers as rational? *Exp(B)*
Article Attributes						
Date	.980	.928	.738	.651	1.066	.199**
Length	1.356	1.835**	1.568*	1.785*	1.271	.852
Proximity (CO)	.588**	.813	.730	.578*	.441**	.539*
Sources[1]						
Students	1.576*	1.736**	1.371	1.390	1.364	1.243
Politicians	1.218	1.330	.877	1.290	.799	.868
General public	.892	.838	.988	.790	.624	.710
Family members	1.441	1.036	.912	.842	1.178	.892
Churchill						
# quoted words	151.734***	2.471*	1.597*	1.731*	1.463	1.042
Scholarship	.701	.690	.713	.729	1.373	.997
Media Reference						
News coverage	1.062	1.145	1.199	1.383	2.064**	1.058
Talk radio	1.113	1.210	.939	.855	.960	.924

Continued

Appendix Table 7.2 Continued

	Does article describe essay beyond Eichmann? *Exp(B)*	Does article convey blowback perspective? *Exp(B)*	Does article reference foreign policy? *Exp(B)*	Does article reference civilian deaths? *Exp(B)*	Does article refer to US citizens in denial? *Exp(B)*	Does article express view of attackers as rational? *Exp(B)*
R^2 Nagelkerke	.493	.364	.258	.356	.396	.311
	$\chi^2 = 92.19$, $df = 11$, $p < .001$	$\chi^2 = 61.43$, $df = 11$, $p < .001$	$\chi^2 = 38.61$, $df = 11$, $p < .001$	$\chi^2 = 44.72$, $df = 11$, $p < .001$	$\chi^2 = 38.34$, $df = 11$, $p < .001$	$\chi^2 = 27.52$, $df = 11$, $p < .01$

Note: Date indicates day at T1; length is measured by word count; and # quoted words refers to the Churchill essay.

$N = 200$. * $p < .05$; ** $p < .01$; *** $p < .001$.

1. A measure for faculty proved unreliable due to difficulty in determining whether a source represented faculty or university administration.

Content Attributes That Accompany De-contextualization

This supplemental analysis identifies elements of news production that accompany or counteract proximity in idea suppression. The research team determined whether articles included views of politicians, members of the general public, and individuals who lost family members on 9/11—all non-academic sources who could serve a latent goal of portraying public outrage.[1] Inside the university, students could represent sources more likely to contextualize the Eichmann trope. Content analysis also accounted for publication date and word length.

We coded for presence or absence of a quote or paraphrase from politicians, members of the public, family members of 9/11 victims, and students. Churchill is a possible source, of course, and we determined the number of words quoted from the essay. Coders also assessed whether an article made any reference to Churchill's scholarship beyond the 9/11 essay.

Finally, we were curious whether reporters would acknowledge the media's role in amplifying the controversy. Churchill was a popular target of bloggers and speared daily on talk radio. Journalistic references to media might demonstrate a reflexive orientation, perhaps working against idea rendering. Coders assessed whether an article mentioned the amount of news coverage about Churchill and whether an article referred to talk radio.

Appendix Table 7.2 summarizes results from logistic regression in which I entered the following predictors of de-contextualization: publication date (coded 1-32 for day at T1), article length (word count), proximity, four sources, number of quoted words from the essay, whether the reporter referred to Churchill's scholarship, and two indicators of media recognition. A value over 1 for an odds ratio indicates an increase in odds of a content element appearing given a 1-unit increase in the independent variable. A value less than 1 indicates a decrease in odds.

The perspective of attackers as rational was less likely to appear later in the time frame, but otherwise publication date failed to predict de-contextualization. Word length was positively related to articles with references to blowback, foreign policy, and civilian deaths. Proximity (Colorado) remained fairly robust despite the inclusion of 10 other predictors. Proximity increased the odds of de-contextualization for every outcome except blowback and foreign policy. Among source variables, students stood out as the only significant predictor. Student voices contributed to contextualized coverage for describing the essay beyond Eichmann and blowback. Quoted words from the essay increased odds of appearance for all content elements except citizens in denial and attackers as rational, but reporters' reference to Churchill's scholarship failed as a predictor. Reporters were more likely to include a view of citizens in denial if they mentioned news coverage. Reference to talk radio was not predictive.

Interviews of Colorado Newspaper Journalists

We achieved a sample of male and female journalists with professional experience from 5 to 40 years and contributions to the coverage ranging from 1 to 21 articles. We included wire correspondents who occupy a role as insiders of the Colorado press yet retain some distance as correspondents writing for a national (and beyond) audience. We oversampled reporters from the *Rocky Mountain News*, the paper with the most articles devoted to the coverage. Interviewees included five reporters from the *Rocky*, one editor and one reporter from *The Denver Post*, one reporter and one editorial writer from the *Boulder Daily Camera*, one reporter from the *Longmont Daily Times-Call*, one correspondent/editor from the AP, and a correspondent for Reuters.

We conducted in-depth, semi-structured, face-to-face interviews averaging 61 minutes, asking reporters and editors to reflect back two years earlier on the initial month of the Churchill coverage. Questions solicited thoughts about the process of news writing and editing, including any internal and/or external influences and organizational constraints; the cultural context of the story and perceptions of the public response; principles guiding the reporting; and sense-making of Churchill's ideas and his rhetorical style. In the consent form and interviews, we avoided conceptual language that would cue journalists to adopt our interpretive frame. However, at the end of interviews we asked respondents to consider results from the content analysis showing infrequent contextualization of Churchill's ideas. We digitally recorded and transcribed the interviews. The chapter does not provide full identification for excerpted quotes from interviews and news articles, nor list articles in Notes, to honor confidentiality and anonymity agreements with the journalists interviewed. I indicate whether the reporter or editor quoted is from Boulder or Denver newspapers. Wire reporters were based in Denver.

8 Closing of the Journalism Mind: Anti-intellectualism among College Students

Development of Measures

In the fall of 2014, Jesse Benn and I were eager to launch a survey that would identify the precursors to journalistic anti-rationalism and anti-elitism in educational experiences. We recognized, however, the need for extensive measurement development. The earlier interviews of Colorado reporters and editors suggested that journalists develop complex and sometimes contradictory attitudes toward the suppression of intellectual dissent, evident in denial, ambivalence, regret, and resistance (Chapter 7). Apart from SAIS, all of the cultural and professional measures of anti-intellectualism are used for the first time in the present project.[2]

We recruited journalism and mass communication students from our home campus, CU Boulder, for pilot surveys in the fall of 2014 (T1, $N = 417$) and spring 2015 (T2, $N = 171$). We formulated questions in ways that limit social desirability bias. This required that we withhold some information from respondents about the study purpose. The preliminary results allowed us to evaluate the reliability and construct validity of the new measures. Results reported in this chapter are derived from a larger sample recruited for a survey in fall 2015 (T3, $N = 1,472$).

Recruitment, Response Rates, and Sample Demographics

Student research pools established at the University of Wisconsin, Michigan State (MSU), and the University of Georgia (UGA) allowed us to administer questionnaires with a web-based data-collection system. The research pool at MSU is primarily populated with students in advertising and public relations. A team member consequently also recruited respondents for the online questionnaire by visiting a large introductory journalism course. A colleague at Marist distributed paper-and-pencil questionnaires to six journalism and communication courses and four political science courses open to non-majors. At CU, I relied on web-based data collection for a large introductory advertising course supplemented with paper-and-pencil questionnaires distributed in five journalism courses and two media studies courses. (I did not teach any of these courses.)

Response rate for the online questionnaires is 41.7%, and the rate for in-class participation is 57%. The overall response rate is 44%. Mode of response is not predictive of SAIS scores or the new indices for anti-intellectualism. Non-respondents include students who did not convey consent or opted to not participate online or in class; students who did not complete questionnaires; and those absent when we visited courses with questionnaires. The response rate compares favorably to rates reported for questionnaire administration in journalism courses in the United States and other nations.[3]

Ethnicity in the CU sample is marginally more diverse than the population as reported by a site visit of the Accrediting Council on Education in Journalism and Mass Communications.[4] The CU sample is 76.6% white, 6.3% Hispanic, 5.9% Asian, 2.4% black, 4.1% multi-ethnic, and .3% Native American. A female majority is common in journalism and mass communication (JMC) programs, but the UGA sample shows a pronounced majority: 74.2% are female in the student population as reported by UGA, while our sample shows the majority at 82.8%. Appendix Table 8.1 provides the breakdowns by college for response rates and subsample socio-demographics.

As for political identity, the sample profile is most liberal at the University of Wisconsin, with the partisan divide at 42% Democrat, 28% Republican. The GOP holds a majority in our sample only at UGA: 35.8% Republican, 24.1% Democrat. Religious beliefs are most important to students at UGA and least important at CU Boulder ($M_{\text{diff}} = 1.05, p < .001$).

Appendix Table 8.1 College response rates, sample socio-demographics, and student majors

	Response rates		Socio-demographics and majors
	Online	In class	
University of Wisconsin ($n = 242$)	67%		65.3% female
			88.5% white, 4.5% Asian, 1.2% black, 2.1% Hispanic, 2.5% multi-ethnic, .8% Native American
			42% Democrat, 28% Republican
			13.2% advertising, 12% public relations, 8.3% media and information, 13.6% communication, 2.1% broadcast news, 1.7% broadcast production, 2.9% online/news-editorial, 1.2% visual communication, 9.5% liberal arts, 35.5% non-media pre-professional

Continued

Appendix Table 8.1 Continued

	Response rates		Socio-demographics and majors
	Online	In class	
University of Georgia ($n = 274$)	31.8%		82.8% female
			82.5% white, 4% Asian, 8% black, 2.9% Hispanic, 2.2% multi-ethnic
			24.1% Democrat, 35.8% Republican
			27.4% advertising, 33.2% public relations, 6.9% media and information, 6.2% communication, 4% broadcast news, 1.1% broadcast production, 5.8% online/news-editorial, 1.1% visual communication, 2.9% liberal arts, 11.3% non-media pre-professional
University of Colorado ($n = 288$)	64.7%	31.2%	70.2% female
			76.6% white, 5.9% Asian, 2.4% black, 6.3% Hispanic, 4.1% multi-ethnic, .3% Native American
			39.9% Democrat, 20.3% Republican
			36.8% advertising, 17.4% public relations, 11.5% media and information, 6.3% communication, 4.9% broadcast news, 2.1% broadcast production, 7.6% online/news-editorial, 3.8% visual communication, 5.9% liberal arts, 3.8% non-media pre-professional
Michigan State ($n = 423$)	36.3%		69.6% female
			70.5% white, 15.5% Asian, 6.6% black, 4% Hispanic, 2.8% multi-ethnic
			28.5% Democrat, 25.4% Republican
			60% advertising, 7.1% public relations, 7.8% media and information, 5.2% communication, 4.5% broadcast news, .9% broadcast production, 4.5% online/news-editorial, 1.2% visual communication, 1.4% liberal arts, 7.3% non-media pre-professional
Marist College ($n = 245$)		79.1%	51.5% female
			83.8% white, 3.4% Asian, 3% black, 5.5% Hispanic, 1.7% multi-ethnic, 1.3% Native American
			33.1% Democrat, 23.9% Republican
			6.9% advertising, 18.8% public relations, 3.7% media and information, 24.1% communication, 9.4% broadcast news, 4.5% broadcast production, 5.3% online/news-editorial, 1.6% visual communication, 18.4% liberal arts, 7.3% non-media pre-professional

Measures

Student anti-intellectualism ($M = 3.65$, *SD* $= .75$, $\alpha = .87$). We relied on the 25 items developed by Eigenberger and Sealander and used subsequently in samples of students in social science, professional, and technical fields.[5] Students responded with a 1 (*strongly disagree*) to 7 (*strongly agree*) scale for student anti-intellectualism and the other measures of anti-intellectualism. The SAIS battery includes positively and negatively worded items to reduce response set. To facilitate comparisons, we calculated average scores for support of both cultural and journalistic anti-intellectualism.

"I see college as a 'necessary evil'—it's the price I have to pay to find a job."

"Many of my college courses are a waste of time for me."

"I would like to deepen my intellectual pursuits after graduation."

"I don't like taking courses that are not directly related to my goals after college."

"I enjoy researching new topics and solving intellectual problems."

"I prefer courses offering practical skills over 'liberal arts' kinds of courses."

"I would rather just pay money for a diploma than have to take so many useless courses."

"It is always worthwhile to study subjects like philosophy, history, and educational theory."

"A *big* reason I'm in college is that I value learning for its own sake."

"Some college professors are alright, but as a whole I don't care much for them."

"I enjoy courses that require research, writing, and critical evaluation."

"Learning a lot of theories is fine for some people, but I'd rather just go out and *do* things."

"Some professors are too 'intellectual' and often bore me with their abstractions."

"The *main* problems in life require clear and direct answers, not intellectual theorizing."

"Requirements to take humanities and liberal arts courses should be reduced or eliminated."

"Generally speaking, professors need to be more interesting."

"I prefer classes where thought-provoking issues are discussed with the professor."

"I prefer classes *without* a lot of critical thinking or analytical activities."

"I become bored in my classes when discussions seem to get too abstract and hypothetical."

"Overall, I find my college courses stimulating and rewarding."

"I pay tuition and feel it is the professor's job to give me what I need to graduate."

"I often feel angry toward many of my professors."

"I appreciate a teacher's depth of knowledge more than how entertaining they are."

"I am *not* interested in hearing students and the professor discuss philosophical issues."

"I'm in a hurry to get my education over with."

Anti-rationalism (M = 3.48, SD = 1.02, α = .67). Students estimated how much they agreed with five statements: "Research can only go so far; sometimes you just know something," "You can learn as much from your religion about the world as you can from academic research," "I trust my gut as much as any professor or academic research," "Creationism is as valid an explanation for the universe as any," and "Sometimes the way I feel about a subject overrides cold hard facts."

Anti-elitism (M = 4.04, SD = 1.00, α = .72). Students responded to three items: "A lot of professors think they're better than everyone," "Academics are often pretentious in the way that they talk and write," and "Tenure at universities protects radical professors from being held accountable to the public."

Journalistic anti-rationalism (M = 3.44, SD = 1.27, α = .72). We operationalized anti-rationalism in journalism with three items that invoke a need for balance when covering science and religion: "Journalists should include religious beliefs as much as science in debates about public policy ... balance scientific expertise with religious expertise when the two conflict ... recognize that intelligent design is a theory just like the theory of evolution."

Journalistic anti-elitism (M = 4.19, SD = .95, α = .73). We developed six statements to measure support for news that protects the public from politicized academics while valuing the opinion of average citizens. "Journalists should acknowledge that all opinions are equal in a democracy," "Journalists should expose professors who ridicule American values," "Journalists should expose professors who undermine American values in their instruction," "Journalists should focus on stories that average citizens care about," "Journalists should recognize that social scientists are politically biased," and "The interests of average citizens rather than experts should guide journalists."

Role identity, support for transparency, and the remaining measures join cultural anti-intellectualism as predictors of journalistic anti-rationalism and anti-elitism. For measures of role identity, we used a 1–5 response scale, with 1 indicating "not important at all" and 5 corresponding to "extremely important." Weaver et al. used a 1–7 scale for the 2002 survey of professional journalists,[6] but we opted for the 1–5 scale to facilitate comparisons with Mellado et al.'s survey of college students in the United States and six other countries.[7]

Interpretive role (M = 3.90, SD = .90). "How important is it for journalists to provide analysis and interpretation of complex problems?"

Disseminator role (M = 3.68, SD = .97). "How important is it for journalists to concentrate on news that's of interest to the widest possible audience?"

Adversary role (M = 3.49, SD = .93). "How important is it for journalists to be an adversary of public officials by being constantly skeptical of their actions?"

Populist mobilizer role (M = 4.04, SD = .90). "How important is it to give ordinary people a chance to express their views on public affairs?"

Loyal role (M = 3.10, SD = 1.09). "How important is it for journalism to cultivate patriotism?"

Transparency (M = 5.05, SD = 1.02, α = .74). We calculated the average score for three items. Students responded with the 1 (strongly disagree) to 7 (strongly agree) scale. In news reports, journalists should acknowledge "the values that influence how they cover issues" and "how their reporting methods shape coverage." "Journalists must ultimately answer to the public when questions arise about reporting methods."

College major. JMC programs at the five colleges collectively offer 10 majors, and we recognized the possibility of ambiguity depending on terms used to describe course sequences. We prefaced a question about major with: "Students often take courses in multiple tracks, but choose the category that best represents your area of study." Students chose from advertising; public relations; media studies and information; communication; broadcast and electronic news; broadcast production; online news and news-editorial; visual communication and design: video, documentary, photography; liberal arts major but not in media; and pre-professional major not in media. For predictors in the regression models, we created dummy measures (coded 0 1) for the three news majors: broadcast and electronic news, broadcast production, and online news and news-editorial.

Ethnicity. "What is your ethnic background?" Hispanic/Latino, black/African American, Asian, Native American, other, multi-ethnic = 0, white/Anglo = 1.

Gender. "What is your gender?" Female = 0, male = 1.

Grade level. (M = 2.69, SD = 1.11). "What is your grade level?" Freshmen = 1, sophomore = 2, junior = 3, senior = 4.

Grade point average (M = 3.91, SD = .83). "What is your overall GPA?" 2.2 or lower = 1, 2.3 to 2.6 = 2, 2.7 to 3.1 = 3, 3.2 to 3.6 = 4, 3.7 or higher = 5.

Strength of religious identity (M = 2.99, SD = 1.43). "How important is religion or religious beliefs to you?" Students used the 1 (not important at all) to 5 (extremely important) scale.

Ideological identity (M = 4.36, SD = 1.34). "Place yourself on a 1–7 scale with 1 meaning extremely liberal and 7 meaning extremely conservative." We reverse coded the responses toward liberal orientation.

Analysis Strategy

After the comparison of journalism and mass communication undergraduates with majors from other fields (Table 8.1), I focused on processes in professional development, in particular associations of role identity and reflexivity with anti-intellectualism. Hierarchical multiple regression accounts for variance in journalistic anti-rationalism and anti-elitism. I considered multi-level modeling to account for the nesting of student respondents at the college level. A two-level model, however, assumes that the identifiable clusters are drawn randomly from a population, in this case colleges. The presence of only five colleges is also unlikely to generate an accurate estimate of variability with respect to support for journalistic anti-intellectualism. Raudenbush and Bryk tracked the socioeconomic status-achievement relationship in journalism schools to illustrate the logic of hierarchical linear modeling (HLM).[8] They assumed random sampling of schools (J) from a population where J is a larger number. Nevertheless, to explore multi-level influence, I ran empty models in ordinary least squares to assess variability of journalistic anti-rationalism and anti-elitism. Campus location accounts for .028 percent of variance in the former and .011 percent in the latter, suggesting marginal within-cluster homogeneity.

Multiple indicators of cultural anti-intellectualism and role identity raise collinearity as an issue, but diagnostics revealed that variance inflation factors were less than 2.3 for all predictors of journalistic anti-rationalism and anti-elitism.

Model 1 in Appendix Table 8.2 establishes linkages between support for cultural and journalistic anti-intellectualism. Model 2 then enters ethnicity, gender, religious and

Appendix Table 8.2 Influences of educational experiences and attitudes on student support for journalistic anti-intellectualism

	Journalistic anti-rationalism		Journalistic anti-elitism	
	Full sample B (SE)	Journalism majors B (SE)	Full sample B (SE)	Journalism majors B (SE)
Cultural anti-intellectualism				
Anti-rationalism	.479*** (.032)	.387*** (.092)	.157*** (.023)	.109 (.072)
Anti-elitism	.027 (.033)	.057 (.089)	.151*** (.024)	.251*** (.070)
Model 1 R^2	.282***	.304***	.230***	.253***
Demographics, ideology, education				
Ethnicity (white)	−.122 (.070)	−.287 (.193)	.041 (.050)	−.133 (.150)
Gender (male)	−.015 (.035)	−.097 (.169)	−.077 (.044)	−.063 (.132)
Strength of religious identity	.201*** (.023)	.200** (.064)	.022 (.016)	.007 (.050)
Ideological ID (liberal)	−.024 (.026)	−.076 (.077)	−.033 (.019)	−.088 (.060)
Wisconsin	.092 (.104)	−.287 (.301)	−.037 (.074)	−.144 (.244)
Michigan State	.243** (.089)	.186 (.239)	−.115 (.064)	.093 (.187)
Georgia	.074 (.096)	−.346 (.244)	−.087 (.069)	−.259 (.190)
Colorado	.000 (.098)	−.425 (.217)	−.024 (.070)	−.247 (.169)
Grade level	.014 (.028)	−.050 (.080)	−.001 (.020)	.116 (.063)
Grade point average	−.015 (.035)	−.083 (.101)	−.062* (.025)	−.004 (.138)
News-editorial/online news	−.191 (.135)		−.109 (.096)	
Broadcast/electronic news	−.201 (.136)		.164 (.097)	
Broadcast production	−.070 (.212)		−.050 (.153)	

Interpretive role	.015 (.033)	.085 (.084)	−.018 (.024)	.056 (.067)
Dissemination role	.020 (.032)	.076 (.085)	.187*** (.023)	.253*** (.066)
Adversary role	−.052 (.031)	−.061 (.084)	−.053* (.022)	−.115 (.066)
Populist mobilizer role	.037 (.035)	.104 (.101)	.068** (.025)	.094 (.079)
Loyal role	.093** (.030)	.078 (.073)	.166*** (.021)	.093 (.057)
Transparency	.118** (.031)	.019 (.092)	.241*** (.022)	.153* (.072)
Model 2 R^2	.097***	.200***	.219***	.238***
Total R^2	.380***	.504***	.448***	.491***

Note: Cell entries report coefficients in the final model of hierarchical multiple regression. Data are weighted to account for unequal sampling probabilities for majors. News majors are coded 0–1. Marist is removed as the base category for campus location.

$N = 1,472$ for full sample; $n = 206$ for journalism majors. *SE*: standard error.

*$p < .05$, **$p < .01$, ***$p < .001$.

political identity, campus location, grade level, grade point average, major, support for journalistic roles, and transparency. Model specification assumes that influence from anti-intellectualism at the cultural level precedes student experiences and attitude crystallization within a college setting. I interpret endorsement of transparency as an expression of reflexivity and presume that role identity contributes to evaluation of the news as it confronts intellect and intellectuals in contentious scenarios.

Supplemental Results

This analysis looks for differences between news and non-news majors vis-à-vis variables predictive of journalistic anti-intellectualism. A lack of differences would suggest that suspicion and resentment toward intellect is an obstinate disposition, ingrained in youth enculturation and resistant to the best intentions of instructors. If, on the other hand, factors such as role identity and support for transparency are stronger predictors of journalistic anti-intellectualism among news majors, we might conclude that professional instruction offers a fast track to antipathy. In a more optimistic scenario, journalism education would inoculate majors.

The survey findings discussed in Chapter 8 are derived from the full sample. This analysis again accounts for influence of news majors in relationship to other predictors of journalistic anti-rationalism and anti-elitism. Appendix Table 8.2, however, reports supplemental findings in comparisons of the full sample with the subsample confined to news majors. Hierarchical multiple regression provides an efficient scheme to determine whether major, role identity, and support for transparency correlate with journalistic anti-intellectualism while accounting for cultural anti-intellectualism and other factors.

In the baseline equation, anti-rationalism generates a significant coefficient for the full sample ($B = .48$, $SE = .03$, $p < .001$) and news majors ($B = .39$, $SE = .09$, $p < .001$) as a correlate of journalistic anti-rationalism. Also as expected, anti-elitism is a robust correlate of journalistic anti-elitism (full sample: $B = .15$, $SE = .02$, $p < .001$; news majors: $B = .25$, $SE = .07$, $p < .001$).

In model 2, strength of religious identity accounts for variance in journalistic anti-rationalism in the full sample ($B = .20$, $SE = .02$, $p < .001$) and among news majors ($B = .20$, $SE = .06$, $p < .01$). Liberal identity, by contrast, generates negative coefficients for both dimensions of journalistic anti-intellectualism, although these associations are not significant. College campus is inconsequential with the exception of MSU producing a positive coefficient for journalistic anti-rationalism in the full sample ($B = .24$, $SE = .09$, $p < .01$). The failure of college site in accounting for variance among news majors implies that attitudes toward intellect are in some respect generally inculcated in journalism education. While GPA associates negatively with journalistic anti-intellectualism, the result is only significant in the full sample for anti-elitism. As reported in the chapter, journalism major fails to guard against support for journalistic anti-intellectualism.

The dissemination of information role is a strong predictor of journalistic anti-elitism in both samples. However, the populist mobilizer ($B = .07$, $SE = .03$, $p < .01$) and loyal roles ($B = .17$, $SE = .02$, $p <. 001$) are significant predictors of journalistic anti-elitism only in the full sample. The loyalty role is also only predictive of journalistic anti-rationalism in the full sample ($B = .09$, $SE = .03$, $p < .01$). This pattern implies that journalism education is at least somewhat protective against the infiltration of antipathy toward intellect. Number of respondents increases the predictive power of role identity in the full sample, but a scan of the coefficients and standard errors suggests that this pattern is noteworthy.

Support for transparency, however, predicts journalistic anti-elitism among news major (B = .15, SE = .07, p < .05) along with the two dimensions of journalistic anti-intellectualism in both samples.

These results replicate across questionnaire administration (in class or online). The study relied on a large set of self-report items, but the findings establish a foothold for future study of anti-intellectualism among college students. In retrospect, I also recognize that some items in the student anti-rationalism and anti-elitism scales arguably confound structure of attitudinal stance with content. For example, the question on creationism as a valid explanation for the universe is not balanced by an item on suspicion of scientific findings that fail to affirm left-wing beliefs.

10 What Intellectual Journalism Would Look Like

Lead Exercise

The following excerpt comes from Prof. Ward Churchill's essay, *Some People Push Back: On the Justice of Roosting Chickens*. The essay was published online the day after the terrorist attacks of September 11, 2001. In this paragraph, Churchill questions the innocence of those who perished in the World Trade Center:

> Well, really. Let's get a grip here, shall we? True enough, they were civilians of a sort. But innocent? Gimme a break. They formed a technocratic corps at the very heart of America's global financial empire—the "mighty engine of profit" to which the military dimension of US policy has always been enslaved—and they did so both willingly and knowingly. Recourse to "ignorance"—a derivative, after all, of the word "ignore"—counts as less than an excuse among this relatively well-educated elite. To the extent that any of them were unaware of the costs and consequences to others of what they were involved in—and in many cases excelling at—it was because of their absolute refusal to see. More likely, it was because they were too busy braying, incessantly and self-importantly, into their cell phones, arranging power lunches and stock transactions, each of which translated, conveniently out of sight, mind and smelling distance, into the starved and rotting flesh of infants. If there was a better, more effective, or in fact any other way of visiting some penalty befitting their participation upon the little Eichmanns* inhabiting the sterile sanctuary of the twin towers, I'd really be interested in hearing about it.

*[In Nazi Germany, Adolf Eichmann managed logistics of the mass deportation of Jews to extermination camps during World War II.]

1. What would you say is the theme of this paragraph?
2. Imagine that you are asked to write a newspaper story about this essay and you want to focus on this paragraph. Write a one- or two-sentence lead for the article. The assignment calls for a news article, not a commentary.

Appendix Table 10.1 Themes and leads from students asked to read excerpt from Ward Churchill essay in 2014

What would you say is the theme of the essay?	*Imagine that you are asked to write a newspaper story about this essay and you want to focus on this paragraph. Write a one- or two-sentence lead for the article.*
The fact that those involved in the "technocratic corps" in the Twin Towers got what they deserved. Churchill is questioning the innocence of the victims of 9/11.	After the terrorist attacks of September 11, 2001, Professor Ward Churchill released a controversial essay entitled "Some People Push Back: On the Justice of Roosting Chickens" questioning the innocence of the victims of 9/11.
Ward Churchill is elaborating on the idea that the people in the WTC were partially responsible for suffering throughout the world, and couldn't plead innocence.	Shortly after the attacks on the World Trade Center, Ward Churchill, a tenured professor at the University of Colorado, has released an essay criticizing the victims, calling them "little Eichmanns."
The theme is criticizing the people who worked in the World Trade Center.	The release of an editorial essay written by University of Colorado Ethnic Studies Professor Ward Churchill has received criticism for being insensitive to the victims of the terrorist attacks on Sept. 11, for instance, by calling them "little Eichmanns."
The people that died in the twin towers were not innocent.	The citizens in the twin towers were innocent, or were they? According to Professor Ward Churchill, the group in the Twin Towers were the "might engine of profit" even going as far as calling them little Eichmanns.
The theme of this paragraph would be a false sense of innocence the author thinks Americans have. He does not see them as victims.	After 9/11 grief was felt throughout America for the losses of many Americans lost in the destruction of the twin towers. The question is whether those lives lost in the destruction were really innocent lives or if they were part of their own self demise.
The people at the World Trade Center were elitist business-people who knew that their business and negotiations had a dark side to them, but they just turned their cheek the other way and continued doing what they did best.	As the aftermath of September 11 seeps into the hearts of the citizens of the US, Professor Ward Churchill argues the innocence of those who died in the World Trade Center that day.
The victims of the terrorist attacks on the World Trade Center were "guilty" of wrongdoings by the way they conducted their daily lives and business, so therefore were not innocents who perished.	On Sept. 11, 2001, many perished in the World Trade Center due to terrorist attacks against the United States of America, however, it could be said that the victims of the attack could have shared part of the blame which was addressed in Prof. Ward Churchill's essay "Some People Push Back: On the Justice of Roosting Chickens."

What would you say is the theme of the essay?	*Imagine that you are asked to write a newspaper story about this essay and you want to focus on this paragraph. Write a one- or two-sentence lead for the article.*
The theme is almost justifying what happened in 9/11 and put blame on the victims.	Innocence is questioned and blame directed towards the mass number of 9/11 victims in Prof. Ward Churchill's controversial article. Ward Churchill holds nothing back in his article directly following the 9/11 terrorist attacks, labeling the number of victims "little Eichmanns."
That the finance specialists at W.T.C. were guilty/culpable for the destruction of the world.	Even in the immediate wake of tragedy, political perspectives arise quickly to blame, as exemplified by Ward Churchill's recent essay on the WTC attacks. Churchill finds the civilians slaughtered to be equally at fault, noting the part they played in a biased global economy.
9/11 was inevitable due to the fact that people working at the twin towers were enacting some sort of genocide.	University of Colorado Ethnic Studies Professor Ward Churchill compared financiers and victims of the 9/11 terrorist attacks to Nazis in a controversial online essay published a day after the tragedy unfolded.
The theme of the paragraph is that those who died on 9/11 deserved it as punishment for perpetuating the damaging effects of US capitalism.	In the wake of the attacks on the Twin Towers in New York, not everyone is mourning. University of Colorado Professor Ward Churchill published an essay one day later justifying the attack as a necessary "penalty" against people who worked in the World Trade Center—people, in Churchill's view who may as well be more murderous than the terrorists who crashed the planes.
September 11th controversy.	Prof. Ward Churchill, a past professor at the University of Colorado Boulder expressed his thoughts on the events of September 11th just 24 hours after the terrorist attacks, bringing most to shock after what he had to say about the innocent.
That although it's a tragedy that all of these people died, he makes the point that they're not innocent, and in fact, some have also acted harmfully towards others, just in a different way.	University of Colorado Professor Ward Churchill unsympathetically calls into question the innocence of those who perished within the twin towers just one day after the September 11th terrorist attack.
The people who died in the WTC attack weren't as innocent as we believe.	Innocence is one trait of being that is not permanent. Ward Churchill would argue we are not as innocent as we believe, and in his essay, he discusses how innocence can be lost.

Continued

Appendix Table 10.1 Continued

What would you say is the theme of the essay?	*Imagine that you are asked to write a newspaper story about this essay and you want to focus on this paragraph. Write a one- or two-sentence lead for the article.*
Arguing that Americans are not innocent, had it comin.'	Following the attacks of 9/11, CU Professor Ward Churchill expressed his controversial opinion in an article published online, where he argues karmic revenge as the motive behind the attacks.
Churchill's essay is discussing whether or not those who died in 9/11 were truly innocent. The theme might be interpreted as innocence.	Days after the terrorist attacks of September 11, 2001, CU Professor Ward Churchill published a controversial essay questioning the true innocence of the American citizens who lost their lives in the World Trade Centers.
Cruelty—telling that Americans are not innocent.	The terror attack of September 11, 2001 was a huge tragedy for United States of America and those who got killed. According to the CU professor Ward Churchill those who got killed, overall Americans in the global financial empire, "deserved it."
The theme is that those working in the twin towers were not innocent, but deserving of what happened on September 11.	CU Professor Ward Churchill is drawing harsh criticism after an essay referring to victims as "little Eichmanns" surfaced online less than 48 hours after Tuesday's attacks on the world trade center.
Explaining the lack of innocence that the workers of the world trade center inhibited.	Despite the grief that many Americans feel over 9/11, evidence shows that although the victims were civilians they were not innocent.
9/11 terrorist attacks were a consequence of the "financial empire" and the people who died were not innocent victims.	Professor Ward Churchill takes a controversial look at the 9/11 terrorist attacks, questioning whether the deaths of the victims were in vain, or just a consequence of their role in "America's financial empire."
Americans provoked the attacks of 9/11.	Ward Churchill, former CU college professor, writes a controversial article questioning the innocence of those whose lives were taken in the World Trade Center on September 11.
Anger at the elitist and so called ignorant nature of the American financial system and that they got what they deserved.	The American financial system was elitist, "ignorant," and got what it deserved, wrote CU professor Ward Churchill in a scathing essay published in response to the 9/11 terrorist attacks.
twin tower employees deserved to die for their "ignorance."	The day after the greatest terrorist attacks of this century, a CU Ethnic Studies professor asserted the victims deserved to die because the glory of their power lunches and high-flying trade allowed them to turn a blind eye to society.
His theme is that the financial workers in the Twin Towers were knowingly exploiting people and they got what they were asking for.	In a shocking essay released the day after the 9/11 terrorist attacks, Ward Churchill criticizes who he believes are the not so innocent victims, the Twin Tower bankers.

Notes

Preface

1. Richard Hofstadter, *Anti-intellectualism in American Life* (New York: Alfred A. Knopf, 1963), 7.
2. Michael McDevitt, "When an Advisory Board Turns on Its School," *Academe* 100, no. 3 (May/June 2014): 21–25.

Chapter 1

1. Jonathan Haidt, *The Righteous Mind: Why Good People Are Divided by Politics and Religion* (New York: Pantheon Books, 2012).
2. Theodore L. Glasser and Marc Gunther, "The Legacy of Autonomy in American Journalism," in *The Press: Institutions of American Democracy*, ed. Geneva Overholser and Kathleen Hall Jamieson (Oxford: Oxford University Press, 2005), 392.
3. Richard Hofstadter begins *Anti-intellectualism in America Life* with a series of exhibits to establish a spectrum of antipathy, with most examples drawn from the 1950s. Much of the structure and interpretations of the present volume draw from Hofstadter's landmark analysis. Richard Hofstadter, *Anti-intellectualism in American Life* (New York: Alfred A. Knopf), 1963.
4. Raymond Hernandez, "MAKING IT WORK: The Marxist Professor," *The New York Times*, October 29, 1995.
5. Daniel M. Gold, "Noam Chomsky Focuses on Financial Inequality in 'Requiem for the American Dream,'" *The New York Times*, January 29, 2016.
6. Evan Kindley, "Growing Up in Public: Academia, Journalism, and the New Public Intellectual," *PMLA* 13, no. 2 (2015): 467–73.
7. Ibid., 469.
8. Stephen D. Reese, August Grant, and Lucig H. Danielian, "The Structure of News Sources on Television: A Network Analysis of 'CBS News,' 'MacNeil/Lehrer,' and 'This Week with David Brinkley,'" *Journal of Communication* 44, no. 2 (1994): 84–107.
9. Ibid., 92.
10. Quoted in Joe Moran, "The Fall and Rise of the Expert," *Critical Quarterly* 53, no. 1 (2011): 6–22.
11. Ibid., 13–14.
12. Jannie Møller Hartley, "When Homo Academicus Meets Homo Journalisticus: An Inter-field Study of Collaboration and Conflict in the Communication of Scientific Research," *Journalism* 18, no. 2 (2017): 211–25.

13. Ibid., 220.

14. Dane Claussen, personal correspondence, August 2, 2018.

15. Graham Ambrose, "These Coloradans Say Earth Is Flat. And Gravity's a Hoax. Now, They're Being Persecuted," *The Denver Post*, July 7, 2017.

16. Claussen, personal correspondence, August 2, 2018.

17. Jean-Paul Sartre, *Humanism and Existentialism* (London: Methuen, 1973).

18. Susie Cook, a professor at Metro State University of Denver, asked the listserv for the National Communication Association for advice on how to cope with a particular type of student. "I've been wondering (as I prepare for the spring term courses), if any of you are confronting the same conundrum in the classroom that I am—namely that I have students who want concrete learning with a predetermined outcome when the topics we're teaching may be open-ended, amorphous, and more journey-like than outcome-focused." Chapter 8 reports findings from a survey of journalism and mass communication students at five colleges, revealing connections between the unreflective instrumentalism that Cook alludes to and support for journalistic anti-rationalism and anti-elitism.

19. George Kennedy, Daryl R. Moen, and Don Ranly, *Beyond the Inverted Pyramid: Effective Writing for Newspapers, Magazines and Specialized Publications* (New York: St. Martin's Press, 1993).

20. Matthew S. McGlone, "Quoted Out of Context: Contextomy and its Consequences," *Journal of Communication* 55, no. 2 (2005): 330–56.

21. Brian S. Brooks, George Kennedy, Daryl Moen, and Don Ranly, *Telling the Story: The Convergence of Print, Broadcast and Online Media* (Boston: Bedford/St. Martin's Press, 2013).

22. Ibid., 234.

23. Hofstadter, *Anti-intellectualism in American Life*, 22.

24. David Rowe, "Working Knowledge Encounters: Academics, Journalists and the Conditions of Cultural Labour," *Social Semiotics* 15, no. 3 (2005): 269–88.

25. Charles H. T. Lesch, "Democratic Solidarity in a Secular Age? Habermas and the 'Linguistification of the Sacred,'" *The Journal of Politics* 81, no. 3 (2019): 862–77.

26. John Nerone, *The Media and Public Life: A History* (Cambridge: Polity, 2015), 222.

27. Matt Carlson, "Metajournalistic Discourse and the Meanings of Journalism: Definitional Control, Boundary Work, and Legitimation," *Communication Theory* 26, no. 4 (2016): 349–68.

28. A critique of the news as *non*-intellectual resonates with Herman and Chomsky's portrayal of the press as passive and propagandistic, but *anti*-intellectualism is the more frequent complaint in the academy. Edward S. Herman and Noam Chomsky, *Manufacturing Consent: The Political Economy of the Mass Media* (New York: Pantheon Books, 1988).

29. Hofstadter, *Anti-intellectualism in American Life*; Daniel Rigney, "Three Kinds of Anti-intellectualism: Rethinking Hofstadter," *Sociological Inquiry* 61 (1991): 434–51.

30. Andrew Rich and R. Kent Weaver, "Think Tanks in the U.S. Media," *The Harvard International Journal of Press/Politics* 5, no. 4 (2000): 81–103.

31. Herbert J. Gans, *Deciding What's News: A Study of CBS Evening News, NBC Nightly News, Newsweek and Time* (New York: Vintage/Random House, 1979).

32. Christopher H. Achen and Larry M. Bartels, *Democracy for Realists: Why Elections Do Not Produce Responsive Governance* (Princeton: Princeton University Press, 2016).

33. Pamela J. Shoemaker, "Hardwired for News: Using Biological and Cultural Evolution to Explain the Surveillance Function," *Journal of Communication* 46, no. 3 (1996): 32–47; Haidt, *The Righteous Mind*.

34. H. L. Mencken, "Bayard vs. Lionheart," *Baltimore Evening Sun*, July 26, 1920.

35. Maureen Dowd, "Washington Chainsaw Massacre," *The New York Times*, August 3, 2011.

36. George A. Donohue, Phillip J. Tichenor, and Clarice N. Olien, "A Guard Dog Perspective on the Role of Media," *Journal of Communication* 45, no. 2 (1995): 115–32.

37. Daniel C. Hallin, *The Uncensored War* (New York: Oxford University Press, 1986); Ian Taylor, "Local Press Reporting of Opposition to the 2003 Iraq War in the UK and the Case for Reconceptualizing the Notions of Legitimacy and Deviance," *Journal of War & Culture Studies* 7, no. 1 (2014): 36–53.

38. Michael McDevitt, Marco Briziarelli, and Brian Klocke, "Social Drama in the Academic-Media Nexus: Journalism's Strategic Response to Deviant Ideas," *Journalism* 14, no. 1 (2013): 111–28.

39. Joseph Turow, Arthur L. Caplan, and John S. Bracken, "Domestic 'Zealotry' and Press Discourse: Kevorkian's Euthanasia Incident," *Journalism* 1, no. 2 (2000): 197–216.

40. Dane S. Claussen, *Anti-intellectualism in American Media: Magazines and Higher Education* (New York: Peter Lang, 2004).

41. Walter Lippmann, *Public Opinion* (New York: Harcourt, Brace, 1922), 364.

42. Ibid.

43. Walter Lippmann, *The Phantom Public* (New York: Harcourt, Brace, 1925).

44. Paul Hollander, "Popular Culture, The *New York Times* and the *New Republic*," *Culture and Society* 51 (2014): 288–96.

45. Claussen, *Anti-intellectualism in American Media*.

46. Phillip MacGregor, "Journalism, Public Imagination and Cultural Policy," *International Journal of Cultural Policy* 15, no. 2 (2009): 231–44.

47. Margaret Canovan, "Trust the People! Populism and the Two Faces of Democracy," *Political Studies* 47 (1999): 2–16; Cas Mudde, "The Populist Zeitgeist," *Government and Opposition* 39, no. 4 (2004): 542–63; Paul A. Taggart, *Populism* (Buckingham, UK: Open University Press, 2000).

48. Peter Wiles, "A Syndrome, Not a Doctrine: Some Elementary Theses on Populism," in *Populism. Its Meanings and National Characteristics*, ed. Ghita Ionescu and Ernest Gellner (London: Weidenfeld and Nicolson, 1969), 166–79.

49. Benjamin Krämer, "Media Populism: A Conceptual Clarification and Some Theses on Its Effects," *Communication Theory* 24, no. 1 (2014): 42–60.

50. Ibid., 49.

51. Kira Hall, Donna M. Goldstein, and Matthew B. Ingram, "The Hands of Trump: Entertainment, Gesture, Spectacle," *HAU: Journal of Ethnographic Theory* 6, no. 2 (2016): 71.

52. "Politics with Pork Chops: Presidential Candidates Flock to Iowa State Fair," *PBS News Hour Weekend*, August 16, 2015, https://www.pbs.org/newshour/politics/photos-presidential-candidates-iowa-state-fair.

53. Thomas E. Patterson, "Pre-Primary News Coverage of the 2016 Presidential Race: Trump's Rise, Sanders' Emergence, Clinton's Struggle," Harvard Kennedy School Working Paper No. 16-023. Retrieved from http://ssrn.com/abstract=2798258.

54. Jim Holt, *Why Does the World Exist? An Existential Detective Story* (New York: Liveright).

55. Elihu Katz and Tamar Liebes, "'No More Peace': How Disaster, Terror and War Have Upstaged Media Events," *International Journal of Communication* 1 (2007): 157–66.

56. Claussen, *Anti-intellectualism in American Media.*

57. Reporters and editors are more likely to recognize hostility toward intellect when they can place the phenomenon outside journalism, but even then there is little consensus on how to proceed. On July 17, 2015, *HuffPost* announced it would no longer cover candidate Trump as political news and would consign him to the entertainment section: Ryan Grim and Danny Shea, "A Note About Our Coverage of Donald Trump's 'Campaign,'" *HuffPost*, July 17, 2015. Retrieved from http://www.huffingtonpost.com. Media mesmerized by Trump were unlikely to coordinate a news boycott, although an editor for the *Daily Beast* called for a boycott of his businesses: Dylan Byers, "*Daily Beast* Editor Calls for Trump Boycott," *CNN Money*, November 23, 2015. Retrieved from http://money.cnn.com.

58. Shanto Iyengar, *Media Politics: A Citizen's Guide* (New York: W. W. Norton, 2019).

59. Richard Hofstadter, "The Paranoid Style in American Politics," *Harper's Magazine*, November 1964, 77.

60. Hofstadter, *Anti-intellectualism in American Life.*

61. Claussen, *Anti-intellectualism in American Media*; Rigney, "Three Kinds of Anti-intellectualism."

62. Nancy Bermeo, "On Democratic Backsliding," *Journal of Democracy* 27, no. 1 (2016): 5–19; David Waldner and Ellen Lust, "Unwelcome Change: Coming to Terms with Democratic Backsliding," *Annual Review of Political Science* 21 (2018): 93–113.

63. Ashley Muddiman and Natalie Jomini Stroud, "News Values, Cognitive Biases, and Partisan Incivility in Comment Sections," *Journal of Communication* 67 (2017): 586–609.

64. Ibid., 588.

65. Steven Levitsky and Daniel Ziblatt, *How Democracies Die* (New York: Crown, 2018). The "norm breaking" comment is quoted from "A Conversation with Steven Levitsky and Daniel Ziblatt," retrieved from http://riseupandread.com/books/how-democracies-die-tr/how-democracies-die-hc.

66. Jay G. Blumler and Dennis Kavanagh, "The Third Age of Political Communication," *Political Communication* 16, no. 3 (1999): 209–30.

67. Victor Turner, "Social Drama and Stories About Them," *Critical Inquiry* 7, no. 1 (1980): 141–68.

68. For example, Christopher Meyers, *Journalism Ethics: A Philosophical Approach* (Oxford: Oxford University Press, 2010); Patrick Lee Plaisance, *Media Ethics: Key Principles for Responsible Practice* (Thousand Oaks, CA: SAGE, 2014).

Chapter 2

1. Perry Parks, "Textbook News Values: Stable Concepts, Changing Voices," *Journalism & Mass Communication Quarterly* 96, no. 3 (2019): 784–810.

2. Benjamin Krämer, "Media Populism: A Conceptual Clarification and Some Theses on Its Effects," *Communication Theory* 24, no. 1 (2014): 42–60.

3. Risto Kunelius and Esa Reunanen, "Changing Power of Journalism: The Two Phases of Mediatization," *Communication Theory* 26 (2016): 374.

4. Henrik Bødker and Chris Anderson, "Digital Media and Populist Time—Trump, Twitter, and Realtimeness," paper presented at the Global Perspectives on Populism and the Media Preconference, International Communication Association, Budapest (May 2018).

5. William Mazzarella, "The Anthropology of Populism: Beyond the Liberal Settlement," *Annual Review of Anthropology* 48 (2019): 45–60.

6. Ernesto Laclau, *On Populist Reason* (London: Verso, 2005), 224.

7. Theodor Adorno, *The Stars Down to Earth and Other Essays on the Irrational in Culture*, ed. Stephen Cook (1994; London: Routledge, 2001).

8. Two prominent political scientists title a chapter on the rationalizing voter: "It Feels Like We're Thinking." Christopher H. Achen and Larry M. Bartels, *Democracy for Realists: Why Elections Do Not Produce Responsive Governance* (Princeton: Princeton University Press, 2016).

9. Steven Levitsky and Daniel Ziblatt, *How Democracies Die: What History Reveals about our Future* (New York: Penguin Random House, 2018); Pippa Norris, "Is Western Democracy Backsliding?" *Journal of Democracy* 28 (2017), http://www.journalofdemocracy.org/articles-files/foa-mounk-exchange/norris.

10. W. Lance Bennett and Steven Livingston, "The Disinformation Order: Disruptive Communication and the Decline of Democratic Institutions," *European Journal of Communication* 33, no. 2 (2018): 122–39.

11. Personal correspondence, September 26, 2019.

12. Jean Folkerts, "History of Journalism Education," *Journalism & Communication Monographs* 16, no. 4 (2014): 227.

13. Betty Houchin Winfield, *Journalism in 1908: Birth of a Profession* (Columbia: University of Missouri Press, 2008), 6.

14. James R. Boylan, *Pulitzer's School: Columbia University's School of Journalism, 1903–2003* (New York: Columbia University Press, 2003), 4.

15. Herbert J. Gans, *Deciding What's News: A Study of CBS Evening News, NBC Nightly News, Newsweek and Time* (New York: Vintage/Random House, 1979).

16. Michael Schudson, "The Concept of Politics in Contemporary U.S. Journalism," *Political Communication* 24, no. 2 (2007): 140. Earlier in this essay, Schudson notes, "If partisanship is contemptible to American journalists, personal political ambition is even worse. The satirical weekly, *The Onion*, got this just right in a mock headline: 'Critics Accuse Joe Biden of Running for President for Political Reasons,'" 134.

17. Betty H. Winfield, *Journalism 1908: Birth of a Profession* (Columbia: University of Missouri Press, 2008), 11.

18. Folkerts, "History of Journalism Education," 237.

19. Commission on Freedom of the Press, *A Free and Responsible Press* (Chicago: University of Chicago Press, 1947), 3.

20. Ibid., 21.

21. Stephen Bates, "The Commission and Its Lessons," *Communication Law and Policy* 3, no. 2 (1998): 146.

22. Chilton Rowlette Bush, *Newspaper Reporting of Public Affairs* (New York: Appleton-Century, 1940).

23. Jerilyn S. McIntyre, "Repositioning a Landmark: The Hutchins Commission and Freedom of the Press," *Critical Studies in Mass Communication* 4, no. 2 (1987): 130–60.

24. Walter Lippmann, *Public Opinion* (New York: Harcourt, Brace, 1922).

25. Quoted in Folkerts, "History of Journalism Education," 262.

26. Michael Schudson, "The 'Lippmann-Dewey Debate' and the Invention of Walter Lippmann as an Anti-Democrat 1986–1996," *International Journal of Communication* 2 (2008): 1031–42.

27. Usher observes that journalists are more likely to translate academic research if it is *not* in journalism studies. Nikki Usher, "Does Anyone Care about Journalism Research? (No, Not Really)," Poynter Institute, April 5, 2017, https://www.poynter.org/news/does-anyone-care-about-journalism-research-no-really.

28. Ian W. Macdonald, "Mindset and Skillset: The Persistence of Division in Media Education," *International Journal of Technology Management & Sustainable Development* 7, no. 2 (2008): 135–42.

29. Stephen D. Reese, "Journalism in Times of Creative Destruction: Revisiting the Academic/Professional Debate," lecture at the University of Colorado Boulder, March 10, 2011.

30. Howard Finberg, "Journalism Education Cannot Teach Its Way to the Future," Poynter Institute, June 15, 2012, https://www.poynter.org/news/journalism-education-cannot-teach-its-way-future.

31. Eric Newton, "Journalism Education Reform: How Far Should It Go?" Keynote address to Middle Tennessee State University, May 11, 2012, https://knightfoundation.org/speeches/journalism-education-reform-how-far-should-it-go.

32. Robert Hernandez, "Reboot Journalism School? Take Control of Your Education Instead," Nieman Journalism Lab, September 24, 2012, http://www.niemanlab.org/2012/09/robert-hernandez-reboot-journalism-school-take-control-of-your-education-instead/.

33. Scratching for academic status and representing a profession in crisis, journalism faculty often lack the presumption of expertise enjoyed in other disciplines. As I write in *Academe*, new-media entrepreneurs goad us to stay "agile" and "nimble." [Michael McDevitt, "When an Advisory Board Turns on Its School," *Academe* 100, no. 3 (2014): 21–25]. Be prepared, they tell us, to "blow up the curriculum" and embrace "creative destruction" in the rapid adoption of new technology. On my campus, an advisory board took the pyrotechnics a bit further in seeking to blow up an entire school. On April 23, 2010, the board presented the CU Boulder chancellor with a letter advocating closure of the School of Journalism and Mass Communication, the school it was established to support. With a stab to the dean's back, the board exploited a zeitgeist of technological disruption and populist suspicion of a plodding,

obstructionist faculty. The assault on the school illustrates the damaged standing of journalism in higher education and a resulting threat to academic freedom.

34. Richard Hofstadter, *Anti-intellectualism in American Life* (New York: Alfred A. Knopf, 1963): 74.

35. Ibid., 323.

36. Ibid., 22–23.

37. Ibid., 7.

38. Richard Hofstadter, "The Paranoid Style in American Politics," *Harper's Magazine*, November 1964, 81.

39. Hofstadter, *Anti-intellectualism in American Life*, 7.

40. Daniel Rigney, "Three Kinds of Anti-intellectualism: Rethinking Hofstadter," *Sociological Inquiry* 61 (1991): 343–51.

41. Achen and Bartels, *Democracy for Realists*.

42. Fabiana Zollo, Petra Kralj Novak, Michela Del Vicario, Alessandro Bessi, Igor Mozetič, Antonio Scala, Guido Caldarelli, and Walter Quattrociocchi, "Emotional Dynamics in the Age of Misinformation," *PLoS ONE* 10, no. 9 (2015), https://doi.org/10.1371/journal.pone.0138740.

43. Rigney, "Three Kinds of Anti-intellectualism," 441.

44. Lawrence Goodwyn, *Democratic Promise: The Populist Movement in America* (New York: Oxford University Press, 1976); Laura Grattan, *Populism's Power: Radical Grassroots Democracy in America* (Oxford: Oxford University Press, 2016).

45. Catherine Liu, *American Idyll: Academic Antielitism as Cultural Critique* (Iowa City: University of Iowa Press, 2011).

46. James Hay, "'Popular Culture' in a Critique of the New Political Reason," *Cultural Studies* 25, nos. 4–5 (2011): 659–84.

47. Rigney, "Three Kinds of Anti-intellectualism," 444.

48. Ibid., 448.

49. Anna Feigenbaum, "Resistance Matters: Tents, Tear Gas and the 'Other Media' of Occupy," *Communication and Critical/Cultural Studies* 11, no. 1 (2014): 15–24; Hallin, *The Uncensored War*; Edward S. Herman and Noam Chomsky, *Manufacturing Consent: The Political Economy of the Mass Media* (New York: Pantheon Books, 1988); Robert M. McChesney, *Rich Media, Poor Democracy: Communication Politics in Dubious Times* (New York: New Press, 2015); Douglas M. McLeod and James K. Hertog, "The Manufacture of 'Public Opinion' by Reporters: Informal Cues for Public Perceptions of Protest Groups," *Discourse and Society* 3, no. 3 (1992): 259–75.

50. Steven Connor, *Postmodernist Culture* (Cambridge, UK: Blackwell, 1989); Liu, *American Idyll*; Snyder, *On Tyranny*.

51. Rigney, "Three Kinds of Anti-intellectualism," 448.

52. Dane S. Claussen, *Anti-intellectualism in American Media: Magazines and Higher Education* (New York: Peter Lang, 2004).

53. Jeff Rutenbeck, "The Triumph of News Over Ideas in American Journalism: The Trade Journal Debate, 1872–1915," *Journal of Communication Inquiry* 18 (1994): 63.

54. Ellen Schrecker, "McCarthyism: Political Repression and the Fear of Communism," *Social Research* 71, no. 4 (2004): 1041–86. Unmasking is manifest, for instance, in the journalistic trope of belittling professors. Nuance is dismissed as "dodging questions."

Dana L. Cloud, "Foiling the Intellectuals: Gender, Identity, Framing, and the Rhetoric of the Kill in Conservative Hate Mail," *Communication, Culture & Critique* 2, no. 4 (2009): 465.

55. Gans, *Deciding What's News*, 68.

56. Ibid., 204.

57. Cas Mudde, "The Populist Zeitgeist," *Government and Opposition* 39, no. 4 (2004): 541–63.

58. Senja Post, "Scientific Objectivity in Journalism? How Journalists and Academics Define Objectivity, Assess Its Attainability, and Rate Its Desirability," *Journalism* 16, no. 6 (2015): 730–49.

59. Michael Schudson, *Discovering the News: A Social History of American Newspapers* (New York: Basic Books, 1978).

60. J. Michael Hogan, "Persuasion in the Rhetorical Tradition," in *The Sage Handbook of Persuasion: Developments in History and Practice*, ed. James Price Dillard and Lijiang Shen (Thousand Oaks, CA: Sage, 2013), 10.

61. For example, see Bødker and Anderson, "Digital Media and Populist Time"; Bernat Ivancsics, "Uncomfortable Symbiosis: Attention Capture, Normalization, and Criticism in the News Coverage of Fringe Social Groups and Populist Movements," paper presented at the Global Perspectives on Populism and the Media Preconference, International Communication Association, Budapest (May 2018); Krämer, "Media Populism."

62. University experts, I should add, are attractive to the quality press and viewed as useful by television news producers. As Shoemaker and Reese observe, "Although few of these academics provoke or challenge, seeing them gives the impression that something important has been said." Pamela J. Shoemaker and Stephen D. Reese, *Mediating the Message in the 21st Century: A Media Sociology Perspective* (New York: Routledge, 2014), 189–90]. The academic-media nexus as a public good remains mostly neglected and undeveloped, largely due to the incompatibility of scientific and journalistic objectivity (Chapter 4).

63. For examples of the political economy approach to news media, see Daniel C. Hallin, *The Uncensored War* (New York: Oxford University Press, 1986); Herman and Chomsky, *Manufacturing Consent*; Robert E. Gutsche, Jr., *Media Control: News as an Institution of Power and Social Control* (New York: Bloomsbury, 2017); Ian Taylor, "Local Press Reporting of Opposition to the 2003 Iraq War in the UK and the Case for Reconceptualizing the Notions of Legitimacy and Deviance," *Journal of War & Culture Studies* 7, no. 1 (2014): 36–53.

64. Michael McCluskey and Young Mie Kim, "Moderatism or Polarization? Representation of Advocacy Group's Ideology in Newspapers," *Journalism & Mass Communication Quarterly* 89, no. 4 (2012): 565–84.

65. Michael W. Wagner and Mike Gruszczynski, "Who Gets Covered? Ideological Extremity and News Coverage of Members of the U.S. Congress, 1993 to 2013," *Journalism & Mass Communication Quarterly* 95, no. 3 (2018): 670–90.

66. Daniel C. Hallin, *We Keep America on Top of the World: Television Journalism and the Public Sphere* (London: Routledge, 1994).

67. Hofstadter, *Anti-intellectualism in American Life*, 45.

68. Hofstadter, "The Paranoid Style in American Politics," 85.

69. Mudde, "The Populist Zeitgeist."

70. A citizen is unlikely to classify her political identity as "instrumentalist" or "hedonist," but over time the life priorities given over to these orientations accrue sensibilities easily offended by intellect, the purpose of which is, after all, to unsettle the unreflective mind. The hedonist and instrumentalist realize their political edge when goaded by the punitive populist.

71. Liu, *American Idyll.*

72. Adorno, *The Stars Down to Earth and Other Essays on the Irrational in Culture.* Liu notes the newspaper advised that the feature "should be read for entertainment only," *American Idyll,* 104. In retrospect, we might read the caution as recognition, at some level of awareness, that the press was letting down its guard as a custodian of reason.

73. Liu, *American Idyll,* 107.

74. Ibid., 121.

75. Ibid., 1.

76. Andrew Ross, *No Respect: Intellectuals and Popular Culture* (New York: Routledge, 1989). I recognize that anarchic elements can confront the managed consensus of technocratic governance, but the purpose of conflict in a public sphere is ultimately to test whether norms and institutions can survive rational scrutiny.

77. Douglass Cater, *The Fourth Branch of Government* (Boston: Houghton Mifflin, 1959).

78. Timothy E. Cook, *Governing with the News: The News Media as a Political Institution* (Chicago: University of Chicago Press, 1998).

79. Ibid., 163.

80. Martin Wettstein, Frank Esser, Florin Büchel, Christian Schemer, Dominique S. Wirz, Anne Schulz, Nicole Ernst, Sven Engesser, Philipp Müller, and Werner Wirth, "What Drives Populist Styles? Analyzing Immigration and Labor Market News in 11 Countries," *Journalism & Mass Communication Quarterly* 96, no. 2 (2019): 516–36.

81. Benedict Anderson, *Imagined Communities: Reflections on the Rise and Spread of Nationalism* (London: Verso, 1987).

82. Eden Litt, "Knock, Knock. Who's There? The Imagined Audience," *Journal of Broadcasting & Electronic Media* 56, no. 3 (2012): 330–45.

83. Rogers Brubaker, "Populism and Nationalism," *Nations and Nationalism* (2019): 10, https://onlinelibrary.wiley.com/doi/full/10.1111/nana.12522.

84. David Lebow, "Trumpism and the Dialectic of Neoliberal Reason," *Perspectives on Politics* 17, no. 2 (2019): 380–98.

85. Ibid., 15.

86. William Mazzarella, "The Anthropology of Populism: Beyond the Liberal Settlement," *Annual Review of Anthropology* 48 (2019): 45–60.

87. All other actors in media politics rely on public attention as a scarce resource, ensuring substantial influence of news media even in an age of digital disruption. Journalists certify authority by "deciding who should speak on what subjects under what circumstances," Cook, *Governing with the News,* 6. That said, news production is largely fueled by subsidies from other political institutions.

88. Lebow, "Trumpism and the Dialectic of Neoliberal Reason"; Levitsky and Ziblatt, *How Democracies* Die; Snyder, *On Tyranny*.

89. Bødker and Anderson, "Digital Media and Populist Time."

90. Krämer, "Media Populism"; Ov Cristian Norocel and Gabriella Szabó, "Mapping the Discursive Opportunities for Radical-Right Populist Politics across Eastern Europe," *Problems of Post-Communism* 66, no. 1 (2019): 1–7.

91. Bødker and Anderson, "Digital Media and Populist Time."

92. Hofstadter, *Anti-intellectualism in American Life*, 407–8.

93. Morton White, "Reflections on Anti-Intellectualism," *Daedalus* 91, no. 3 (1962): 457–68.

94. Tom Lutz, "Antielitism Left and Right: An Interview with Catherine Liu," *Los Angeles Times Review of Books*, January 8, 2012, https://lareviewofbooks.org/article/antielitism-left-and-right-an-interview-with-catherine-liu/.

95. Robert Manoff, "Democratic Journalism and the Republican Subject: Or, the Real American Dream and What Journalism Educators Can Do About It," *Zoned for Debate*, September 16, 2002, https://journalism.nyu.edu/publishing/archives/debate/forum.1.essay.manoff.html.

96. Barbara Ehrenreich, *Nickle and Dimed: On (Not) Getting by in America* (New York: Henry Holt, 2001).

97. Jay Rosen, *What Are Journalists For?* (New Haven, CT: Yale University Press, 1999), 66.

98. Sandra L. Borden, "Communitarian Journalism and Flag Displays After September 11: An Ethical Critique," *Journal of Communication Inquiry* 29, no. 1 (2005): 30–46.

99. David A. Craig, "Communitarian Journalism(s): Clearing Conceptual Landscapes," *Journal of Mass Media Ethics* 11, no. 2 (1996): 107–18; Michael McDevitt, "In Defense of Autonomy: A Critique of the Public Journalism Critique," *Journal of Communication* 53, no. 1 (2003): 155–64.

100. David S. Allen, "The Trouble with Transparency: The Challenge of Doing Journalism Ethics in a Surveillance Society," *Journalism Studies* 9, no. 3 (2008): 323–40; Kristy Hess, "Shifting Foundations: Journalism and the Power of the 'Common Good,'" *Journalism* 18, no. 7 (2017): 801–16.

101. Patrick Ferrucci and Jacob Nelson, "The Dewey Problem: Public Journalism, Engagement and More than Two Decades of Denigrating Discourse," paper presented at the annual conference of the Association for Education in Journalism and Mass Communication, Toronto, August 7–10, 2019.

102. Achen and Bartels, *Democracy for Realists*.

103. Michael Schudson, *Why Democracies Need an Unlovable Press* (Cambridge: Polity, 2011),

104. Silvio Waisbord, "Why Populism Is Troubling for Democratic Communication," Communication Culture & Critique 11 (2018): 21–34.

105. Liu, *American Idyll*.

106. Jill A. Edy and Shawn M. Snidow, "Making News Necessary: How Journalism Resists Alternative Media's Challenge," *Journal of Communication* 61, no. 5 (2011): 829.

Chapter 3

1. James W. Carey, "The Press and Public Discourse," *The Center Magazine* 20, no. 2 (1987): 4–32.
2. Dane S. Claussen, *Anti-intellectualism in American Media: Magazines and Higher Education* (New York: Peter Lang, 2004); Benjamin Krämer, "Media Populism: A Conceptual Clarification and Some Theses on its Effects," *Communication Theory* 24, no. 1 (2014): 42–60; Daniel Rigney, "Three Kinds of Anti-intellectualism: Rethinking Hofstadter," *Sociological Inquiry* 61 (1991): 434–51.
3. Gianpietro Mazzoleni, Julianne Stewart, and Bruce Horsfield, *The Media and Neo-Populism: A Contemporary Analysis* (Westport, CT: Praeger, 2003).
4. Elena Block and Ralph Negrine, "The Populist Communication Style: Toward a Critical Framework," *International Journal of Communication* 11 (2017): 179.
5. Thomas E. Patterson, "Pre-Primary News Coverage of the 2016 Presidential Race: Trump's Rise, Sanders' Emergence, Clinton's Struggle," Harvard Kennedy School Working Paper No. 16-023, June 20, 2016, https://ssrn.com/abstract=2798258.
6. While these latter principles certainly influence how correspondents evaluate a candidate on any given day, the concern here is more basic: the amount of attention allocated in the news, i.e., space controlled by journalists.
7. Patterson, "Pre-Primary News Coverage of the 2016 Presidential Race," 5.
8. Cas Mudde, "The Populist Zeitgeist," *Government and Opposition* 39, no. 4 (2004): 543.
9. Stephanie Craft, "Distinguishing Features: Reconsidering the Link Between Journalism's Professional Status and Ethics," *Journalism & Communication Monographs* 19, no. 4 (2017): 260–301; Risto Kunelius and Esa Reunanen, "Changing Power of Journalism: The Two Phases of Mediatization," *Communication Theory* 26 (2016): 369–88.
10. Matthew Cecil, "Bad Apples: Paradigm Overhaul and the CNN/Time 'Tailwind' Story," *Journal of Communication Inquiry* 26, no. 1 (2002): 46–58.
11. Elizabeth Blanks Hindman, "Jayson Blair, *The New York Times*, and Paradigm Repair," *Journal of Communication* 55, no. 2 (2006): 225–41.
12. Russell Frank, "'These Crowded Circumstances': When Pack Journalists Bash Pack Journalism," *Journalism* 4, no. 4 (2003): 441–58.
13. Laura Ahva, "Public Journalism and Professional Reflexivity," *Journalism* 14, no. 6 (2012): 791.
14. Claussen, *Anti-intellectualism in American Media*, 23.
15. Frank, "'These Crowded Circumstances.'"
16. Rigney, "Three Kinds of Anti-intellectualism."
17. Colleen J. Shogan, "Anti-intellectualism in the Modern Presidency: A Republican Populism," *Perspectives on Politics* 5, no. 2 (2007): 295–303.
18. Todd Gitlin, "The Renaissance of Anti-intellectualism," *Chronicle of Higher Education*, December 8, 2000.
19. Frank, "'These Crowded Circumstances.'"
20. Michael McDevitt and Patrick Ferrucci, "Populism, Journalism, and the Limits of Reflexivity: The Case of Donald J. Trump," *Journalism Studies* 19, no. 4: (2018): 512–26.

21. Matt Carlson, "Metajournalistic Discourse and the Meanings of Journalism: Definitional Control, Boundary Work, and Legitimation," *Communication Theory* 26, no. 4 (2016): 350.

22. Ida Schultz, "The Journalistic Gut Feeling: Journalistic Doxa, News Habitus and Orthodox News Values," *Journalism Practice* 1, no. 2 (2007): 190–207.

23. Darren G. Lilleker, Daniel Jackson, Einar Thorsen, and Anastasia Veneti, *US Election Analysis 2016: Media, Voters, and the Campaign: Early Reflections from Leading Academics* (Bournemouth, UK: Bournemouth University Press, 2016).

24. Lilleker et al. explain that the purpose of the publication is "is to capture immediate thoughts, reflections and early research of leading academics in media and politics in the United States and around the globe; and in this way contribute to public understanding of the contest whilst it is fresh in the memory and help shape the path ahead," 8.

25. Editors and contributors represent the following disciplines: advertising, American studies, communication, cyber security, English, ethnic and gender studies, film studies, geography, Germanic studies, government, history, information studies, journalism studies, literary studies, marketing, media studies, philological studies, political science, psychology, public policy, statistics, and women's studies. Most of the contributors work at universities in Britain and the United States. Here is the breakdown: US (45), Britain (22), Australia (4), Belgium (3), Canada (3), Russia (2), Greece (2), Croatia (2), Czech Republic (1), Italy (1), Ireland (1), China (1), Slovenia (1), and Norway (1).

26. We removed duplicate articles from wire services and culled articles not about the election. We then read through the remaining content and removed articles that did not include any reflections about the election. This left us with 212 articles.

27. Tara Trower Doolittle, "During Farewell, a Lament for Public Discourse's Sad Spiral," *Austin American-Statesman*, November 13, 2016.

28. Maggie Haberman, "Alex Jones, Host and Conspiracy Theorist, Says Donald Trump Called to Thank Him," *The New York Times*, November 16, 2016.

29. John Herrman, "What We've Learned about the Media Industry During This Election," *The New York Times Magazine*, November 8, 2016.

30. Dana Milbank, "Trump's Campaign Made It Safe to Hate Again. Will He Turn that Around?" *The Washington Post*, November 15, 2016.

31. Terrence McCoy, "For the 'New Yellow Journalists,' Opportunity Comes in Clicks and Bucks," *The Washington Post*, November 20, 2016.

32. Jim Rutenberg, "Mark Zuckerberg and Facebook Must Defend the Truth," *The New York Times*, November 21, 2016.

33. Zeynep Tufekci, "Mark Zuckerberg Is in Denial," *The New York Times*, November 15, 2016.

34. Elizabeth Dwoskin, Caitlin Dewey, and Craig Timberg, "Why Facebook and Google Are Struggling to Purge Fake News," *The Washington Post*, November 15, 2016.

35. Liz Spayd, "One Thing Voters Agree On: Better Campaign Coverage Was Needed," *The New York Times*, November 19, 2016.

36. Jim Rutenberg, "A 'Dewey Defeats Truman" Lesson for the Digital Age," *The New York Times*, November 9, 2016.

37. Michael Wolff, "Media Has Itself to Blame for Such an Epic Election Fail; Botched Coverage Similar to that of '07 Financial Meltdown," *USA Today*, November 15, 2016.

38. For example, Benjamin Toff, "Polls May Be Making Voters Worse at Predicting Elections," *The Washington Post*, November 18, 2016.

39. Jack Kelly, "The Press Lost the Election Too: Mainstream Journalists Are Totally Out of Touch," *The Pittsburgh Post-Gazette*, November 19, 2016.

40. Chris Cillizza, "How Hillary Clinton Won," *The Washington Post*, November 10, 2016.

41. Brian McNair, "After Objectivity," in Lilleker et al., *US Election Analysis 2016*, 12.

42. Svenja Ottovordemgentschenfelde, "Tweeting the Election: Political Journalists and a New Privilege of Bias," *US Election Analysis* 2016, 77.

43. Gianpietro Mazzoleni, "Did the Media Create Trump?," *US Election Analysis*, 2016, 21.

44. Alfred Hermida, "Trump and the Triumph of Affective News When Everyone Is the Media," *US Election Analysis*, 2016, 76.

45. Alex Marland, "Trying to Avoid Trump: A Canadian Experience," *US Election Analysis*, 2016, 71.

46. Peter Van Aelst, "The 2016 Election and the Success of Fact Free Politics," *US Election Analysis*, 2016, 16.

47. W. Lance Bennett, "Democracy Trumped," *US Election Analysis*, 2016, 98.

48. Eric P. Bucy, "Image Bites, Voter Enthusiam, and the 2016 Presidential Election," *US Election Analysis*, 2016, 32.

49. Seth Lewis and Matt Carlson, "The Dissolution of News: Selective Exposure, Filter Bubbles, and the Boundaries of Journalism," *US Election Analysis*, 2016, 78.

50. Denis Muller, "Trump, Truth and the Media," *US Election Analysis*, 2016, 17.

51. Lewis and Carlson, "The Dissolution of News."

52. Robert McChesney, "Reflections on the 2016 US Election," *US Election Analysis*, 2016, 104.

53. Hermida, "Trump and the Triumph of Affective News When Everyone Is the Media," 76.

54. Geoffrey Baym, "Trump and Mediatization," *US Election Analysis*, 2016, 15.

55. Jenna Johnson, "Donald Trump Says Tough Gun Control Laws in Paris Contributed to Tragedy," *The Washington Post*, November 14, 2015.

56. Patterson, "Pre-Primary News Coverage of the 2016 Presidential Race."

57. Krämer, "Media Populism."

58. Brian Klocke and Michael McDevitt, "Foreclosing Deliberation: Journalists' Lowering of Expectations in the Marketplace of Ideas," *Journalism Studies* 14, no. 6 (2013): 891–906.

59. I would like to thank an anonymous reviewer for this insight.

60. Ian Taylor, "Local Press Reporting of Opposition to the 2003 Iraq War in the UK and the Case for Reconceptualizing the Notions of Legitimacy and Deviance," *Journal of War & Culture Studies* 7, no. 1 (2014): 36–53

61. Gaye Tuchman, "Objectivity as Strategic Ritual: An Examination of Newsmen's Notions of Objectivity," *American Journal of Sociology* 77, no. 4 (1972): 666–79.

62. Taylor, "Local Press Reporting of Opposition to the 2003 Iraq War."

63. Commission on Freedom of the Press, *A Free and Responsible Press* (Chicago: University of Chicago Press, 1947).

64. Krämer, "Media Populism"; Silvio Waisbord, "Democracy, Journalism, and Latin American Populism," *Journalism* 14, no. 4 (2012): 504–21; Martin Wettstein, Frank Esser, Florin Büchel, Christian Schemer, Dominique S. Wirz, Anne Schulz, Nicole Ernst, Sven Engesser, Philipp Müller, and Werner Wirth, "What Drives Populist Styles? Analyzing Immigration and Labor Market News in 11 Countries," *Journalism & Mass Communication Quarterly* 96, no. 2 (2019): 516–36.

65. Wettstein et al., "What Drives Populist Styles?"

66. Elihu Katz and Tamar Liebes, "'No More Peace': How Disaster, Terror and War Have Upstaged Media Events," *International Journal of Communication* 1 (2007): 157–66.

67. Perry Parks, "The Discipline-Autonomy Paradox: How U.S. Journalism Textbooks Construct Reporters' Freedom Just to Tear It Down," *Journalism Studies* (2018): 1, https://www.tandfonline.com/doi/full/10.1080/1461670X.2018.1541755.

68. Michel Foucault, *Discipline and Punish: The Birth of the Prison* (New York: Vintage, 1975, 1995).

69. Simon Cottle, "Mediatized Ritual: Beyond Manufacturing Consent," *Media, Culture & Society* 28, no. 3 (2006): 411–32.

70. Schultz, "The Journalistic Gut Feeling."

71. Parks, "The Discipline-Autonomy Paradox."

Chapter 4

1. Daniel C. Hallin, *The Uncensored War* (New York: Oxford University Press, 1986); Gaye Tuchman, "Objectivity as Strategic Ritual: An Examination of Newsmen's Notions of Objectivity," *American Journal of Sociology* 77, no. 4 (1972): 666–79.

2. Edward Shils, "The Intellectuals and the Powers: Some Perspectives for Comparative Analysis," in *On Intellectuals: Theoretical Studies, Case Studies*, ed. Philip Rieff (Garden City, NY: Doubleday, 1969), 30.

3. Ellen Schrecker, "McCarthyism: Political Repression and the Fear of Communism," *Social Research* 71, no. 4 (2004): 1041–86.

4. Ian Taylor, "Local Press Reporting of Opposition to the 2003 Iraq War in the UK and the Case for Reconceptualizing the Notions of Legitimacy and Deviance," *Journal of War & Culture Studies* 7, no. 1 (2014): 36–53.

5. David Rowe, "Working Knowledge Encounters: Academics, Journalists and the Conditions of Cultural Labour," *Social Semiotics* 15, no. 3 (2005): 269–88.

6. Shaeda Isani, "Journalism FASP & Fictional Representations of Journalists in Popular Contemporary Literature," *ILCEA* 11 (2009): 4, http://ilcea.revues.org.

7. Tuchman, "Objectivity as Strategic Ritual."

8. Pierre Bourdieu, *On Television and Journalism* (London: Pluto, 1998).

9. Georgy Levit, "The Biosphere and the Noosphere Theories of V. I. Vernadsky and P. Teilhard de Chardin: A Methodological Essay," *International Archives on the History of Science/Archives Internationales D'Histoire des Sciences* 50, no. 144 (2000): 160–76.

10. Ruud Koopmans, "Movements and Media: Selection Processes and Evolutionary Dynamics in the Public Sphere," *Theory and Society* 33 (2004): 372.

11. Kevin Coe, David Domke, Erica S. Graham, Sue Lockett John, and Victor W. Pickard, "No Shades of Gray: The Binary Discourse of George W. Bush and an Echoing Press," *Journal of Communication* 54, no. 2 (2004): 234–52.

12. Max McCombs, "A Look at Agenda-Setting: Past, Present and Future," *Journalism Studies* 6, no. 4 (2005): 549.

13. In an era of media abundance, public attention remains a limited resource. Issue agendas are themselves subject to market pressure, producing winners and losers in the battle for attention.

14. Jay G. Blumler and Dennis Kavanagh, "The Third Age of Political Communication: Influences and Features," *Political Communication* 16, no. 3 (1999): 209–30; Michael Crozier, "Recursive Governance: Contemporary Political Communication and Public Policy," *Political Communication* 24, no. 1 (2007): 1–18.

15. Seth Lewis and Stephen Reese, "What Is the War on Terror? Framing through the Eyes of Journalists," *Journalism & Mass Communication Quarterly* 86, no. 1 (2009): 85–102.

16. Spiro Kiousis, Jesper Strömbäck, and Michael McDevitt, "Influence of Issue Decision Salience on Vote Choice: Linking Agenda Setting, Priming, and Issue Ownership," *International Journal of Communication* 9 (2015): 3347–68.

17. Robert M. Entman, "Cascading Activation: Contesting the White House Frame After 9/11," *Political Communication* 20 (2003): 417.

18. Henry A. Giroux, "Cultural Studies, Public Pedagogy, and the Responsibility of Intellectuals," *Communication and Critical/Cultural Studies* 1, no. 1 (2004): 59–79; Evan Kindley, "Growing Up in Public: Academia, Journalism, and the New Public Intellectual," *PMLA* 13, no. 2 (2015): 467–73; Michael McDevitt, Marco Briziarelli, and Brian Klocke, "Social Drama in the Academic-Media Nexus: Journalism's Strategic Response to Deviant Ideas," *Journalism* 14, no. 1 (2013): 111–28.

19. Antonio Gramsci, "The Intellectual," in *Selections from Prison Notebooks*, ed. Quintin Hoare and Geoffrey Nowell Smith (New York: International, 1971).

20. Bourdieu, *On Television and Journalism*.

21. Thomas Hanitzsch, "Deconstructing Journalism Culture: Toward a Universal Theory," *Communication Theory* 17, no. 4 (2007): 367–85.

22. Michael Brüggemann, "Between Frame Setting and Frame Sending: How Journalists Contribute to News Frames," *Communication Theory* 24, no. 1 (2014): 61–82.

23. Shanto Iyengar, *Media Politics: A Citizen's Guide* (New York: London, 2019).

24. Coe et al., "No Shades of Gray."

25. Jesper Strömbäck and Daniela V. Dimitrova, "Mediatization and Media Interventionism: A Comparative Analysis of Sweden and the United States," *The International Journal of Press/Politics* 16, no. 1 (2011): 30–49.

26. Rodney Benson, "News Media as a 'Journalistic Field': What Bourdieu Adds to New Institutionalism, and Vice Versa," *Political Communication* 23, no. 2 (2006): 187–202; Bourdieu, *On Television and Journalism*; David M. Ryfe, *Journalism and the Public* (Cambridge: Polity, 2017).

27. Jesper Strömbäck, "Four Phases of Mediatization: An Analysis of the Mediatization of Politics," *The International Journal of Press/Politics* 13, no. 3 (2008): 228–46.

28. Michael Welch, Melissa Fenwick, and Meredith Roberts, "State Managers, Intellectuals, and the Media: A Content Analysis of Ideology in Experts' Quotes in Feature Newspaper Articles on Crime," *Justice Quarterly* 15, no. 2 (1998): 219–41.

29. Stephen D. Reese, August Grant, and Lucig H. Danielian, "The Structure of News Sources on Television: A Network Analysis of 'CBS News,' 'MacNeil/Lehrer,' and 'This Week with David Brinkley,'" *Journal of Communication* 44, no. 2 (1994): 84–107.

30. Jean-François Lyotard, *The Postmodern Condition: A Report on Knowledge* (Minneapolis: University of Minnesota Press, 1979, 1984), 26.

31. Ibid., 27–28.

32. Clyde W. Barrow, *Universities and the Capitalist State: Corporate Liberalism and the Reconstruction of American Higher Education, 1894–1928* (Madison: University of Wisconsin Press, 1990), 10.

33. Talcott Parsons, "The Intellectuals: A Social Role Category," in *On Intellectuals: Theoretical Studies, Case Studies*, ed. Philip Rieff (Garden City, NY: Doubleday, 1969), 17.

34. Amitai Etzioni and Alyssa Bowditch, *Public Intellectuals: An Endangered Species?* (Lanham, MD: Rowman and Littlefield, 2006).

35. Steven Best and Douglas Kellner, *Postmodern Theory: Critical Interrogations* (New York: Guilford, 1991).

36. Pierre Bourdieu, *The Intellectual Field: A World Apart in Other Words: Essays Towards a Reflexive Sociology* (Stanford, CA: Stanford University Press, 1985).

37. Lewis A. Coser, *Men of Ideas: A Sociologist's View* (New York: Free Press, 1997).

38. Thomas Molnar, *The Decline of the Intellectual: History of Philosophy and Ethics* (New Rochelle, NY: Arlington House, 1961).

39. Edward W. Said, *Culture and Imperialism* (London: Chatto and Windus, 1993).

40. Theodor W. Adorno, *Minima Moralia: Reflections on a Damaged Life* (London: New Left Books, 1974); Noam Chomsky, "Paths Taken, Tasks Ahead," *Profession* (2000): 32–39; Henry A. Giroux, "Academic Freedom Under Fire: The Case for Critical Pedagogy," *College Literature* 33, no. 4 (2006): 1–42; C. Wright Mills, *Mass Society and Liberal Education* (Chicago: Center for the Study of Liberal Education for Adults, 1954).

41. Catherine Liu, *American Idyll: Academic Antielitism as Cultural Critique* (Iowa City: University of Iowa Press, 2011), 223.

42. Allan Bloom, *The Closing of the American Mind: How Higher Education Has Failed Democracy and Impoverished the Souls of Today's Students* (New York: Simon & Schuster, 1987).

43. Jules Henry, *Culture Against Man* (New York: Alfred A. Knopf, 1963).

44. David Isaacson, "Anti-intellectualism in American Libraries," *Library Journal* 107 (1982): 227–32.

45. Dane S. Claussen, *Anti-intellectualism in American Media: Magazines and Higher Education* (New York: Peter Lang, 2004).

46. Henry A. Giroux, *Dangerous Thinking in the New Authoritarianism* (New York: Routledge, 2015), 21.

47. Gerald A. Hauser, "Observations on Being a Public Intellectual in a Post-Westphalian Public Sphere," presented at the National Communication Association Workshop on Public Intellectuals, Las Vegas, NV, 2015, 1.

48. Ibid., 2.

49. C. Wright Mills, *Power, Politics, and the People* (New York: Oxford University Press, 1963), 299.

50. Thomas Poell and Erik Borra, "Twitter, YouTube, and Flickr as Platforms of Alternative Journalism: The Social Media Account of the 2010 Toronto G20 Protests," *Journalism* 13, no. 6 (2012): 695–713.

51. Kevin M. DeLuca, Sean Lawson, and Ye Sun, "Occupy Wall Street on the Public Screens of Social Media: The Many Framings of the Birth of a Protest Movement," *Communication, Culture & Critique* 5, no. 4 (2012): 483–509.

52. Jeffrey C. Alexander, *The Civil Sphere* (Oxford: Oxford University Press, 2006).

53. Mills, *Power, Politics, and the People.*

54. Hannah Arendt, *Eichmann in Jerusalem: A Report on the Banality of Evil* (New York: Penguin Books, 1963).

55. Said, *Culture and Imperialism.*

56. Joseph G. Peschek, "C. Wright Mills and American Democracy," *New Political Science* 30, no. 3 (2008): 403.

57. Sid Bedingfield, "Culture, Power, and Political Change: Skeptics and the Civil Sphere," *Journal of Communication Inquiry* 39, no. 2 (2015): 158–69.

58. Bruce Robbins, *Secular Vocations: Intellectuals, Professionalism and Culture* (London: Verso, 1993).

59. Liu, *American Idyll*, 4–5.

60. Ibid., 220.

61. Stewart M. Hoover and Lynn S. Clark, "Event and Publicity as Social Drama: A Case Study of the RE-Imaging Conference 1995," *Review of Religious Studies* 39, no. 2 (1997): 155.

62. Victor Turner, "Social Drama and Stories about Them," *Critical Inquiry* 7, no. 1 (1980): 141–68.

63. David Horowitz, *The Professors: The 101 Most Dangerous Academics in America* (Washington, DC: Regnery, 2006).

64. Aberjhani, "Guerilla Decontextualization and the 2012 Presidential Election Campaign," accessed November 24, 2018, http://1guerrilla-decontextualization.weebly.com.

65. Walter Lippmann, *Public Opinion* (New York: Harcourt, Brace, 1922).

66. Christopher Mele, "Professor Watchlist Is Seen as Threat to Academic Freedom," *The New York Times*, November 28, 2016.

67. Turning Point USA, accessed November 14, 2018, http://www.professorwatchlist.org.

68. John Fritch, Catherine Helen Palczewski, Jennifer Farrell, and Eric Short, "Disingenuous Controversy: Responses to Ward Churchill's 9/11 Essay," *Argumentation and Advocacy* 42, no. 4 (2006): 201.

69. George F. Will, "After the Paris Attacks, We Should Turn to Chris Christie," *Business Insider*, November 19, 2015.

70. Igor Volsky, "Arizona Bill to Force Students to Take Loyalty Oath," AlterNet, January 26, 2013.

71. Richard Hofstadter, *Anti-intellectualism in American Life* (New York: Alfred A. Knopf, 1963), 35.

72. David Rowe and Kylie Brass, "The Uses of Academic Knowledge: The University in the Media," *Media, Culture & Society* 30, no. 5 (2008): 677. Rowe, a cultural studies scholar at Western Sydney University, was the first to recognize the significance of the academic-media nexus for the fate of intellect. Exchanges between reporters and professors highlight a struggle over which ideas already salient in scholarly discourse can circulate more broadly in the public sphere. Idea brokering of some sort is inevitable. Journalism typically does not seek intellectual engagement but packaged expertise. In the first study, Rowe interviewed academics and journalists in Australia, Britain, and the United States. The editor of a British broadsheet recalled his strategy for scholars when working as a reporter. He looked for somebody "who was going to be instantly on the end of the phone, who was going to give a pithy quote straight away on an issue." Rowe, "Working Knowledge Encounters," 275. See also Kylie Brass and David Rowe, "Knowledge Limited: Public Communication, Risk, and University Media Policy," *Continuum: Journal of Media & Cultural Studies* 23, no. 1 (2009): 53–76; David Rowe and Kylie Brass, "'We Take Academic Freedom Seriously': How University Media Offices Manage Academic Public Communication," *International Journal of Media and Cultural Politics* 7, no. 1 (2011): 3–20; David Rowe, "The University as a 'Giant Newsroom': The Uses of Academic Knowledge Revisited," *Culture Unbound* 9, no. 3 (2017): 228–39.

73. Matthew S. McGlone, "Contextomy: The Art of Quoting Out of Context," *Media, Culture & Society* 2, no. 4 (2005): 511–22.

74. Hoover and Clark, "Event and Publicity as Social Drama."

75. Risto Kunelius, "Journalism as Robust Secular Drama: Reading the Future by Amplifying the Present," *Journalism* 10, no. 3 (2009): 343–46.

76. Bourdieu, *On Television and Journalism.*

77. Kunelius, "Journalism as Robust Secular Drama," 345.

78. Rowe, "Working Knowledge Encounters," 270.

79. Ibid., 275.

80. Michael Roberts, "4/20 at CU-Boulder: Fish Fertilizer Used on Norlin Quad a Favorite of Pot Growers," *Westword*, April 20, 2012.

81. "Nation's 10-Year-Old Boys: 'If You See Someone Raping Us, Please Call the Police,'" *The Onion*, December 1, 2011.

82. http://www.museumofpoliticalcorruption.org/about.html.

83. Chris Churchill, "Albany Needs Political Corruption Museum," *Times Union*, August 1, 2013.

84. See, for example, Bloom, *The Closing of the American Mind*; Giroux, "Academic Freedom Under Fire"; Molnar, *The Decline of the Intellectual*; Said, *Culture and Imperialism.*

85. Brass and Rowe, "Knowledge Limited," 56.

86. Ibid., 53.

87. Michael McDevitt, "When an Advisory Board Turns on Its School," *Academe* 100, no. 3 (May/June 2014): 25.

88. American Association of University Professors, *Academic Freedom and Electronic Communication* (Washington, DC: AAUP, 2004).

89. Stanford News Service, "Bob Beyers, Longtime Stanford News Service Director, Dies at 71," October 21, 2002, http://www.news.stanford.edu.

90. Chris Quintana, "If There's an Organized Outrage Machine, We Need an Organized Response," *Chronicle of Higher Education*, July 18, 2017.

91. Claussen, *Anti-intellectualism in American Media*.

92. By contrast, consider the intense interest in how news outlets should negotiate relationships with social media and amateur journalists. For example, see Christopher Meyers, Wendy N. Wyatt, Sandra L. Borden, and Edward Wasserman, "Professionalism, Not Professionals," *Journal of Mass Media Ethics* 27, no. 3 (2012): 189–205.

Chapter 5

1. Benjamin Krämer, "Media Populism: A Conceptual Clarification and Some Theses on Its Effects," *Communication Theory* 24, no. 1 (2014): 42–60

2. Michael Billig, *Banal Nationalism* (London: Sage, 1995).

3. CW Anderson, "Between Creative and Quantified Audiences: Web Metrics and Changing Patterns of Newswork in US Local Newsrooms," *Journalism* 12, no. 5 (2011): 550–66.

4. James A. Danowski and David W. Park, "Networks of the Dead or Alive in Cyberspace: Public Intellectuals in the Mass and Internet Media," *New Media & Society* 11, no. 3 (2009): 338.

5. Richard Hofstadter, *Anti-intellectualism in American Life* (New York: Alfred A. Knopf, 1963), 25.

6. Gaye Tuchman, *Making News: A Study in the Construction of Reality* (New York: Free Press, 1978).

7. Michael P. Boyle, Michael R. McCluskey, Narayan Devanathan, Susan E. Stein, and Douglas McLeod, "The Influence of Level of Deviance and Protest Type on Coverage of Social Protest in Washington from 1960 to 1999," *Mass Communication & Society* 7, no. 1 (2004): 43–60; Anna Feigenbaum, "Resistance Matters: Tents, Tear Gas and the 'Other Media' of Occupy," *Communication and Critical/Cultural Studies* 11, no. 1 (2014): 15–24; Douglas M. McLeod and James K. Hertog, "The Manufacture of 'Public Opinion' by Reporters: Informal Cues for Public Perceptions of Protest Groups," *Discourse and Society* 3, no. 3 (1992): 259–75.

8. David A. Weaver and Joshua M. Scacco, "Revisiting the Protest Paradigm: The Tea Party as Filtered through Prime-Time Cable News," *The International Journal of Press/Politics* 8, no. 1 (2013): 61–84.

9. Feigenbaum, "Resistance Matters," 15.

10. Luis Duno Gottberg, "Mob Outrages: Reflections on the Media Construction of the Masses in Venezuela (April 2000–January 2003)," *Journal of Latin American Cultural Studies* 13, no. 1 (2004), 131.

11. Martin Heidegger, *The Question Concerning Technology* (New York: Harper & Row, 1971).

12. *Concise Oxford Dictionary* (Oxford: Oxford University Press, 1999).

13. Precious N. Chatterje-Doody and Rhys Crilley, "Populism and Contemporary Global Media: Populist Communication Logics and the Co-construction of Transnational Identities," in *Populism and World Politics: Exploring Inter- and Transnational Dimensions*, ed. Frank Stengel, David B. MacDonald, and Dirk Nabers (New York: Palgrave Macmillan, 2019); Michael Crozier, "Recursive Governance: Contemporary Political Communication and Public Policy," *Political Communication* 24 (2007): 1–18; Don J. Waisanen, "(Trans)national Advocacy in the Ousting of Milošević: The Otpor Movement's Glocal Recursions," *Communication Studies* 64, no. 2 (2013): 158–77.

14. Daniel Rigney, "Three Kinds of Anti-intellectualism: Rethinking Hofstadter," *Sociological Inquiry* 61 (1991): 434–51.

15. Michael Welch, Melissa Fenwick, and Meredith Roberts, "State Managers, Intellectuals, and the Media: A Content Analysis of Ideology in Experts' Quotes in Feature Newspaper Articles on Crime," *Justice Quarterly* 15, no. 2 (1998): 219–41.

16. Ibid., 234.

17. Ibid., 237.

18. Ibid., 235.

19. Alessandra Stanley, "Not Speaking for Obama, Pastor Speaks for Himself, at Length," *The New York Times*, April 29, 2008.

20. In another example from *The New York Times*, columnist Nicholas Kristof argued that professors exclude themselves from national debates in a culture of unintelligible discourse. ("Professors, We Need You!" *The New York Times*, February 15, 2014.)
The most stinging dismissal of a point is to say: "That's academic." In other words, to be a scholar is, often, to be irrelevant.
One reason is the anti-intellectualism in American life, the kind that led Rick Santorum to scold President Obama as "a snob" for wanting more kids to go to college, or that led congressional Republicans to denounce spending on social science research. Yet it's not just that America has marginalized some of its sharpest minds. They have also marginalized themselves.

21. Robert E. Gutsche, Jr., *Media Control: News as an Institution of Power and Social Control* (New York: Bloomsbury, 2017), 98.

22. Ibid., 109.

23. Edward Caudill, *Darwinism in the Press: The Evolution of an Idea* (Hillsdale, NJ: Lawrence Erlbaum, 1989). Quoted in Dane S. Claussen, *Anti-intellectualism in American Media: Magazines and Higher Education* (New York: Peter Lang, 2004), 52–53.

24. Pamela J. Shoemaker and Stephen D. Reese, *Mediating the Message: Theories of Influence on Mass Media Content* (White Plains, NY: Longman, 1996).

25. Tuchman, "Objectivity as Strategic Ritual," 661.

26. Kevin Coe, David Domke, Erica S. Graham, Sue Lockett John, and Victor W. Pickard, "No Shades of Gray: The Binary Discourse of George W. Bush and an Echoing Press," *Journal of Communication* 54, no. 2 (2004): 234–52; Ian Taylor, "Local Press Reporting of Opposition to the 2003 Iraq War in the UK and the Case for Reconceptualizing the Notions of Legitimacy and Deviance," *Journal of War & Culture Studies* 7, no. 1 (2014): 36–53.

27. Erika G. King and Mary deYoung, "Imag(in)ing September 11: Ward Churchill, Frame Contestation, and Media Hegemony," *Journal of Communication Inquiry* 32, no. 2 (2008): 123–39.

28. Philip MacGregor, "Journalism, Public Imagination and Cultural Policy," *International Journal of Cultural Policy* 15, no. 2 (2009): 231–44.

29. Ibid., 233.

30. Ibid., 238.

31. Jeffrey C. Alexander, *The Civil Sphere* (Oxford: Oxford University Press, 2006).

32. Matthew S. McGlone, "Quoted Out of Context: Contextomy and Its Consequences," *Journal of Communication* 55, no. 2 (2005): 330.

33. Karen S. Johnson-Cartee, *News Narratives and News Framing* (Lanham, MD: Rowman & Littlefield, 2005), 133.

34. Gaye Tuchman, "Objectivity as Strategic Ritual: An Examination of Newsmen's Notions of Objectivity," *American Journal of Sociology* 77, no. 4 (1972): 663–64.

35. Ibid., 660.

36. Barbie Zelizer, "Journalists as Interpretive Communities," *Critical Studies in Mass Communication* 10, no. 3 (1993): 219–37.

37. Heidi K. Goar, "Anti-intellectualism as a Social Control: Reflexivity and Conformity," MA thesis, Mankato State University, 1992, 60.

38. Michael McCluskey, Susan E. Stein, Michael P. Boyle, and Douglas M. McLeod, "Community Structure and Social Protest: Influences on Newspaper Coverage," *Mass Communication and Society* 12, no. 3 (2009): 353–71.

39. Damon T. Di Cicco, "The Public Nuisance Paradigm: Changes in Mass Media Coverage of Political Protest Since the 1960s," *Journalism & Mass Communication Quarterly* 87, no. 1 (2010): 135–53.

40. MacGregor, "Journalism, Public Imagination and Cultural Policy," 231.

41. Hofstadter, *Anti-intellectualism in American Life*.

42. Mat Ekström and Bengt Johansson, "Talk Scandals," *Media, Culture & Society* 30, no. 1 (2008): 61–79.

43. Caroline Rizza, Ângela Guimarães Pereira, and Paula Curvelo, "'Do-it-Yourself Justice': Considerations of Social Media Use in a Crisis Situation: The Case of the 2011 Vancouver Riots," *International Journal of Information Systems for Crisis Response and Management* 6, no. 4 (2014): 42–59.

44. Ann Telnaes, "The Red, White and Blue Palette," *Nieman Reports* 58, no. 4 (2004): 28.

45. Victor Turner, "Social Drama and Stories about Them," *Critical Inquiry* 7, no. 1 (1980): 141–68.

46. Simon Cottle, "Mediatized Ritual: Beyond Manufacturing Consent," *Media, Culture & Society* 28, no. 3 (2006): 411–32.

47. Dana White, "The Right to Die Debate: The Demonization of Dr. Kevorkian and the Creation of a Moral Panic Surrounding Physician-Assisted Suicide in the United States," Honors scholar theses, University of Connecticut, 2009.

48. Joseph Turow, Arthur L. Caplan, and John S. Bracken, "Domestic 'Zealotry' and Press Discourse: Kevorkian's Euthanasia Incident," *Journalism* 1, no. 2 (2000): 197–216.

49. David Rowe, "Working Knowledge Encounters: Academics, Journalists and the Conditions of Cultural Labour," *Social Semiotics* 15, no. 3 (2005): 269–88.

50. McGlone, "Quoted Out of Context."

51. Dana L. Cloud, "Foiling the Intellectuals: Gender, Identity, Framing, and the Rhetoric of the Kill in Conservative Hate Mail," *Communication, Culture & Critique* 2, no. 4 (2009): 465.

52. Rita Colistra, "Shaping and Cutting the Media Agenda: Television Reporters' Perceptions of Agenda—and Frame-Building and Agenda-Cutting influences," *Journalism & Communication Monographs* 14, no. 2 (2012): 85–146.

53. Michael Brüggemann, "Between Frame Setting and Frame Sending: How Journalists Contribute to News Frames," *Communication Theory* 24, no. 1 (2014): 68.

54. Jay G. Blumler and Dennis Kavanagh, "The Third Age of Political Communication: Influences and Features," *Political Communication* 16, no. 3 (1999): 209–30.

55. Robert Entman, "Cascading Activation: Contesting the White House Frame After 9/11," *Political Communication* 20 (2003): 415–32.

56. Cas Mudde, "The Populist Zeitgeist," *Government and Opposition* 39, no. 4 (2004): 543.

57. Crozier, "Recursive Governance."

58. Charles Horton Cooley, *Human Nature and the Social Order* (New York: Charles Scribner's Sons, 1902).

59. Pamela J. Shoemaker, "Hardwired for News: Using Biological and Cultural Evolution to Explain the Surveillance Function," *Journal of Communication* 46, no. 3 (1996): 32–47.

60. Heejo Keum, Elliott D. Hillback, Hernando Rojas, Homero Gil de Zuniga, Dhavan V. Shah, and Douglas M. McLeod, "Personifying the Radical: How News Framing Polarizes Security Concerns and Tolerance Judgments," *Human Communication Research* 31, no. 3 (2005): 337–64.

61. David H. Weaver, Randal A. Beam, Bonnie J. Brownlee, Paul S. Voakes, and G. Cleveland Wilhoit, *The American Journalist in the 21st Century: U.S. News People at the Dawn of the New Millennium* (Mahwah, NJ: Lawrence Erlbaum, 2007).

62. McLeod and Hertog, "The Manufacture of 'Public Opinion' by Reporters."

63. Ida Schultz, "The Journalistic Gut Feeling: Journalistic Doxa, News Habitus and Orthodox News Values," *Journalism Practice* 1, no. 2 (2007).

64. David M. Ryfe, *Journalism and the Public* (Cambridge: Polity, 2017).

65. Eden Litt, "Knock, Knock. Who's There? The Imagined Audience," *Journal of Broadcasting & Electronic Media* 56, no. 3 (2012): 330–45.

Chapter 6

1. Ward Churchill, *On the Justice of Roosting Chickens: Reflections on the Consequences of U.S. Imperial Arrogance and Criminality* (Edinburgh, Scotland: AK Press, 2003).
2. Ward Churchill, "'Some People Push Back': On the Justice of Roosting Chickens. A Supplement of Dark Night Field Notes," *Pockets of Resistance* 11, September 12, 2001, http://www.darknightpress.org/index.php?i=print&article=9.
3. Stanley Cohen, *Folk Devils and Moral Panics* (London: Routledge, 1972); Michael Welch, Melissa Fenwick, and Meredith Roberts, "Primary Definitions of Crime and Moral Panic: A Content Analysis of Experts' Quotes in Feature Newspaper Articles on Crime," *Journal of Research in Crime and Delinquency* 34, no. 4 (1997): 474–94.
4. Simon Cottle, "Mediatized Ritual: Beyond Manufacturing Consent," *Media, Culture & Society* 28, no. 3 (2006): 415.
5. Henrik Ibsen, *An Enemy of the People* (Leipzig: Reclams Universal Bibliothek, 1882).
6. Arthur Miller, *The Crucible* (Oxford: Heinemann Educational, 1953).
7. Robert Darnton, "Writing News and Telling Stories," *Daedalus* 104, no. 2 (1975): 193.
8. Pamela J. Shoemaker, Jong Hyuk Lee, Gang (Kevin) Han, and Akiba A. Cohen, "Proximity and Scope as News Values," in *Media Studies: Key Issues and Debates*, ed. Eoin Devereux (London: Sage, 2007).
9. Ellen Schrecker, "McCarthyism: Political Repression and the Fear of Communism," *Social Research* 71, no. 4 (2004): 1041–86.
10. Victor Turner, "Symbols in African Ritual," *Science* 179, no. 4078 (1972): 1100–5; Victor Turner, *Dramas, Fields, and Metaphors: Symbolic Action in Human Society* (Ithaca, NY: Cornell University Press, 1974).
11. Victor Turner, "Social Drama and Stories about Them," *Critical Inquiry* 7, no. 1 (1980): 149.
12. Ibid., 149.
13. Ibid., 142.
14. Cohen, *Folk Devils and Moral Panics*.
15. Turner, "Social Drama and Stories about Them," 151.
16. Emile Durkheim, *The Elementary Forms of Religious Life* (New York: Free Press, 1965, 1915).
17. Turner, "Social Drama and Stories about Them," 162.
18. James S. Ettema, "Press Rites and Race Relations: A Study of Mass Mediated Ritual," *Critical Studies in Mass Communication* 7, no. 4 (1990): 309–31.
19. Nicole L. Muller, "As the [Sports] World Turns: An Analysis of the Montana-49er Social Drama," *Journal of Sport and Social Issues* 19, no. 2 (1995): 157–79.
20. Stewart M. Hoover and Lynn S. Clark, "Event and Publicity as Social Drama: A Case Study of the RE-Imaging Conference 1995," *Review of Religious Studies* 39, no. 2 (1997): 153–71.
21. Ronald Bishop, "If You Build It, We Won't Leave: Turner's Social Drama in Newspaper Coverage of Stadium Construction Controversies," *Journalism Studies* 2, no. 3 (2011): 373–92.

22. Bradford Scott Simon, "Entering the Pit: Slam-Dancing and Modernity," *The Journal of Popular Culture* 31, no. 1 (1997): 149–76.

23. Ettema, "Press Rites and Race Relations," 312.

24. John Fritch, Catherine Helen Palczewski, Jennifer Farrell, and Eric Short, "Disingenuous Controversy: Responses to Ward Churchill's 9/11 Essay," *Argumentation and Advocacy* 42, no. 4 (2006): 190–205.

25. David P. Schulz and G. Mitchell Reyes, "Ward Churchill and the Politics of Public Memory," *Rhetoric & Public Affairs* 11, no. 4 (2008): 631–58.

26. Kevin Coe, David Domke, Erica S. Graham, Sue Lockett John, and Victor W. Pickard, "No Shades of Gray: The Binary Discourse of George W. Bush and an Echoing Press," *Journal of Communication* 54, no. 2 (2004): 234–52.

27. Judith Butler, "Explanation and Exoneration, or What We Can Hear," *Social Text* 20, no. 3 (2002): 177.

28. Henry A. Giroux, "Academic Freedom Under Fire: The Case for Critical Pedagogy," *College Literature* 33, no. 4 (2006): 1–42.

29. Gaye Tuchman, "Objectivity as Strategic Ritual: An Examination of Newsmen's Notions of Objectivity," *American Journal of Sociology* 77, no. 4 (1972): 663–64.

30. Elfriede Fürsich, "In Defense of Textual Analysis: Restoring a Challenged Method for Journalism and Media Studies," *Journalism Studies* 10, no. 2 (2009): 245.

31. The "Eichmann" passage is provided here:
Well, really. Let's get a grip here, shall we? True enough, they were civilians of a sort. But innocent? Gimme a break. They formed a technocratic corps at the very heart of America's global financial empire—the "mighty engine of profit" to which the military dimension of U.S. policy has always been enslaved—and they did so both willingly and knowingly. Recourse to "ignorance"—a derivative, after all, of the word "ignore"—counts as less than an excuse among this relatively well-educated elite. To the extent that any of them were unaware of the costs and consequences to others of what they were involved in—and in many cases excelling at—it was because of their absolute refusal to see. More likely, it was because they were too busy braying, incessantly and self-importantly, into their cell phones, arranging power lunches and stock transactions, each of which translated, conveniently out of sight, mind and smelling distance, into the starved and rotting flesh of infants. If there was a better, more effective, or in fact any other way of visiting some penalty befitting their participation upon the little Eichmanns inhabiting the sterile sanctuary of the twin towers, I'd really be interested in hearing about it.

32. Erika G. King and Mary deYoung, "Imag(in)ing September 11: Ward Churchill, Frame Contestation, and Media Hegemony," *Journal of Communication Inquiry* 32, no. 2 (2008): 123–39.

33. George W. Bush, remarks by the president in photo opportunity with the National Security Team, September 12, 2001, http://georgewbush-whitehouse.archives.gov/news/releases/2001/09/20010912-4.html.

34. King and deYoung, "Imag(in)ing September 11," 127.

35. Schulz and Reyes, "Ward Churchill and the Politics of Public Memory," 631.

36. Hoover and Clark, "Event and Publicity as Social Drama."

37. Kylie Brass and David Rowe, "Knowledge Limited: Public Communication, Risk, and University Media Policy," *Continuum: Journal of Media & Cultural Studies* 23, no. 1 (2009): 53–76.

38. Tuchman, "Objectivity as Strategic Ritual."

39. Coe et al., "No Shades of Gray."

40. Seth Lewis and Stephen D. Reese, "What Is the War on Terror? Framing Through the Eyes of Journalists," *Journalism & Mass Communication Quarterly* 86, no. 1 (2009): 86.

41. In the aftermath of September 11, 2001, the Bush administration deployed rhetorical strategies designed to unify the country, foster a sense of security, and pave the way for military excursions in Afghanistan and Iraq. See John Hutcheson, David Domke, Andre Billeaudeaux, and Philip Garland, "U.S. National Identity, Political Elites, and a Patriotic Press Following September 11," *Political Communication* 21 (2004): 27–50. Journalists transmitted, reified, and naturalized the War on Terror frame as "a socially shared organizing principle." Lewis and Reese, "What Is the War on Terror?," 86. A traumatized public was likewise receptive to the clear-cut language of good and evil pronounced by the Bush administration and reinforced by an echoing press. By contrast, commentators outside mainstream media and the policy/military complex—activists, academics, unaffiliated intellectuals, and so on—were more likely to challenge a moralistic binary.

42. This interpretation resonates with a textual analysis of press response to the "Mohammed cartoon affair." Berkowitz and Eko argue that coverage of the controversy in France and the United States became a ritual to "restate and maintain" core values of distinct journalistic paradigms "as well as the national cultures from which those paradigms evolved." Dan Berkowitz and Lyombe Eko, "Blasphemy as Sacred Rite/Right: 'The Mohammed Cartoons Affair' and Maintenance of Journalistic Ideology," *Journalism Studies* 8, no. 5 (2007): 779.

43. Simon, "Entering the Pit," 154.

44. Schrecker, "McCarthyism."

45. The editor of the *Rocky* at the time, John Temple, teaches investigative reporting at the University of California, Berkeley, as I write this, suggesting that a lustful assault on academic dissent does not raise a red flag at US journalism schools.

46. In late winter of 2005, Churchill upped the ante in an ongoing scandal frame that was, at the time, plaguing the Boulder campus. The university had received negative press for allegations of its football program using sex to recruit athletes; episodes of undergraduate binge drinking accompanied by ritualistic couch burnings; and a *Princeton Review* ranking as the Number 1 party school. Churchill himself was an established local figure in the scandal frame, having been arrested for protesting a Columbus Day parade in Denver, about 25 miles southeast from Boulder. Churchill seems to enjoy his role as a provocateur. It is one of his modes of activism, and the same abrasive, unapologetic attitude that so irritates his detractors just as effectively endears him to supporters. So it was perhaps not surprising when media and ideological opportunists seized on Churchill's persona as an icon for a range of contentious issues: academic freedom, free speech, the "liberal agenda," racial identity, and tenure.

47. Felisa Cardona, "Ex-Gov. Owens Denies 'Plan' to Fire Churchill," *The Denver Post*, March 11, 2009.

48. Colorado is not an epicenter for anti-intellectualism in news media, but there is little affection for the "People's Republic of Boulder" in most regions of the state outside Denver and the ski resorts. Editors at the *Post* and the *Rocky* encouraged student interns at CU to be on the lookout for "only in Boulder stories," features that would reinforce regional stereotypes about the People's Republic. Campus administrators sought protection from the hostile press by erecting an aggressive public relations staff that would stomp out brush fires. Some faculty believed that at least a few CU administrators changed their party membership to GOP to show state legislators that Republicans do hold offices on campus.

49. The purpose of this chapter is not to evaluate CU's investigation and firing of Churchill but to understand how media ritual functions in the social control of an intellectual breach. A faculty committee at CU found Churchill guilty of research misconduct in 2006 (Appendix Table 6.1) but did not recommend termination. Regents nevertheless fired him based on charges of plagiarism, fabrication, and falsification of evidence. The American Association of University Professors concluded: "It is obvious that the University would never have begun its investigation of Ward Churchill were it not for his 'little Eichmanns' comment, which he made as a citizen, not as a scholar or as a representative of the University. It is also obvious that dismissing Churchill from his position as a professor at the University violated his First Amendment rights." Colorado Conference of the American Association of University Professors, *Report on the Termination of Ward Churchill*, November 1, 2011, 6.

50. Turner, "Social Drama and Stories about Them," 152.

51. Ettema, "Press Rites and Race Relations," 327.

52. On four consecutive days in early February 2005, the *Rocky* questioned Churchill's ethnicity following charges that he manufactured his Native American identity to advance his career. On March 29, a CU committee received allegations that Churchill committed research misconduct, prompting the *Rocky* to publish a multiweek series giving its conclusions on charges pending before the committee.

53. Ettema, "Press Rites and Race Relations," 312.

54. Gaye Tuchman, *Making News: A Study in the Construction of Reality* (New York: Free Press, 1978); Tuchman, "Objectivity as Strategic Ritual."

55. Matthew C. Ehrlich, "Using "Ritual" to Study Journalism," *Journal of Communication Inquiry* 20, no. 2 (1996): 3–17.

56. Tuchman, *Making News*, 41.

57. Ettema, "Press Rites and Race Relations," 312.

58. Fürsich, "In Defense of Textual Analysis," 245.

59. Diane L. Carter, Ryan J. Thomas, and Susan Dente Ross, "You Are Not a Friend: Media Conflict in Times of Peace," *Journalism Studies* 12, no. 4 (2011): 456–73.

60. Michael P. Boyle, Michael R. McCluskey, Narayan Devanathan, Susan E. Stein, and Douglas McLeod, "The Influence of Level of Deviance and Protest Type on Coverage of Social Protest in Washington from 1960 to 1999," *Mass Communication and Society* 7, no. 1 (2004): 43–60.

61. Turner, "Symbols in African Ritual," 1100.

62. The author acknowledges Nancy K. Thorwardson and Katie Pickrell for the design of Figure 6.2.

63. Melita Poler Kovačič and Karmen Erjavec, "Construction of Semi-Investigative Journalism: Journalists' Discourse Strategies in the Slovenian Daily Press," *Journalism Studies* 12, no. 3 (2011): 328–43.

64. Hannah Arendt, *Eichmann in Jerusalem: A Report on the Banality of Evil* (New York: Penguin Books, 1963).

65. Matthew S. McGlone, "Quoted Out of Context: Contextomy and Its Consequences," *Journal of Communication* 55, no. 2 (2005): 330; Matthew S. McGlone, "Contextomy: The Art of Quoting Out of Context," *Media, Culture & Society* 2, no. 4 (2005): 511–22.

66. Lane Van Ham, "Reading Early Punk as Secularized Scared Clowning," *The Journal of Popular Culture* 42, no. 2 (2009): 330.

67. Victor Turner, *The Ritual Process: Structure and Anti-Structure* (Chicago: Aldine, 1969), 27.

68. David Rowe, "Working Knowledge Encounters: Academics, Journalists and the Conditions of Cultural Labour," *Social Semiotics* 15, no. 3 (2005): 269–88.

69. Turner, *Dramas, Fields, and Metaphors*, 42.

70. Carter et al., "You Are Not a Friend."

71. Steven Livingston and W. Bennett, "Gatekeeping, Indexing, and Live-Event News: Is Technology Altering the Construction of News?," *Political Communication* 20 (2003): 359–62.

72. Lewis and Reese, "What Is the War on Terror?"

73. W. Lance Bennett, "An Introduction to Journalistic Norms and Representations of Politics," *Political Communication* 13 (1996): 373–84.

74. Cottle, "Mediatized Ritual."

Chapter 7

1. David P. Schulz and G. Mitchell Reyes, "Ward Churchill and the Politics of Public Memory," *Rhetoric & Public Affairs* 11, no. 4 (2008): 631–58.

2. George A. Donohue, Phillip J. Tichenor, and Clarice N. Olien, "A Guard Dog Perspective on the Role of Media," *Journal of Communication* 45, no. 2 (1995): 116.

3. Howard S. Becker, *Outsiders: Studies in the Sociology of Deviance* (New York: Free Press, 1963).

4. Complex ideas undergo simplification as regular practice in journalism. There is no benchmark available to evaluate how much explication of an idea is reasonable in a particular episode. I also acknowledge that Churchill sought to provoke through invective; no one should be surprised by a hostile response. I do believe, though, that comparisons between Colorado and non-local content highlight a prominent role for proximate media in the control of ideational dissent. A characterization of news production as inherently reductionist vis-à-vis intellectual discourse does not account for any effect of proximity.

5. Pamela J. Shoemaker, Jong Hyuk Lee, Gang (Kevin) Han, and Akiba A. Cohen, "Proximity and Scope as News Values," in *Media Studies: Key Issues and Debates*, ed. Eoin Devereux (London: Sage, 2007).

6. Stanley Cohen, *Folk Devils and Moral Panics* (London: Routledge, 1972).

7. Hindman concluded that local newspapers are likely to cover conflict only when community leaders initiate controversy. "Local mass media serve a system maintenance role that is supportive of community norms and social arrangements." Douglas Blanks Hindman, "Community Newspapers, Community Structural Pluralism, and Local Conflict with Nonlocal Groups," *Journalism & Mass Communication Quarterly* 73, no. 3 (1996): 709.

8. Kristie Bunton, "Social Responsibility in Covering Community: A Narrative Case Analysis," *Journal of Mass Media Ethics* 13, no. 4 (1998): 242.

9. Pamela J. Shoemaker and Stephen D. Reese, *Mediating the Message in the 21st Century: A Media Sociology Perspective* (New York: Routledge, 2014), 189–90.

10. The media spectacle of pathologist Jack Kevorkian in the 1990s foreshadows the Churchill case in some respects in the foreclosing of deliberation. Reporters preferred to focus on the "suicide machine" of "Dr. Death" rather than open up dialogue on a patient's right to die. The Churchill case is instructive due to the absence of a criminal or behavioral component, allowing us to concentrate on how journalism confronts deviance when confined to intellectual discourse. Joseph Turow, Arthur L. Caplan, and John S. Bracken, "Domestic 'Zealotry' and Press Discourse: Kevorkian's Euthanasia Incident," *Journalism* 1, no. 2 (2000): 197–216.

11. Ian Taylor, "Local Press Reporting of Opposition to the 2003 Iraq War in the UK and the Case for Reconceptualizing the Notions of Legitimacy and Deviance," *Journal of War & Culture Studies* 7, no. 1 (2014): 36–53.

12. Daniel C. Hallin, *We Keep America on Top of the World: Television Journalism and the Public Sphere* (London: Routledge, 1994).

13. Michael McCluskey, Susan E. Stein, Michael P. Boyle, and Douglas M. McLeod, "Community Structure and Social Protest: Influences on Newspaper Coverage," *Mass Communication and Society* 12, no. 3 (2009): 353–71.

14. Alternative interpretations of the results are possible. De-contextualization practiced by the large, Denver dailies implies that proximity can override countervailing influences that might engender relative tolerance for dissent, such as the size of a newsroom or ideological diversity in a cosmopolitan readership. The current sample provides only so much leverage for disentangling proximity from newspaper circulation. Nearly all (92%) of the newspapers below circulation of 100,000 exist in Colorado. A related concern is that the content analysis fails to account for news quality. In a supplemental analysis, I expected that elite media would be more tolerant of Churchill's ideas. Populist sentiment—actual or perceived—should be less consequential at these papers. The T1 sample includes a small number of articles in this category: five from *The New York Times*, one from *The Washington Post*, and one from the *Christian Science Monitor*. In Chi square tests, elite media were more likely to convey content beyond Eichmann ($p < .05$), blowback ($p < .01$), foreign policy ($p < .01$), civilian deaths ($p < .001$), and citizens in denial ($p < .001$). Nevertheless, non-Colorado

media remained more tolerant of Churchill's ideas with elite newspapers removed from the sample.

15. The test for correspondence, Spearman rank-order correlation, is used most often in media effects research to test the agenda-setting hypothesis, which predicts similarity of issue salience between news content and public opinion.

16. Mirroring is not entirely explained vis-à-vis general-to-specific orientations. I would expect a relatively large percentage of articles to mention *some aspect* of foreign policy, but general-to-specific distinctions are less obvious when comparing, for instance, reference to civilian deaths and attackers as rational. The ratios of non-Colorado to Colorado percentages for the ideational elements increase substantially for the most incendiary items. This implies an interaction between proximity and level of deviance, although the content measures are not coded by degree of deviance to test an interaction statistically. For the least sensitive element (essay content beyond Eichmann), the ratio is 1.99. Ratios for the most controversial ideas are 5.52 (citizens in denial) and 4.29 (attackers as rational).

17. Hannah Arendt, *Eichmann in Jerusalem: A Report on the Banality of Evil* (New York: Penguin Books, 1963).

18. Robert E. Gutsche, Jr., *Media Control: News as an Institution of Power and Social Control* (New York: Bloomsbury, 2017).

19. Barbie Zelizer, Journalists as Interpretive Communities," *Critical Studies in Mass Communication* 10, no. 3 (1993): 219–37.

20. Linda Steiner, Jing Guo, Raymond McCaffrey, and Paul Hills, "*The Wire* and Repair of the Journalistic Paradigm," *Journalism* 14, no. 6 (2013): 703–20.

21. Laura Ahva, "Public Journalism and Professional Reflexivity," *Journalism* 14, no. 6 (2012): 790–806.

22. Brian Klocke and Michael McDevitt, "Foreclosing Deliberation: Journalists' Lowering of Expectations in the Marketplace of Ideas," *Journalism Studies* 14, no. 6 (2013): 891–906.

23. The Appendix provides more detail on the sample.

24. Comparisons between news content and interview transcripts also assisted in the refinement of emergent themes from interviews.

25. I recognized that journalists could perceive the interviews as confrontational. Qualitative researchers have argued, however, that questioning interview subjects of similar social status to points of disagreement will bring out more clarity of empirical understanding. Plesner notes that "research dealing with journalists . . . produce[s] overly smooth interactions . . . [that] can cause a problem in relation to learning anything new or unexpected," and calls for "more confrontational types of interview[s]." Ursula Plesner, "Studying Sideways: Displacing the Problem of Power in Research Interviews with Sociologists and Journalists," *Qualitative Inquiry* 17, no. 6 (2011): 471–82.

26. Theodore Glasser, "The Puzzle of Objectivity I: Objectivity Precludes Responsibility," *Quill*, February 1984, 15.

27. Gaye Tuchman, "Objectivity as Strategic Ritual: An Examination of Newsmen's Notions of Objectivity," *American Journal of Sociology* 77, no. 4 (1972): 663–64.

28. Matt Carlson, "'Where Once Stood Titans': Second-Order Paradigm Repair and the Vanishing Newspaper," *Journalism* 13, no. 3 (2012): 269.

29. Warren Breed, "Social Control in the Newsroom: A Functional Analysis," *Social Forces* 33, no. 4 (1955): 326–35.

30. Elisabeth Noelle-Neumann, "The Spiral of Silence: A Theory of Public Opinion," *Journal of Communication* 24, no. 2 (1974): 43–51.

31. Silvio Waisbord, "Why Populism Is Troubling for Democratic Communication," *Communication, Culture & Critique* 11, no. 1 (2018): 21–34.

32. Hernando Rojas, "'Corrective' Actions in the Public Sphere: How Perceptions of Media and Media Effects Shape Political Behaviors," *International Journal of Public Opinion Research* 22, no. 3 (2010), 343–63.

33. Henry A. Giroux, "Cultural Studies, Public Pedagogy, and the Responsibility of Intellectuals," *Communication and Critical/Cultural Studies* 1, no. 1 (2004): 59–79.

34. Front Range newspapers constitute a diverse group of newspapers. Prior to the *Rocky*'s demise, they included competitive, Denver dailies with distinct ideological identities. The tabloid-format *Rocky* was recognized as more conservative editorially than the *Post*. Two smaller newspapers circulate in a college town known for its progressive politics, and the Longmont paper covers a middle-class suburb. Despite this diversity, the local press clustered in context inclusion consistently lower than the range for non-Colorado media at T1 (Appendix Table 7.1).

35. Hindman, "Community Newspapers, Community Structural Pluralism, and Local Conflict with Nonlocal Groups."

36. Donohue et al., "A Guard Dog Perspective on the Role of Media."

Chapter 8

1. Walter Lippmann, *Public Opinion* (New York: Harcourt, Brace, 1922).

2. Sidney Blumenthal, "Walter Lippmann and American Journalism Today," openDemocracy, October 31, 2007, https://www.opendemocracy.net/article/walter_lippmann_and_american_journalism_today.

3. Dane S. Claussen, *Anti-intellectualism in American Media: Magazines and Higher Education* (New York: Peter Lang, 2004).

4. Michael McDevitt, "Political Socialization and Child Development," in *The SAGE Handbook of Political Sociology*, ed. William Outhwaite and Stephen Turner (London: Sage, 2018).

5. Richard Hofstadter, *Anti-intellectualism in American Life* (New York: Alfred A. Knopf, 1963); Daniel Rigney, "Three Kinds of Anti-intellectualism: Rethinking Hofstadter," *Sociological Inquiry* 61 (1991): 434–51.

6. Andrew J. Perrin, J. Micah Roos, and Gordon W. Gauchat, "From Coalition to Constraint: Modes of Thought in Contemporary American Conservatism," *Sociological Forum* 29, no. 2 (2014): 290.

7. Martin E. Eigenberger and Karen A. Sealander, "A Scale for Measuring Students' Anti-Intellectualism," *Psychological Reports* 89 (2001): 387–402.

8. The 25-item scale demonstrated a fundamentally unidimensional structure with samples at universities in Wisconsin, Indiana, and Arizona.

9. Antonio Laverghetta, "The Relationship Between Student Anti-Intellectualism and Proneness to Boredom in a Sample of College Students," *College Student Journal* 49, no. 4 (2015): 487–90.

10. Rafik Z. Elias, "Anti-Intellectualism Attitudes and Academic Self-Efficacy among Business Students," *Journal of Education for Business* 84, no. 2 (2008): 110–16.

11. Antonio Laverghetta and J. Kathleen Nash, "Student Anti-Intellectualism and College Major," *College Student Journal* 44, no. 2 (2010): 528–32.

12. Antonio Laverghetta, Juliana Stewart, and Lawrence Weinstein, "Anti-Intellectualism and Political Ideology in a Sample of Undergraduate and Graduate Students," *Psychological Reports* 101 (2007): 1050–56.

13. Claudia Mellado, Folker Hanusch, María Luisa Humanes, Sergio Roses, Fábio Pereira, Lyuba Yez, Salvador De León, Mireya Márquez, Federico Subervi, and Vinzenz Wyss, "The Pre-Socialization of Future Journalists: An Examination of Journalism Students' Professional Views in Seven Countries," *Journalism Studies* 14, no. 6 (2013): 857–74.

14. Daniel C. Hallin, *The Uncensored War* (New York: Oxford University Press, 1986), 117.

15. Mellado et al., "The Pre-Socialization of Future Journalists," 864.

16. Eigenberger and Sealander, "A Scale for Measuring Students' Anti-Intellectualism."

17. Steven Knowlton and J. Christopher McKinley, "There's More to Ethics than Justice and Harm: Teaching a Broader Understanding of Journalism Ethics," *Journalism & Mass Communication Educator* 71, no. 2 (2016): 133–45.

18. Jean Piaget, *Intellectual Evolution from Adolescence to Adulthood* (Cambridge: Cambridge University Press, 1977); Lawrence Kohlberg, *The Philosophy of Moral Development: Moral Stages and the Idea of Justice* (Cambridge, MA: Harper & Row, 1981).

19. John W. C. Johnstone, Edward J. Slawski, and William W. Bowman, *The News People: A Sociological Portrait of American Journalists and Their Work* (Urbana: University of Illinois Press, 1976); David H. Weaver, Randal A. Beam, Bonnie J. Brownlee, Paul S. Voakes, and G. Cleveland Wilhoit, *The American Journalist in the 21st Century: U.S. News People at the Dawn of the New Millennium* (Mahwah, NJ: Lawrence Erlbaum, 2007).

20. Hofstadter, *Anti-intellectualism in American Life.*

21. John H. McManus, *Market-Driven Journalism: Let the Citizen Beware?* (Thousand Oaks, CA: Sage, 1994).

22. Mellado et al., "The Pre-Socialization of Future Journalists," 864.

23. Masahiro Yamamoto and Matthew J. Kushin, "More Harm Than Good? Online Media Use and Political Disaffection among College Students in the 2008 Election," *Journal of Computer-Mediated Communication* 19, no. 3 (2014): 430–45.

24. Gene Allen, Stephanie Craft, Chrisopther Waddell, and Mary Lynn Young, *Toward 2020: New Directions in Journalism Education* (Toronto, Canada: Ryerson Journalism Research Center, 2015).

25. We should resist blaming youth for the culture in which they are socialized, but some students presumably self-select to a profession prone to distraction. The reading and news consumption divide between young adults and previous generations is well documented, as is the unreflective hedonism of students entering college. For the reading/news divide, see Yoojung Kim, Dongyoung Sohn, and Sejung Marina Choi, "Cultural Differences in Motivations for Using Social Network Sites: A Comparative Study of American and Korean College Students," *Computers in Human Behavior* 27, no. 1 (2011): 365–72. For unreflective hedonism, see Victora J. Rideout, Ulla G. Foehr, and Donald F. Roberts, *Generation M2: Media in the Lives of 8- to 18-Year-Olds. A Kaiser Family Foundation Study* (Menlo Park, CA: The Henry J. Kaiser Family Foundation, 2010).

26. David H. Weaver and G. Cleveland Wilhoit, *The American Journalist in the 1990s: U.S. News People at the End of an Era* (Mahwah, NJ: Lawrence Erlbaum, 1996); Weaver et al., *The American Journalist in the 21st Century*; Lars Willnat, David H. Weaver, and G. Cleveland Wilhoit, *The American Journalist in the Digital Age: A Half-Century Perspective* (New York, Peter Lang, 2017).

27. David H. Weaver, Lars Willnat, and G. Cleveland Wilhoit, "The American Journalist in the Digital Age: Another Look at U.S. News People," *Journalism & Mass Communication Quarterly* 96, no. 1 (2019): 101–30.

28. Theodore L. Glasser, "Professionalism and the Derision of Diversity: The Case of the Education of Journalists," *Journal of Communication* 42, no. 2 (1992): 134.

29. Laura Ahva, "Public Journalism and Professional Reflexivity," *Journalism* 14, no. 6 (2012): 790–806; Matt Carlson, "Metajournalistic Discourse and the Meanings of Journalism: Definitional Control, Boundary Work, and Legitimation," *Communication Theory* 26, no. 4 (2016): 349–68.

30. David A. Craig, "Communitarian Journalism(s): Clearing Conceptual Landscapes," *Journal of Mass Media Ethics* 11, no. 2 (1996): 107–118; Theodore L. Glasser and James S. Ettema, "Ethics and Eloquence in Journalism: An Approach to Press Accountability," *Journalism Studies* 9, no. 4 (2008): 512–31.

31. Benedict Anderson, *Imagined Communities: Reflections on the Rise and Spread of Nationalism* (London: Verso, 1987); Kevin M. Carragee and Wim Roefs, "The Neglect of Power in Recent Framing Research," *Journal of Communication* 54, no. 2 (2004): 214–33; Perry Parks, "The Discipline-Autonomy Paradox: How U.S. Journalism Textbooks Construct Reporters' Freedom Just to Tear It Down," *Journalism Studies* 20, no. 13 (2019): 1903–19.

32. Tanni Hass and Linda Steiner, "Public Journalism as a Journalism of Publics: Implications of the Habermas-Fraser Debate for Public Journalism," *Journalism* 2, no. 2 (2001): 123–47; Gaye Tuchman, "Objectivity as Strategic Ritual: An Examination of Newsmen's Notions of Objectivity," *American Journal of Sociology* 77, no. 4 (1972): 663–64.

33. Sample demographics are similar to those reported by the corresponding school/ college and by data, when available, from sites visits of the Accrediting Council on Education in Journalism and Mass Communications. The overall sample break-down for gender is 68.5% female, 31.5% male. Gotlieb, McLaughlin, and Cummins

reported that women comprised 65.8 percent of undergraduate students in the Annual Survey of Journalism and Mass Communication Enrollments. The ethnic profile for this chapter, however, is less diverse: 79.5% white/Anglo, 7.7% Asian, 4.7% black/African American, 4.2% Hispanic/Latino, 2.7% multi-ethnic, 1% Native American, and 1% other. While 20.5% of students in this study report ethnic identity other than white/Anglo, 33.7% of the Gotlieb et al. sample identify as members of a US minority group. Melissa R. Gotlieb, Bryan McLaughlin, and R. Glenn Cummins, "Enrollments: Challenges and Opportunities for a Changing and Diverse Field," *Journalism & Mass Communication Educator* 72, no. 2 (2017): 139–53.

34. Elias, "Anti-Intellectualism Attitudes and Academic Self-Efficacy among Business Students."

35. Laverghetta and Nash, "Student Anti-Intellectualism and College Major."

36. Melanie Killen and Judith G. Smetana, *Handbook of Moral Development* (Mahwah, NJ: Lawrence Erlbaum., 2013). Indicators of anti-intellectualism also relate to each other in predictable ways. The correlation for journalistic anti-rationalism and anti-elitism ($r = 37, p < .001$) is consistent with the expectation that response to provocative ideas is accompanied by suspicion of intellectuals themselves.

37. Philip M. Fernbach, Nicholas Light, Sydney E. Scott, Yoel Inbar, and Paul Rozin, "Extreme Opponents of Genetically Modified Foods Know the Least but Think They Know the Most," *Nature Human Behavior*, January 14, 2019, https://www.nature.com/articles/s41562-018-0520-3.

38. For example, Sandra L. Borden, "Communitarian Journalism and the Common Good: Lessons from the *Catholic Worker*," *Journalism* 15, no. 3 (2014): 273–88; Dennis D. Cali, "Journalism after September 11: Unity as Moral Imperative," *Journal of Mass Media Ethics* 17, no. 4 (2002): 290–303; Clifford G. Christians, John P. Ferré, and P. Mark Fackler, *Good News: Social Ethics and the Press* (Oxford: Oxford University Press, 1993).

39. Dane S. Claussen, "A Truly Bold Idea for U.S. J&MC Education: Sincerely Trying True Excellence for Once," *Journalism & Mass Communication Educator* 67, no. 3 (2012): 211–17; Dane S. Claussen, "Book Review: *Toward 2020: New Directions in Journalism Education*, by Gene Allen, Stephanie Craft, Christopher Waddell, & Mary Lynn Young eds.," *Journalism & Mass Communication Educator* 71, no. 4 (2016): 487–89.

40. McDevitt, "Political Socialization and Child Development."

41. Claussen, *Anti-intellectualism in American Media*; Paul Hollander, "Popular Culture, *The New York Times* and the *New Republic*," *Culture and Society* 51 (2014): 288–96.

42. Renita Coleman and Lee Wilkins, "The Moral Development of Journalists: A Comparison with Other Professions and a Model for Predicting Quality Ethical Reasoning," *Journalism & Mass Communication Quarterly* 81, no. 3 (2004): 511–27.

43. Kohlberg, *The Philosophy of Moral Development*.

44. A more definitive interpretation of the relationships among reflexivity, role identity, and support for journalistic anti-intellectualism will require replication with a larger number of colleges, ideally in a panel design to document stability or changes in the

same students. A longitudinal study that tracks curricular experiences might challenge the finding that JMC instruction over time fails to alter attitudes toward intellect. Future research would improve generalizability through multistage sampling, with regions of the country sampled first followed by schools, majors, and students.

45. Leon V. Sigal, "Sources Make the News," in *Reading the News*, ed. R K. Manoff and Michael Schudson (New York: Pantheon, 1986), 9–37.

46. Glasser and Ettema, "Ethics and Eloquence in Journalism," 512.

47. Clifford G. Christians, Mark Fackler, Kathy Brittain Richardson, Peggy J. Kreshel, and Robert H. Woods, *Media Ethics: Cases and Moral Reasoning* (New York: Routledge, 2017); Patrick Lee Plaisance, *Media Ethics: Key Principles for Responsible Practice* (Thousand Oaks, CA: SAGE, 2004).

48. Parks, "The Discipline-Autonomy Paradox."

49. David Nolan, "Journalism, Education and the Formation of 'Public Subjects,'" *Journalism* 9, no. 6 (2008): 733–49.

50. Robert Manoff, "Democratic Journalism and the Republican Subject: Or, the Real American Dream and What Journalism Educators Can Do About It," *Zoned for Debate* (blog), New York University, September16, 2002, https://journalism.nyu.edu/publishing/archives/debate/forum.1.essay.manoff.html.

51. Patrick Ferrucci and Jacob Nelson, "The Dewey Problem: Public Journalism, Engagement and More than Two Decades of Denigrating Discourse," paper presented at the annual conference of the Association for Education in Journalism and Mass Communication, Toronto, August 7–10, 2019. Anti-elitism in the academy, anti-professionalism, and disregard for institutions mingle in a repudiation of journalistic authority. While this confluence is not a coordinated alliance, enthusiasm of these projects for the dismantling of professional autonomy deserves scrutiny in a period in which journalists have become enemies of the people.

52. Pamela J. Shoemaker and Stephen D. Reese, *Mediating the Message in the 21st Century: A Media Sociology Perspective* (New York: Routledge, 2014).

53. Catherine Liu, *American Idyll: Academic Antielitism as Cultural Critique* (Iowa City: University of Iowa Press, 2011).

54. Michael Schudson, *Why Democracies Need an Unlovable Press* (Malden, MA: Polity, 2011), 125.

Chapter 9

1. Jannie Møller Hartley, "When Homo Academicus Meets Homo Journalisticus: An Inter-field Study of Collaboration and Conflict in the Communication of Scientific Research," *Journalism* 18, no. 2 (2017): 211–25.

2. Erik Albæk, "The Interaction Between Experts and Journalists in News Journalism," *Journalism* 12, no. 3 (2011): 335–48; Marcel Broersma, Bas den Herder, and Birte Schohaus, "A Question of Power. The Changing Dynamics Between Journalists and Sources," *Journalism Practice* 7, no. 4 (2013): 388–95.

3. David Rowe and Kylie Brass, "The Uses of Academic Knowledge: The University in the Media," *Media, Culture & Society* 30, no. 5 (2008): 677–98; Pamela J. Shoemaker, "Media Treatment of Deviant Political Groups," *Journalism Quarterly* 61, no. 1 (1984): 66–82.

4. William A. Gamson and Gadi Wolfsfeld, "Movements and Media as Interacting Systems," *The ANNALS of the American Academy of Political and Social Science* 528, no. 1 (1993): 115.

5. Albæk, "The Interaction Between Experts and Journalists in News Journalism"; Dahlia K. Remler, Don J. Waisanen, and Andrea Gabor, "Academic Journalism: A Modest Proposal," *Journalism Studies* 15, no. 4 (2014): 357–73.

6. Ian Taylor, "Local Press Reporting of Opposition to the 2003 Iraq War in the UK and the Case for Reconceptualizing the Notions of Legitimacy and Deviance," *Journal of War & Culture Studies* 7, no. 1 (2014): 36–53.

7. Chris Quintana, "If There's an Organized Outrage Machine, We Need an Organized Response," *Chronicle of Higher Education*, July 18, 2017.

8. Robert Jensen, "U.S. Guilty of Committing Own Violent Acts," *Houston Chronicle*, September 14, 2001.

9. Scott Jaschik, "Controversial Professor Placed on Leave," *Inside Higher Ed*, October 11, 2017.

10. Stewart M. Hoover and Lynn S. Clark, "Event and Publicity as Social Drama: A Case Study of the RE-Imaging Conference 1995," *Review of Religious Studies* 39, no. 2 (1997): 153–71.

11. Steven W. Thrasher, "Yes, There Is a Free Speech Crisis. But Its Victims Are Not Men," *The Guardian*, June 5, 2017.

12. Marc Parry, "Nancy MacLean Responds to Her Critics," *Chronicle of Higher Education*, July 19, 2017.

13. Michael McDevitt, "When an Advisory Board Turns on Its School," *Academe* 100, no. 3 (May/June 2014): 21–25.

14. Quintana, "If There's an Organized Outrage Machine, We Need an Organized Response."

15. Pierre Bourdieu, *On Television and Journalism* (London: Pluto, 1998).

16. David M. Ryfe, *Journalism and the Public* (Cambridge: Polity, 2017), 13.

17. Eleanor Townsley, "The Public Intellectual Trope in the United States," *The American Sociologist* 37, no. 3 (2006): 63.

18. Catherine Liu, *American Idyll: Academic Antielitism as Cultural Critique* (Iowa City: University of Iowa Press, 2011).

19. Hartley, "When Homo Academicus Meets Homo Journalisticus," 220.

20. The symbolic capital of news is not always deployed toward benign ends; it can manifest in a predatory rendering of dissent in ways that elevate journalism's cultural standing at the expense of academia (Chapter 4).

21. Gitlow v. New York, 268 U.S. 652 (1925).

22. Marian Meyers, "Reporters and Beats: The Making of Oppositional News," *Critical Studies in Mass Communication* 9, no. 1 (1992): 75–90.

23. Ibid., 84.

24. See, for example, Todd Gitlin, *The Whole World Is Watching* (Berkeley: University of California Press, 1980); Daniel C. Hallin, *The Uncensored War* (New York: Oxford University Press, 1986); Edward S. Herman and Noam Chomsky, *Manufacturing Consent: The Political Economy of the Mass Media* (New York: Pantheon Books, 1988); Shoemaker, "Media Treatment of Deviant Political Groups"; John Zaller and Dennis Chiu, "Government's Little Helpers: U.S. Press Coverage of Foreign Policy Crises, 1945–1991," *Political Communication* 13, no. 4 (1996): 385–405.

25. Quintana, "If There's an Organized Outrage Machine, We Need an Organized Response."

26. Gaye Tuchman, "Objectivity as Strategic Ritual: An Examination of Newsmen's Notions of Objectivity," *American Journal of Sociology* 77, no. 4 (1972): 663–64; Gaye Tuchman, *Making News: A Study in the Construction of Reality* (New York: Free Press, 1978).

27. Hartley, "When Homo Academicus Meets Homo Journalisticus."

28. Townsley, "The Public Intellectual Trope in the United States," 46.

29. David Horowitz, *The Professors: The 101 Most Dangerous Academics in America* (Washington, DC: Regnery, 2006).

30. Ibid., liv.

31. Ibid., xvi.

32. Professor Watchlist, Turning Point USA, accessed November 22, 2018, http://www.professorwatchlist.org.

33. Ibid.

34. John F. Zipp and Rudy Fenwick, "Is the Academy a Liberal Hegemony? The Political Orientations and Educational Values of Professors," *Public Opinion Quarterly* 70, no. 3 (2006): 304–62.

35. The American Association of University Professors, however, unveiled a surveillance-of-surveillance initiative on March 13, 2018 (https://onefacultyoneresistance.org). We have received reports from faculty members about experiences of targeted harassment and intimidation. We want to get a greater sense of the prevalence of this at colleges and universities around the country. If you have been targeted as a result of something you have said in your classroom, in your publications, or outside work (on social media for example), please tell us what happened by filling out the form.

36. Townsley, "The Public Intellectual Trope in the United States," 41.

37. The response rate of 59.5% compares favorably to recent interviews of senior women professors and assistant professors in social work. Paula Burkinshaw and Kate White, "Fixing the Women or Fixing Universities? Women in HE Leadership," *Administrative Sciences* 7, no. 3 (2017): 1–14; Sarah Carter Narendorf, Eusebius Small, Jodi A. Berger Cardoso, Richard W. Wagner, and Sheara Williams Jennings, "Managing and Mentoring: Experiences of Assistant Professors in Working with Research Assistants," *Social Work Research* 40, no. 1 (2016): 19–30. Subjects interviewed for this chapter were eager to share their experiences with reporters. I provided a list of questions for the eight respondents who preferred email, but the 12 Skype and five phone sessions allowed for give-and-take in semi-structured interviews that ranged from 26 to 89 minutes. The invitation to interview explained that the project explores how scholars

interact with journalists to reach citizens beyond academia. Several questions, however, welcomed scenarios in which public scholars might prefer to bypass news media. I initially asked subjects to comment on how they felt about appearing on one (or both) of the watchlists, and whether this fame/infamy affected their work as public scholars. Subsequent items covered rules of engagement with reporters from market-driven and quality media.

38. Mats Lindberg, "Qualitative Analysis of Ideas and Ideological Content," in *Analyzing Text and Discourses: Eight Approaches for the Social Sciences*, ed. Kristina Boréus and Göran Bergström (London: Sage, 2017), 86–121.

39. Horowitz, *The Professors*, 13.

40. Ibid., 254–55.

41. Brendan O'Connor, "There Is No Such Thing as 'White Genocide,'" *Jezebel*, December 26, 2016, https://jezebel.com/there-is-no-such-thing-as-white-genocide-1790500883. Ciccariello-Maher announced his resignation on December 28, 2017, following what he described as "nearly a year of harassment by right-wing, white supremacist media outlets and Internet mobs, after death threats and threats of violence directed against me and my family." Melissa Gray, "Drexel Professor Resigns Amid Threats Over Controversial Tweets," CNN, December 29, 2017, https://www.cnn.com/2017/12/28/us/drexel-university-professor-resigns/index.html.

42. Jerry Lembcke, *The Spitting Image: Myth, Memory and the Legacy of Vietnam* (New York: New York University Press, 1998).

43. David P. Schulz and G. Mitchell Reyes, "Ward Churchill and the Politics of Public Memory," *Rhetoric & Public Affairs* 11, no. 4 (2008): 631–58.

44. David Rowe, "Working Knowledge Encounters: Academics, Journalists and the Conditions of Cultural Labour," *Social Semiotics* 15, no. 3 (2005): 269–88.

45. Philip MacGregor, "Journalism, Public Imagination and Cultural Policy," *International Journal of Cultural Policy* 15, no. 2 (2009): 231–44.

46. Richard Hofstadter, *Anti-intellectualism in American Life* (New York: Alfred A. Knopf, 1963).

47. For example, Gamson and Wolfsfeld, "Movements and Media as Interacting Systems"; Gitlin, *The Whole World is Watching*; Hallin, *The Uncensored War*; Taylor, "Local Press Reporting of Opposition to the 2003 Iraq War in the UK and the Case for Reconceptualizing the Notions of Legitimacy and Deviance"; Zaller and Chiu, "Government's Little Helpers."

48. For a more serious take on the journalistic attraction to sociobiological explanations, see Susan Sperling, "Baboons with Briefcases: Feminism, Functionalism, and Sociobiology in the Evolution of Primate Gender," *Signs: Journal of Women in Culture and Society* 17, no. 1 (1991): 1–27.

49. Rodney Benson, "News Media as a 'Journalistic Field': What Bourdieu Adds to New Institutionalism, and Vice Versa," *Political Communication* 23 (2006): 187–202.

50. Ryfe, *Journalism and the Public*.

51. Ibid., 27.

52. Thomas S. Kuhn, *The Structure of Scientific Revolutions* (Chicago: University of Chicago Press, 1962).

Chapter 10

1. Michael Crozier, "Recursive Governance: Contemporary Political Communication and Public Policy," *Political Communication* 24 (2007): 1–18.
2. Douglas R. Hofstadter, *Gödel, Escher, Bach: An Eternal Golden Braid* (London: Penguin Books, 2000).
3. Crozier, "Recursive Governance," 11.
4. Timothy Snyder, *On Tyranny: Twenty Lessons from the Twentieth Century* (New York: Tim Duggan, 2017).
5. Ibid., 119.
6. Ibid., 124.
7. Thomas E. Patterson, "Pre-Primary News Coverage of the 2016 Presidential Race: Trump's Rise, Sanders' Emergence, Clinton's Struggle," Harvard Kennedy School Working Paper No. 16-023, June 20, 2016, https://ssrn.com/abstract=2798258.
8. Elihu Katz and Tamar Liebes, "'No More Peace': How Disaster, Terror and War Have Upstaged Media Events," *International Journal of Communication* 1 (2007): 157–66.
9. Simone Chambers, "Deliberative Democratic Theory," *Annual Review of Political Science* 6 (2003): 307–26; Michael McDevitt and Ally Ostrowski, "The Adolescent Unbound: Unintentional Influence of Civic Curricula on Ideological Conflict Seeking," *Political Communication* 26, no. 1 (2009): 11–29.
10. Michael McDevitt, "Political Socialization and Child Development," in *The SAGE Handbook of Political Sociology*, ed. William Outhwaite and Stephen Turner (London: SAGE, 2018).
11. Gaye Tuchman, "Objectivity as Strategic Ritual: An Examination of Newsmen's Notions of Objectivity," *American Journal of Sociology* 77, no. 4 (1972): 663–64.
12. Pamela J. Shoemaker, "Hardwired for News: Using Biological and Cultural Evolution to Explain the Surveillance Function," *Journal of Communication* 46, no. 3 (1996): 32–47.
13. Richard Hofstadter, *Anti-intellectualism in American Life* (New York: Alfred A. Knopf, 1963), 7.
14. Victor Turner, "Liminality and the Performance Genres," in *Rite, Drama, Festival, Spectacle: Rehearsals Toward a Theory of Cultural Performance*, ed. John J. MacAloon (Philadelphia: Institute for the Study of Human Issues, 1984), 19–41.
15. David A. Craig, "Communitarian Journalism(s): Clearing Conceptual Landscapes," *Journal of Mass Media Ethics* 11, no. 2 (1996): 107–18.
16. Jay Black, *Mixed News: The Public/Civic/Communitarian Journalism Debate* (Mahwah, NJ: Lawrence Erlbaum, 1997).
17. Mark Deuze and Tamara Witschge, "Beyond Journalism: Theorizing the Transformation of Journalism," *Journalism* 19, no. 2 (2018): 165–81. In media ethics theory, textbooks, and discourse of journalists themselves, audience-facing reflexivity is hailed as conducive to critical thinking. Christopher Meyers, Wendy N. Wyatt, Sandra L. Borden, and Edward Wasserman, "Professionalism, Not Professionals," *Journal of Mass Media Ethics* 27, no. 3 (2012): 189–205; Patrick Lee Plaisance, *Media Ethics: Key Principles for Responsible Practice* (Thousand Oaks,

CA: SAGE, 2004; Matt Carlson, "Metajournalistic Discourse and the Meanings of Journalism: Definitional Control, Boundary Work, and Legitimation," *Communication Theory* 26, no. 4 (2016): 349–68. Craft distills the consensus: autonomy from the market and the state "is integral to journalism's ability to serve the public. Autonomy from the *public*, however, is not." News media demonstrate accountability through transparency, an ethical imperative but also a strategy to rebuild trust in digital platforms. Stephanie Craft, "Distinguishing Features: Reconsidering the Link Between Journalism's Professional Status and Ethics," *Journalism & Communication Monographs* 19, no. 4 (2017): 294.

18. Many instructors would applaud student respondents for their commitment to transparency: the mean is 5.32 on a 1–7 range. The subsample of news majors shows ambivalence toward contextualism ($M = 3.01$), a craft orientation that demands assertion of professional discretion in discernment of meaning. While news majors are more committed to transparency than other students ($M_{diff.} = .32$, $p < .001$), they are less supportive of contextualism compared with majors outside journalism ($M_{diff.} = .49$, $p < .001$).

19. Michael McDevitt, "In Defense of Autonomy: A Critique of the Public Journalism Critique," *Journal of Communication* 53, no. 1 (2003): 155–64.

20. Stewart Hoover, *Religion in the Media Age* (New York: Routledge, 2006), 289.

21. Stephen D. Reese, "Journalism in Times of Creative Destruction: Revisiting the Academic/Professional Debate," Lecture at the University of Colorado Boulder, March 10, 2011.

22. Victor Pickard, "Rediscovering the News: Journalism Studies' Three Blind Spots," in *Remaking the News: Essays on the Future of Journalism in the Digital Age*, ed. Pablo J. Boczkowski and C. W. Anderson (Cambridge, MA: MIT Press, 2017), 47–60.

23. Clifford G. Christians, John P. Ferré, and P. Mark Fackler, *Good News: Social Ethics and the Press* (Oxford: Oxford University Press, 1993); Jill A. Edy and Shawn M. Snidow, "Making News Necessary: How Journalism Resists Alternative Media's Challenge," *Journal of Communication* 61, no. 5 (2011): 816–34.

24. Meyers et al., "Professionalism, Not Professionals."

25. Theodore L. Glasser and Marc Gunther, "The Legacy of Autonomy in American Journalism," in *The Press: Institutions of American Democracy*, ed. Geneva Overholser and Kathleen Hall Jamieson (Oxford: Oxford University Press, 2005), 388.

26. Editorial Page Editor Chuck Plunkett resigned after management spiked another editorial critical of ownership. He has subsequently become a colleague of mine in the Journalism Department at the University of Colorado Boulder.

27. Randal A. Beam, "Journalism Professionalism as an Organizational-Level Concept," *Journalism Monographs* 121 (1990): 1–41.

28. Tracy Callaway Russo, "Organizational and Professional Identification," *Management Communication Quarterly* 12 (1998): 72–111.

29. Plaisance, *Media Ethics*.

30. Catherine Liu, *American Idyll: Academic Antielitism as Cultural Critique* (Iowa City: University of Iowa Press, 2011).

31. Ibid., 221.

32. Natalia Roudakova, *Losing Pravda: Ethics and the Press in Post-Truth Russia* (Cambridge: Cambridge University Press, 2017).

33. Claudia Mellado, Folker Hanusch, María Luisa Humanes, Sergio Roses, Fábio Pereira, Lyuba Yâez, Salvador De León, Mireya Márquez, Federico Subervi, and Vinzenz Wyss, "The Pre-Socialization of Future Journalists: An Examination of Journalism Students' Professional Views in Seven Countries," *Journalism Studies* 14, no. 6 (2013): 857–74; Lars Willnat, David H. Weaver, and G. Cleveland Wilhoit, *The American Journalist in the Digital Age: A Half-Century Perspective* (New York, Peter Lang, 2017).

34. Shanto Iyengar, *Media Politics: A Citizen's Guide* (New York: London, 2019); Thomas E. Patterson, *Out of Order: How the Decline of the Political Parties and the Growing Power of the News Media Undermine the American Way of Electing Presidents* (New York: Alfred A. Knopf, 1993).

35. Karl Popper, *The Open Society and Its Enemies* (Princeton: Princeton University Press, 1945), 439.

36. George Orwell, *Nineteen Eighty-Four* (London: Secker & Warburg, 1949).

37. Philip MacGregor, "Journalism, Public Imagination and Cultural Policy," *International Journal of Cultural Policy* 15, no. 2 (2009): 233.

38. Ibid., 241.

39. Ernesto Laclau, "Totalitarianism and the Moral Imagination," *Diacritics* 20, no. 3 (1990): 88–95.

40. Jennifer Daryl Slack and M. Mehdi Semati, "Intellectual and Political Hygiene: The 'Sokal Affair,'" *Critical Studies in Media Communication* 14, no. 3 (1997): 201–27.

41. In describing the nature of news rules, Ryfe observes: "The rules of how to produce the news are not embedded in journalists themselves but in the practice of news production," *Journalism and the Public*, 136. Thus, overt practice is not necessarily an accurate guide to perspectives and beliefs of individual journalists. "Ideal-typical" traits used by journalists to define professional obligations are sufficiently fluid to defend whatever content is produced. Robert L. Handley, "What Media Critics Reveal about Journalism: Palestine Media Watch and U.S. News Media," *Journal of Communication Inquiry* 36, no. 2 (2012), 131–48. This fluidity allows for strategic adjustments when journalists negotiate between the contradicting communities of the nation/culture (expecting loyalty) and a semi-autonomous profession. Eyal Zandberg and Motti Neiger, "Between the Nation and the Profession: Journalists as Members of Contradictory Communities," *Media, Culture & Society* 27, no. 1 (2005): 131–41. The news paradigm is also flexible enough to allow journalists to accommodate contradictions between personal values and professional roles, without it being in danger of breaking. Stephen D. Reese, "The News Paradigm and the Ideology of Objectivity: A Socialist at the *Wall Street Journal*," *Critical Studies in Mass Communication* 7, no. 4 (1990): 390–409. Thus, reporters felt comfortable about expressing backstage tolerance—in some cases support—for Churchill's thesis on blowback.

42. Christopher Wilson, "The Journalist Who Was Always Late: Time and Temporality in Literary Journalism," *Literary Journalism Studies* 10, no. 1 (2018): 112–39.

43. Tim O'Reilly, "Clay Shirky's Newspapers and Thinking the Unthinkable," March 14, 2009, http://radar.oreilly.com/2009/03/clay-shirkys-newspapers-and-thinking-the-unthinkable.html.

44. John R. Baker, "Fundamentalism as Anti-intellectualism," *Humanist* 46, no. 2 (1986): 26.

45. Hofstadter, *Anti-intellectualism in American Life*; Daniel Rigney, "Three Kinds of Anti-intellectualism: Rethinking Hofstadter," *Sociological Inquiry* 61 (1991): 434–51; Dane S. Claussen, *Anti-intellectualism in American Media: Magazines and Higher Education* (New York: Peter Lang, 2004).

46. Rapid adoption and promotion of new technology come at the cost of a university's reputation as a host for critical and reflective practice. Journalism professors, for their part, have largely failed to elevate the intellectual standing of their programs. A discourse of the digital sublime betrays an eager instrumentalism. Faculty struggle to articulate professional boundaries within a landscape characterized by amateur journalism, blogging, and an erosion of public trust in news media. A profession without boundaries and a distinct body of applied knowledge is a profession without gravitas.

47. Tim Markham, "Journalism and Critical Engagement: Naiveté, Embarrassment, and Intelligibility," *Communication and Critical/Cultural Studies* 11, no. 2 (2014): 158–74.

48. Chris Atton, "Alternative Journalism: Ideology and Practice," in *The Routledge Companion to News and Journalism*, ed. S Allan (London: Routledge, 2010), 169–78.

49. Chantal Mouffe, "Deliberative Democracy or Agonistic Liberalism?," in *The Idea of the Public Sphere: A Reader*, ed. Jostein Gripsrud, Hallvard Moe, Anders Molander, and Graham Murdock (Lanham, MD: Lexington Books, 2010), 270–78.

50. Snyder, *On Tyranny*, 22.

51. Ibid., 38.

52. Ibid., 41.

53. Ibid., 40.

54. Patrick Baert and Marcus Morgan, "A Performative Framework for the Study of Intellectuals," *European Journal of Social Theory* 21, no. 3 (2018): 323–39.

55. Magda Konieczna, *Journalism Without Profit. Making News When Markets Fail* (New York: Oxford University Press, 2018); Ryfe, *Journalism and the Public*.

56. Pickard, "Rediscovering the News."

57. Deuze and Witschge, "Beyond Journalism."

58. Rick Edmonds and Amy Mitchell, "Journalism Partnerships: A New Era of Interest," Pew Research Center, December 4, 2014, http://www.journalism.org/2014/12/04/journalism-partnerships.

59. Glasser and Gunther, "The Legacy of Autonomy in American Journalism"; Meyers et al., "Professionalism, Not Professionals."

60. Sandra L. Borden, "Communitarian Journalism and Flag Displays after September 11: An Ethical Critique," *Journal of Communication Inquiry* 29, no. 1 (2005): 30–46.

61. Bernat Ivancsics, "Uncomfortable Symbiosis: Attention Capture, Normalization, and Criticism in the News Coverage of Fringe Social Groups and Populist Movements,"

paper presented at the Global Perspectives on Populism and the Media preconference, International Communication Association, Budapest, May 2018.

62. Caitlin Petre and Max Besbris, "Hitting a Moving Target: How Journalism Schools Are Adapting to an Unstable Media Job Market," unpublished paper, New York University, 2013, 8.

63. Media sociologist Lewis Friedland distilled the need for institutions "to give force to the force of the better argument." We discussed deinstitutionalization at the Global Perspectives on Populism and the Media preconference in 2018.

64. George Lakoff and Mark Johnson, *Metaphors We Live By* (Chicago: University of Chicago Press, 1980).

65. Dahlia K. Remler, Don J. Waisanen, and Andrea Gabor, "Academic Journalism: A Modest Proposal," *Journalism Studies* 15, no. 4 (2014): 357–73.

66. Thomas E. Patterson, *Informing the News: The Need for Knowledge-Based Journalism* (New York: Vintage Books, 2013).

67. Andrew Jaspan, "Who We Are," The Conversation, accessed November 32, 2018, https://theconversation.com/us/who-we-are.

68. McDevitt, "In Defense of Autonomy."

69. Hofstadter, *Anti-intellectualism in American Life*, 125.

70. Ithiel de Pool and Irwin Shulman, "Newsmen's Fantasies, Audiences, and Newswriting," *Public Opinion Quarterly* 23, no. 2 (1959): 145.

71. David Rowe, "The University as a 'Giant Newsroom': The Uses of Academic Knowledge Revisited," *Culture Unbound* 9, no. 3 (2017): 228.

72. Matthew S. McGlone, "Quoted Out of Context: Contextomy and its Consequences," *Journal of Communication* 55, no. 2 (2005): 330–56.

73. Shoemaker, "Hardwired for News."

74. Seth Lewis and Stephen D. Reese, "What Is the War on Terror? Framing Through the Eyes of Journalists," *Journalism & Mass Communication Quarterly* 86, no. 1 (2009): 85–102.

75. Robert Entman, "Cascading Activation: Contesting the White House Frame After 9/11," *Political Communication* 20 (2003): 415–32.

76. Mark R. Levy, "Disdaining the News," *Journal of Communication* 31, no. 3 (1981): 24–31.

77. Warren Breed, "Social Control in the Newsroom: A Functional Analysis," *Social Forces* 33, no. 4 (1955): 326–35.

78. Quoted in Stephen D. Reese and Jane Ballinger, "The Roots of a Sociology of News: Remembering Mr. Gates and Social Control in the Newsroom," *Journalism & Mass Communication Quarterly*, 78, no, 4 (2001): 652.

79. Edward S. Herman and Noam Chomsky, *Manufacturing Consent: The Political Economy of the Mass Media* (New York: Pantheon Books, 1988); Robert E. Gutsche, Jr., *Media Control: News as an Institution of Power and Social Control* (New York: Bloomsbury, 2017).

80. W. Lance Bennett, "An Introduction to Journalistic Norms and Representations of Politics," *Political Communication* 13 (1996): 373–84.

81. Entman, "Cascading Activation."

82. McDevitt, "In Defense of Autonomy."

83. James S. Ettema and Theodore L. Glasser, "The Irony in—and of—Journalism: A Case Study in the Moral Language of Liberal Democracy," *Journal of Communication* 44, no. 2 (1994): 5.

84. Ibid., 8.

Appendix

1. Michael McCluskey, Susan E. Stein, Michael P. Boyle, and Douglas M. McLeod, "Community Structure and Social Protest: Influences on Newspaper Coverage," *Mass Communication and Society* 12, no. 3 (2009): 353–71.

2. Michael McDevitt and Jesse Benn, "Closing of the Journalism Mind: Anti-intellectualism in the Professional Development of Students," paper presented at the annual meeting of the Association for Education in Journalism and Mass Communication, San Francisco, August 2015.

3. Claudia Mellado, Folker Hanusch, María Luisa Humanes, Sergio Roses, Fábio Pereira, Lyuba Yez, Salvador De León, Mireya Márquez, Federio Subervi, and Vinzenz Wyss, "The Pre-Socialization of Future Journalists: An Examination of Journalism Students' Professional Views in Seven Countries," *Journalism Studies* 14, no. 6 (2013): 857–74.

4. Peter Bhatia, "Accrediting Council on Education in Journalism and Mass Communications Revisit Team Report," University of Colorado, Boulder, 2012.

5. Martin E. Eigenberger and Karen A. Sealander, "A Scale for Measuring Students' Anti-Intellectualism," *Psychological Reports* 89 (2001): 387–402.

6. David H. Weaver, Randal A. Beam, Bonnie J. Brownlee, Paul S. Voakes, and G. Cleveland Wilhoit, *The American Journalist in the 21st Century: U.S. News People at the Dawn of the New Millennium* (Mahwah, NJ: Lawrence Erlbaum, 2007).

7. Mellado et al., "The Pre-Socialization of Future Journalists."

8. Stephen W. Raudenbush and Anthony S. Bryk, *Hierarchical Linear Models: Applications and Data Analysis Methods* (Thousand Oaks, CA: SAGE, 2002).

Index

Note: Tables and figures are indicated by *t* and *f* following the page number